Black Writers and Latin America:

Cross-Cultural Affinities

RICHARD L. JACKSON

 Howard University Press

Washington, DC
1998

Howard University Press, Washington, D.C.20001

Manufactured in the United States of America

This book is printed on acid-free paper.

10   9   8   7   6   5   4   3   2   1

Library of Congress Cataloging-in-Publication Data

Jackson, Richard L., 1937–
    Black writers and Latin America : cross-cultural affinities /
  Richard L. Jackson.
      p. cm.
  Includes bibliographical references and index.
  ISBN 0-88258-039-6 (alk. paper)
    1. American literature—Afro-American authors—History and criticism.   2. Latin American literature—Black authors—History and criticism.   3. Latin American literature—20th century—History and criticism.   4. American literature—20th century—HIstory and criticism.   5. Literature, Comparative—American and Latin American.
6. Literature, Comparative—Latin American and American.   7. American literature—Latin American influences.   8. Latin American literature—American influences.
9. Blacks—Latin America—Intellectual life.   10. Afro-Americans—Intellectual life.
I. Title.
PS153.N5J38 1998
810.9'896073—dc21
                                                               98–17582
                                                                   CIP

To Chris, Sonnie, and Lil

In loving memory

Afro-America constitutes a bridge
between Latin America and the
United States.
—Vera Kutzinski[*]

"The Logic of Wings: Gabriel García Márquez and Afro-American Literature,"
Latin American Literary Review 13 (1985): 143.

Acknowledgments

I started this book, probably as therapy, a few months after the death of my son, Chris, in 1986. I completed it almost ten years later in December 1995. Writing again served as therapy because in July of that year my brother, Sonnie, and my wife, Lil, passed away. She and Chris, like the rest of my family—D. D., Shaw, and Charley—are always my inspiration for everything I do. I also would like to thank the Langston Hughes Society for permission to use material first published in my article: "Langston Hughes and the African Diaspora in South America," *The Langston Hughes Review* 5, no. 1 (1986): 23–33.

Contents

INTRODUCTION

The International Dimension in U.S. Black Writing

> I must go to another place,
> another country.
> —Delores Kendrick[1]

An international dimension has always existed in the writing of U.S. blacks. Despite unrelenting focus on the black experience in the United States, some U.S. black writers have gone beyond our shores to advocate Pan-Africanism—an interest in blacks all over the world and especially in Africa—while others have identified with the worldwide proletariat. Still others have tried to reconcile black nationalism and "red" internationalism.[2] Black writers during the 1930s, 1940s, and 1950s were especially mindful of the increasing involvement of the United States in world events, and they themselves took an interest in other nations and those nations' relations with the United States.[3]

Internationalism, therefore, is not new to U.S. blacks nor is foreign travel. In fact, "present-day pilgrimages of black Americans, West Indians, and Africans to China and Cuba," wrote St. Clair Drake in 1970, "are reminiscent of the Moscow journeys of an earlier period."[4] Drake believed that the dilemmas and contradictions that accompanied attempts to reconcile Marxism and black nationalism were as perplexing to the intellectuals of the 1960s as they were to those of the 1920s and 1930s. Black writers today still face these dilemmas. But not all their travel is in search of identity or ideology, and not all trips are political. The 1980s could well be remembered, in part, as the decade of world outreach for U.S. blacks. During that time we saw the first national holiday celebrating the birthday of Martin Luther King Jr. Also U.S. blacks became concerned about blacks in the Diaspora and in South Africa, a concern that merged with a broader world consciousness and was reinforced daily through television and other media reports of world events. This concern was reinforced through personal travel, some of it to Latin America and Spain.

The Hispanic world and often the black inhabitants of it have had a great impact on the lives and work of several contemporary U.S. black writers. But writers' fascination with Spain and Latin America did not start in our day. Blacks in the United States have long shown such interest. The political activist, the ordinary tourist who dreams of visiting Mexico or even retiring there, and the academic are all aware of Latin America's "mythical" quality on the question. Black scholars and intellectuals have tackled subjects such as the black discovery of America; the African influence on the Olmecs, one of the "mother" cultures of America; and racial discrimination in Cuba since that country's revolution. Brazil is widely popularized, erroneously, as the Western Hemisphere's "racial paradise." This belief about Brazil is regularly exposed as a myth.[5]

Part of the fascination blacks have with Latin America comes from media, books, schools, and geographical studies, especially about Mexico and Brazil. Audre Lorde knew Mexico was "connected"[6] to where she lived and felt she could walk there if necessary. G. C. Oden, in his "Private Letter to Brazil," writes: "The map shows me where it is you are," on the other side of "hopscotching islands that loosely, moors / your continent to mine."[7] This interest in Latin America, however, has come not just from U.S. blacks. It has never been unusual for other writers in the United States to visit or to write about Latin America; American literature using Hispanic background materials exists in abundance.[8] Nor is there a shortage of documentation on the impact, reception, and influence in Latin America of the United States and its literature, especially of major figures such as Poe, Franklin, Longfellow, Whitman, Emerson, Irving, Cooper, Faulkner, and Hemingway.[9] But despite this lengthy list, except for some work on Nicolás Guillén and the Caribbean,[10] little notice has been given to the influence of the United States and its writers on Hispanic black writers. This influence has been ignored even though some writers such as Quince Duncan, Manuel Zapata Olivella, and Adalberto Ortiz openly acknowledge it. The impact of the United States in Latin America has been inevitable in many spheres, including literature. This undeniable influence makes the lack of critical material charting cross-cultural influences all the more remarkable.

Significant cultural and political exchanges have been taking place between black Americans in the United States and black

Latin Americans since the 19th century. For example, musicians such as Marian Anderson, Lionel Hampton, Dizzy Gillespie, and many others appeared at popular concerts in Cuba during the 1930s, 1940s, and 1950s. Their appearances helped bring about the important fusion of Afro-Cuban and jazz rhythms, notably through the efforts of Dizzy Gillespie and the Cuban drummer Chano Pozo. Black baseball teams from the United States played regularly in Cuba during this period, and Cuban boxers and baseball players were frequently stars in the United States.[11] The pair of world developments following World War II that "book-end" the maturation of black writing was the proliferation of claims of the United States as a superpower and the emergence of the concept of the Third World.[12] Both developments affected the cultural and political relations that were taking place between U.S. blacks and Hispanic blacks. The Bay of Pigs invasion in 1961, the blockade of Cuba, and the October Missile Crisis in 1962 interrupted this cross-cultural travel and exchange with Cuba, but not before U.S. blacks more widely recognized that they did share something with other peoples in this hemisphere.

As black writers today reach beyond the black community and their own country, we should remember that Africa was one of the first stopping places on the black journey to world vision. Langston Hughes started this identification with Africa in one of his first poems, "The Negro Speaks of Rivers," and he never stopped. Africa has been in vogue since the 1920s, sparked not only by Langston Hughes and the Harlem Renaissance, but also by W. E. B. Du Bois and Marcus Garvey, and the trend has continued in our time. We saw it in the 1960s, both in "Black Is Beautiful" slogans and in the racial and political identification with Africans abroad. One of the lasting legacies of Langston Hughes and of the 1960s is this identification or re-identification with Africa. Hughes's anthology, *An African Treasury* (1960), and his *Poems from Black Africa* (1963), along with his many trips to Africa during the 1960s, led to what has been called "the recovery of Africa."[13] Frank Yerby's *The Dahomean* (1971), Alex Haley's *Roots* (1976), Toni Morrison's *Song of Solomon* (1977), Alice Walker's *The Color Purple* (1982), and Charles Johnson's *Middle Passage* (1990) are all part of this new positive identification with Africa.

The recovery of Africa, however, was only the first step, as U.S. blacks reached out even further toward a "deeper" redefin-

ition of black American literary expression, namely, identification with the emerging Third World perspective.[14] The relevance
of black America to Africa and the Third World became clearer,
and black writing increasingly reflected this broader perspective. Beginning with Africa in the mid-1950s, Richard Wright
had begun to discover the Third World. He published *Black
Power* in 1955 and *White Man Listen* in 1957. His series of lectures
devoted especially to the Third World was called Wright's "tes-
tament ideologique."[15]

Part of the recovery of Africa was the realization, even among
black nationalists, that resistance against domination existed in
other parts of the world, not just in the United States. The examples of Che, Lumumba, Nkruma, Fanon, and Guillén helped
writers like Amiri Baraka to evolve from a belief in cultural
nationalism to a belief in revolutionary socialism. The celebrated
evolution of Baraka, who "led his verse and that of other poets of
the 1960s and early 1970s in a violent assault on the obsessively
universal in Afro-American writing,"[16] was especially influenced, as we shall see, by his trip to Cuba in 1963. If Africa deep-
ened the self-concept of black writing, the Third World gave it
"fuller dimension."[17] During this period, black America joined
hands with Africa, Asia, and the Caribbean in a common historic
revolt. In short, the writings of black American literary intellectuals showed a global perspective as writers moved beyond "the
first post-war vision of the black man as America's metaphor to
seek a new anchorage in historically ascending cultures."[18]

Politically oriented black writers discovered a Third World
that was, in fact, Afrocentric, "a Third World frontier whose vanguard is modern Africa."[19] Other U.S. blacks traveled and discovered Spain and Latin America, often benefiting from academic
support or from other opportunities. In fact, today's black writers
not only are becoming part of world movements unknown by
earlier black authors but also are "generally better educated than
their literary ancestors; have entered more fully into the higher
echelons of American governmental, academic, and professional
life; and have been given by the Civil Rights Acts and the whole
civil rights movement a broader social experience."[20]

Older black writers like Richard Wright, Chester Himes, Frank
Yerby, and Langston Hughes traveled to and lived in Spain and
Latin America, and Hughes even translated from the Spanish,
but among the new breed of traveling black writers are some

whose major in college was Spanish. Al Young, who earned a B.A. in Spanish at the University of California at Berkeley in 1969, comes to mind, as does Robert Hayden. Young traveled widely throughout the United States, Mexico, and Europe; and Hayden spent a year in Mexico on a Ford Foundation Grant (1954–1955). Michael Harper spent a summer in Mexico and some time in Europe. Clarence Major has spent time in Mexico, as has Charles Wright (Veracruz) and L. V. Mack. Audre Lorde spent a year at the University of Mexico, and Delores Kendrick spent a year in Spain, teaching and writing. More recently, during her postdoctoral Fulbright Fellowship (1985–1986), Carolivia Herron packed her bags and, like her protagonist in the long short story "That Place,"[21] headed for Mexico.

The list could go on to include the trips to Cuba by Lance Jeffers or back in time to mention some of the black expatriates to Europe who also traveled to Latin America. The motivations are as interesting and as varied as the trips themselves. We will see that some of this travel was politically motivated, but much of it was less motivated by ideology and the search for political alternatives than by adventure or romance or by sheer fascination with Latin America or Spain or by a desire just to get away and write. Some wanted simply to vacation; others were impulsively or compulsively in love with the idea of travel. Some were culturally curious and wanted to study; others traveled out of the desire for anonymity and racial freedom, or like Al Young's protagonist, were in search of "unpressured soul space."[22] Some blacks, like Langston Hughes's father, went to another country "where a colored man could get ahead and make money quicker,"[23] considerations of the father that hardly seemed to motivate the son. Hughes's father had taken up residence in Mexico and "wished his handsome, clever son to abandon America and his race . . . to study abroad and return to Mexico where the two would grow prosperous together."[24] But, as history has shown, the son wanted something quite different.

Black writers whose literature is not blatantly involved in the ideological concept of the Third World, then, are also among those whose vision turned international. Today, "not all but many of them are walking boldly in a world that is freer, more sophisticated, more complex, and more cosmopolitan than that of older writers."[25] From the "discretely universalist"[26] poetry of Robert Hayden and Michael Harper to Amiri Baraka, black literature in the United States reflects this travel. Many who went abroad wrote about their experiences immediately. But others who waited some time before writing about their foreign travel seemed to have a better perspective, not only on foreign cultures but also on their own. Some found, in the cultures they were exposed to, reflections of their own culture. Black writers today draw on their experiences abroad by setting some of their literature in Spain and such Latin American countries as Mexico, Cuba, and Brazil. It is this recent literature on Latin America and, to a lesser extent, on Spain that will be highlighted in the first part of this study. The work of Langston Hughes, of course, is pivotal as is the work of other older writers such as Frank Yerby, Claude McKay, Chester Himes, and Richard Wright. All of them have ties to Latin America and certainly to Spain. While I do explore these ties, this study is also comparative and draws rather closely on directions for future study suggested by Vera Kutzinski, Melvin Dixon, Mercer Cook, Thomas Hale, and Edward Ako.

Vera Kutzinski[27] looks for patterns of cross-cultural interpenetration in modern American literature and suggests there are textual relationships among contemporary black writers from the United States whose works reflect an interest in Latin America and Latin American texts. Melvin Dixon[28] focuses on affinities, a black sensibility in literature, and mutual influences. Like Dixon, whose work lends support to the need to give more attention to the international vision of black American authors, Mercer Cook[29] calls for more research on contacts and influences among Caribbean, black American, and African writers. His study, in turn, is similar to Thomas Hale's[30] and Edward Ako's.[31] Hale believes black American, Caribbean, and African writers, beginning in the 1920s, sought inspiration from each other, exchanged visions of ethnic identity, and consciously tried to reestablish contact in the Black Diaspora. Ako specifically set out to examine literary and personal contacts and influence.

Whether they use intertextuality (Dixon), cross-cultural interpenetration (Kutzinski), or influence (Cook, Hale, Ako), these comparatists in one way or another underscore the theoretical approach I follow in the identification of links—both symbolic and real—between U.S. black writers and their counterparts in Latin America. Affinities that form the basis for a black aesthetic crossing national boundaries can be derived from the same shared history of Africa—the common source—and of the common New World experiences of slavery, racism, and colonialism. Such affinities inspire similar work among black writers in Africa and the Americas, and comparative criticism must continue to identify these common elements. Such affinities are often inspired by outlook and not necessarily by literary and personal contacts and relationships established through travel and collegial association. In this study, I try to determine affinities where applicable and patterns of true influence when possible. I go beyond acquaintance and coincidence, however, to explore Langston Hughes's clear influence not only on Nicolás Guillén but also on other writers in Latin America.

Langston Hughes's influence on Nicolás Guillén began in the 1930s. Coming full circle, I will discuss Guillén's own subsequent role as model for and forerunner of the Black Arts Movement in the United States in the 1960s. I will discuss, in turn, the impact of the "Turbulent Sixties" on today's black writers in Latin America. In fact, I will explore the question of influence in several stages beginning with the slave narratives and continuing with Langston Hughes and the Harlem Renaissance in the 1920s and 1930s, to Richard Wright in the 1940s, to James Baldwin in the 1950s, to the New Black Renaissance in the 1960s with the Civil Rights/Black Power/Black Arts Movement, and to Alex Haley's *Roots* in the 1970s. Haley's novel stimulated a widespread search for black ancestral roots and an interest in black history not only in the United States but also in Latin America, especially in Central America among Hispanic writers of West Indian origin.

U.S. black writers like Langston Hughes and Alex Haley appear often in black literature in Latin America, as do other U.S. black figures, from Martin Luther King Jr. and Angela Davis to Emmett Till and the Scottsboro boys. In fact, black Hispanic literature focuses intently on blacks and racism in the United States. Over the years, black writers in Latin America have viewed black Americans in the United States either as symbols and victims of injustice or as model figures in the fight against racism in this hemisphere. This process of influence clearly is a two-way street, and I will explore the effects on both groups. U.S. black writers, for example, have traveled to the Hispanic world. Latin American black writers such as Nicolás Guillén, Quince Duncan, Blas Jiménez, Norberto

James, Carlos Guillermo Wilson, Nancy Morejón, Adalberto Ortiz, Jorge Artel, Manuel Zapata Olivella, Nelson Estupiñán Bass, and Abdias do Nascimento have, in turn, lived or traveled in the United States. As an example of Latin American influence, Nancy Morejón, the African Cuban poet who is continuing the work of her mentor Nicolás Guillén, is now recognized in this country as a spokesperson for feminist, political, and racial causes.

As a corollary to this cross-exchange, I will examine the growing body of black immigration literature, especially on the black Puerto Rican in New York. In exploring the black image in this literature, I will attempt to determine whether conflict, disunity, and alienation among native and immigrant blacks are the exception or the rule. I will also discuss a related topic, namely, autobiographical literature of Hispanic black writers and academics who travel or live in the United States and write of their own black experience either in straight autobiographical accounts or in thinly disguised fiction or other creative literature. The works of the African Panamanian Carlos Guillermo Wilson, the African Chicano poet Guillermo Bowie, and the African Colombian Manuel Zapata Olivella are representative.

This study also requires some discussion of black writers in Latin America today who, like their predecessors, are very much aware of the United States and U.S. blacks. I will discuss as well some of the later literature of earlier writers—the old guard, including Nicolás Guillén whose memoirs appeared in 1982. Guillén's life-long opposition to the United States is a thematic constant in that volume. Many of the Latin American black writers I will discuss are extremely assertive on the question of race and unreservedly outspoken against the mistreatment of blacks both in their homelands and in the United States. This final part of my study relates to and, in a sense, continues the work of Marvin Lewis[32] and Ian Smart.[33] Lewis limited his study to South American poetry written in Spanish and covered only the years up to 1980. Smart limited his book to West Indian or "Pan-Caribbean" themes, language, and religion in Panamanian and Costa Rican black literature.

The black writer in Latin America has gained some recognition in the United States. This recognition has been won through critical works in English, increased study, wider incorporation of black writers in the humanities curriculum, and translations of these writers' works.[34] In addition to the books by Lewis and Smart, William Luis[35] has edited a collection of essays, and several new books on Nicolás Guillén have appeared.[36] While I am encouraged by these books and other fine studies,[37] my work develops ideas broached in my own writings on related matters.[38] Creative literature by blacks continues to appear in Latin America and comparative critical assessments bringing Diaspora literature together must keep pace if we are to increase our understanding of how we blacks see the Latin American world and how blacks are seen by it.

I have divided this study into five chapters. In chapter 1, "U.S. Black Writers and Spain," I will discuss primarily the work of some of the major U.S. black writers who earlier in this century had a good deal to say about Spain as well as Latin America. In chapter 2, "U.S. Black Writers and Latin America," I will return to these earlier figures and also move forward to newer U.S. black writers whose interest in the Hispanic world focuses more on Latin America than on Spain. In chapter 3, "The Influence of U.S. Black Writers," I will focus primarily on the work and example of Langston Hughes in Latin America. In chapter 4, "Hispanic Black Writers and the United States," I will discuss the impact the United States, racism, and black America have had on black writers and black consciousness in Latin America. Chapter 5, "Black Writers in Latin America Today" is, in a sense, a continuation of chapter 4.

In the conclusion and throughout this study, I will draw not only on creative works, reviews, articles, criticisms, and other traditional documentation but also on autobiographies and published conversations and interviews with several writers. Fortunately, there is a tremendous amount of material of this kind available. The interviews, conversations, and autobiographical writings are especially useful for a reader interested as much in what black writers say about literature and experience as in the literature itself. The interview in particular has become a welcome adjunct to an author's work and is a candid and direct source of information about a writer's personal, professional, and creative thinking. In the interview we meet the creative artist and the person. In this study, I will try to bring the two together to better understand U.S. black writers and their interest in Latin America and Spain and to understand the Hispanic black writers' preoccupation with the United States.

Notes

1. Delores Kendrick, *Now Is the Thing to Praise* (Detroit: Lotus Press, 1984): 5.
2. "Margaret Walker," in *Black Women Writers at Work*, ed. Claudia Tate (New York: Continuum, 1983), 199.
3. See Dudley Randall, "The Black Aesthetic of the Thirties, Forties, and Fifties," in *The Black Aesthetic*, ed. Addison Gayle Jr. (Garden City, N.Y.: Doubleday and Co., 1971), 224–34. Also see *Race Relations in the International Arena, 1940–1955*, papers of the NAACP that document black intellectual thought about race relations on a global scale. Now available on microfilm from University Publications of America.
4. St. Clair Drake, "Introduction," *Claude McKay: A Long Way from Home* (New York: Harcourt Brace and World, 1970), ix.
5. "Racial Gap Grows Wider in Brazil," *The Globe and Mail* (Toronto), 24 May 1986, A9.
6. Audre Lorde, *Zami: A New Spelling of My Name* (Trumansburg, N.Y.: Crossing Press, 1982), 147. The idea of being "connected" to some other people is explored by Julianne Malveaux in "Widening the Lens of Black History," *Black Issues in Higher Education* (25 February 1993): 30.
7. G. C. Oden, "A Private Letter to Brazil," *Kaleidoscope: Poems by American Negro Poets*, ed. Robert Hayden (New York: Harcourt Brace and World, 1967), 185.
8. See Sturgiss Leavitt, "Latin American Literature in the United States," in *Revue de littérature comparée* 11 (1931): 126–48, and his *Hispano-American Literature in the United States* (Cambridge: Harvard University Press, 1932). Also see Stanley T. Williams, *The Spanish Background of American Literature*, 2 vols, (New Haven: Yale, 1955); Frederick S. Stimson, *Orígenes del hispanismo norteamericano* (México City: Andrea, 1961); Drewey Wayne Gunn, *American and British Writers in Mexico 1559–1973* (Austin: University of Texas Press, 1974); and Cecil Robinson, *Mexico and the Hispanic Southwest in American Literature* (Tucson: University of Arizona Press, 1977).
9. See, for example, José de Onís, *The United States as Seen by the Spanish American Writers 1776–1890* (New York: Gordon Press, 1975) and John T. Reid, *Spanish American Images of the United States* (Gainesville: University Presses of Florida, 1977). Also see the entire issue: Joaquín Roy, ed., *Los Ensayistas* 12–13 (March 1982), on the image of the United States in Hispanic America, especially its extensive and comprehensive bibliography (pages 87–197); Hector H. Orjuela, *Imagen de los Estados Unidos en la poesía de Hispanoamérica* (Mexico City: UNAM, 1980a) and his follow-up essay, "Imagen de los Estados Unidos en la poesía de Hispanoamérica," *Literatura hispanoamericana: ensayos de interpretación y de crítica* (Bogotá: Publicaciones del Instituto Caro y Cuervo, 1980b), 121–46.
10. See Oscar Rivera-Rodas, "La imagen de los Estados Unidos en la poesía de Nicolás Guillén," *Casa de las Américas* 120 (1980): 154–60; Joseph Pereira, "Raza en la obra de Nicolás Guillén después de 1959," *Sin nombre* 13, no. 3 (1983): 30–38; Constance S. de García-Barrios, "The Black in Post-Revolutionary Cuban Literature," *Revista/Review Interamericana* 8 (1978): 263–70; Miriam DeCosta "Nicolás Guillén and His Poetry for Afro-

Americans" *Black World* (September 1973): 12–16; Renée Larrier, "Racism in the United States: An Issue in Caribbean Poetry," *Journal of Caribbean Studies* 2, no. 1 (Spring 1981): 51–71; and others like Mirta Aguirre, "Un poeta y un continente," in her book titled *Un poeta y un continente* (Havana: Editorial Letras Cubanas, 1982).

11. Robert Chrisman, "Langston Hughes: Six Letters to Nicolás Guillén," trans. Carmen Alegría, *The Black Scholar* 16, no. 4 (1985): 54. Digna Castañeda and Lisa Brock are preparing an anthology of relations between Cubans and African Americans. It will be called *The Unbroken Cord: African-Americans and Cubans in the Nineteenth and Twentieth Centuries*. Tracy Mishkin (Ann Arbor, Mich.), looking at the larger picture, is preparing a collection of essays on literary influences and African-American writers in general. Also see David Hellwig, ed., *African-American Reflections on Brazil's Racial Paradise* (Philadelphia: Temple University Press, 1992), for more on ties among African Americans, Latin Americans, and Afro-Latin Americans.

12. Clyde Taylor, "Black Writing as Immanent Humanism," *The Southern Review* 21, no. 3 (1985): 791.

13. Ibid., 792.

14. Sigmund Ro, "'Desecrators' and 'Necromancers': Black American Writers and Critics in the Nineteen-Sixties and the Third World Perspective," *Callaloo* 8, no. 33 (1985): 567.

15. Michel Faber, "Richard Wright et l'Afrique." *Notre librairie* 77 (November–December 1984): 42. Also see John Reilly, "Richard Wright's Discovery of the Third World," *Minority Voices* (1978): 47–53, and his "Richard Wright and the Art of Non-Fiction: Stepping Out on the Stage of the World," *Callaloo* 9, no. 3 (1986): 507–20. Also useful is Wimal Dissanayake, "Richard Wright: A View from the Third World," *Callaloo* 9, no. 3 (1986). Dissanayake says that Wright is one of the most widely discussed writers in the Third World.

16. Arnold Rampersad, "The Universal and the Particular in Afro-American Poetry," *College Language Association Journal* 25, no. 1 (1981): 14.

17. Taylor, "Black Writing," 794.

18. Sigmund Ro, " 'Desecrators' and 'Necromancers,'" 569.

19. Ibid., 564.

20. Arthur P. Davis, "Novels of the New Black Renaissance (1960–1977): A Thematic Survey," *College Language Association Journal* 21, no. 4 (1978): 490.

21. Carolivia Herron, "That Play," *Callaloo* 10, no. 3 (1987): 391–413.

22. Al Young, *Who Is Angelina?* (New York: Holt, Rinehart, and Winston, 1975), 123.

23. Langston Hughes, *The Big Sea* (New York: A. A. Knopf, 1942), 15.

24. Mary White Ovington, *Portraits in Color* (New York: Viking, 1927), 198. Cited in Edward Mullen, *Langston Hughes in the Hispanic World and Haiti* (Hamden, Conn.: Archon Books, 1977), 17.

25. Davis, "Novels of Black Renaissance," 490.

26. Rampersad, "Universal Poetry," 14.

27. Vera Kutzinski, "The Logic of Wings: Gabriel García Márquez and Afro-American Literature," *The Latin American Literary Review* 13 (1985): 133–46.

28. Melvin Dixon, "Rivers Remembering Their Sources: Comparative Studies in Black Literary History—Langston Hughes, Jácques Roumain, and

Negritude," *Afro-American Literature: The Reconstruction of Instruction*, ed. Dexter Fisher and Robert B. Stepto (New York: Modern Language Association, 1979), 25–43.

29. Mercer Cook, "Some Literary Contacts: African, West Indian, Afro-American," *The Black Writer in Africa and the Americas*, ed. Lloyd W. Brown (Los Angeles: Hennessey and Ingalls, 1973).

30. Thomas Hale, "From Afro-America to Afro-France: The Literary Triangle Trade," *The French Review* 49 (1976): 1089–96.

31. Edward Ako, "Langston Hughes and the Negritude Movement: A Study in Literary Influences," *College Language Association Journal* 28 (1984): 46–56.

32. Marvin Lewis, *Afro-Hispanic Poetry, 1940–1980* (Columbia: University of Missouri Press (1983). Lewis has since published *Treading the Ebony Path: Ideology and Violence in Contemporary Afro-Colombian Prose Fiction* (Columbia: University of Missouri Press, 1987; *Ethnicity and Identity in Contemporary Afro-Venezuelan Literature* (Columbia: University of Missouri Press, 1992); and *Afro-Argentine Discourse: Another Dimension of the Black Diaspora* (Columbia: University of Missouri Press, 1995).

33. Ian Smart, *Central American Writers of West Indian Origin: A New Hispanic Literature* (Washington, D.C.: Three Continents Press, 1984).

34. See, for example, Adalberto Ortiz, *Juyungo*, trans. Susan Hill and Jonathan Tittler (Washington, D.C: Three Continents Press, 1982); Nancy Morejón, *Where the Island Sleeps Like a Wing*, trans. Kathleen Weaver (San Francisco: The Black Scholar Press, 1985); Ann Venture Young, *The Image of Black Women in 20th Century South American Poetry: A Bilingual Anthology* (Washington, D.C.: Three Continents Press, 1987); Carlos Guillermo Wilson, *Short Stories by Cubena*, trans. Ian Smart (Washington, D.C.: The Afro-Hispanic Institute, 1986); Nelson Estupiñán Bass, *When the Guayacans Were in Bloom*, trans. Henry Richards (Washington, D.C.: Afro-Hispanic Institute, 1987); and Manuel Zapata Olivella, *Chambacu: Black Slum*, trans. Jonathan Tittler (Pittsburgh: Latin American Literary Review Press, 1989). Other volumes recently appearing in translation include Carlos Guillermo Wilson's *Black Cubena's Thoughts*, trans. Elba D. Birmingham-Pokorny (Miami: Ediciones Universal, 1991); Nelson Estupiñán Bass, *Curfew*, trans. Henry J. Richards (Washington, D.C.: Afro-Hispanic Institute, 1992); and Nelson Estupiñán Bass, *Pastrana's Last River*, trans. Ian Smart (Washington, D.C.: Afro-Hispanic Institute, 1993).

35. William Luis, ed., *Voices from Under. Black Narrative in Latin America and the Caribbean* (Westport, Conn.: Greenwood Press, 1984). Luis also published *Literary Bondage: Slavery in Cuban Narrative* (Austin: University of Texas Press, 1990).

36. Keith Ellis, *Cuba's Nicolás Guillén. Poetry and Ideology* (Toronto: University of Toronto Press, 1983), and his *Nicolás Guillén, New Love Poetry: Nueva poesía de amor* (Toronto: University of Toronto Press, 1994), which Ellis edited and translated; Lorna Williams, *Self and Society in the Poetry of Nicolás Guillén* (Baltimore: Johns Hopkins University Press, 1982); Ian Smart, *Nicolás Guillén, Popular Poet of the Caribbean* (Columbia: University of Missouri Press, 1990); Josephat B. Kubayanda, *The Poet's Africa: Africanness in the Poetry of Nicolás Guillén and Aimé Césaire* (Westport, Conn.:

Greenwood Press, 1990); and Vera Kutzinski, *Against the American Grain: Myth and History in William Carlos Williams, Jay Wright, and Nicolás Guillén* (Baltimore: Johns Hopkins University Press, 1987), and her *Sugar's Secrets: Race and the Erotics of Cuban Nationalism* (Charlottesville: University Press of Virginia, 1993). Also see Clement White, *Decoding the Word: Nicolás Guillén* (Miami: Ediciones Universal, 1995).

37. For example, Martha Cobb, *Harlem, Haiti, and Havana: A Comparative Critical Survey of Langston Hughes, Jacques Roumain, and Nicolás Guillén* (Washington, D.C.: Three Continents Press, 1979); and Edward Mullen, *Langston Hughes in the Hispanic World and Haiti* (Hamden, Conn.: Archon Books, 1977); Yvonne Captain-Hidalgo, *The Culture of Fiction in the Works of Manuel Zapata Olivella* (Columbia: University of Missouri Press, 1993); Elba Birmingham-Pokorny, ed., *Denouncement and Reaffirmation of the Afro-Hispanic Identity in Carlos Guillermo Wilson's Works* (Miami: Ediciones Universal, 1993). Also see Richard L. Jackson, *The Afro-Spanish American Author II: The 1980s* (West Cornwall, Conn.: Locust Hill Press, 1989b) for other recent titles.

38. See Richard L. Jackson, *The Black Image in Latin American Literature* (Albuquerque: University of New Mexico Press, 1976); *Black Writers in Latin America* (Albuquerque: University of New Mexico Press, 1979); *The Afro-Spanish American Author: An Annotated Bibliography of Criticism* (New York: Garland Publishing Co., 1980); *Black Literature and Humanism in Latin America* (Athens: University of Georgia Press, 1988); and *The Afro-Spanish American Author II—The 1980s: An Annotated Bibliography of Recent Criticism* (West Cornwall, Conn.: Locust Hill Press, 1989). Also see, *Black Writers and the Hispanic Canon in Latin America*, New York, Twayne Publishers, 1997 and *Black Literature and Latin America: Contemporary Issues* forthcoming from Howard University Press.

ONE

U.S. Black Writers and Spain

> Yes, Langston Hughes is the traveling
> star of coloured America.
> —Nancy Cunard[1]

THE SPANISH CIVIL WAR AND ITS AFTERMATH

There are many studies on the black image in Spanish literature, especially of the Golden Age, including bibliographies listing the early black writers in Spain.[2] Not too much, however, has been written about U.S. black writers in our century, some of them expatriates to Europe, who have commented extensively on Spain. Their remarks are especially revealing because they often tell us as much about themselves as U.S. blacks as they do about Spain. The Spanish Civil War (1936–1939) and its aftermath, for the most part, form the basis for many of their reactions to and assessments of that country. Blacks from all over the world participated in that war. Their story is yet to be written, though Langston Hughes did his part to chronicle their history.

Hughes wrote a great deal about Spain, having spent six months there in 1937 covering the Spanish Civil War for the *Baltimore Afro-American*, the *Cleveland Call and Post*, and the *Globe* as the only black newspaper correspondent in Spain. His task ostensibly was to cover U.S. blacks in the International Brigades on the front lines of the Civil War,[3] but he did more than that. Hughes was at great personal risk in Spain, but he was just as brave about going as he was apprehensive about not coming back. His most outspoken prose and poetry are from the 1930s, "a period when many American artists and writers, concerned about the economic depression in America and the rise of fascism in Europe and disillusioned by the values of capitalist society as a whole, were moving toward the left. Hughes's revolutionary writing of that decade was a result not only of those forces but also of his own travels to Russia, China and Spain."[4] Hughes's writings on Spain were not easily accessible to the casual reader until the two publications—Faith Berry (1973) and Edward Mullen (1977)—made them available.

Berry grouped some of Hughes's writings on Spain under the heading "Darkness in Spain" in section 10 of her edition. She includes "Too Much of Race," "Franco and the Moors," "Negroes in Spain," "Madrid," "Laughter in Madrid," "Air Raid: Barcelona," "Moonlight in Valencia: Civil War," "Tomorrow's Seed," and "Hero-International Brigade." Four years later, Mullen includes those same articles in his edition. In addition, he includes the full version of the article "Franco and the Moors" ("Hughes Finds Moors Being Used as Pawns by Fascists in Spain") and several other essays from the *Baltimore Afro-American*: "Hughes Bombed in Spain: Tells of Terror of Fascist Raid"; "Organ Grinder's Swing Heard Above Gunfire in Spain—Hughes"; "Madrid Getting Used to Bombs: It's Food Shortage That Counts"; "Madrid's Flowers Hoist Blooms to Meet Raining Fascist Bombs"; "New York Nurse Wed Irish Fighter in Spain's War"; "Soldiers From Many Lands United in Spanish Fight"; "Milt Herndon Died Trying to Rescue Wounded Pal"; "Fighters From Other Lands Look to Ohio Man For Food"; "Pittsburgh Soldier Hero, But Too Bashful to Talk"; "Walter Cobb, Driving Captured Fascist Truck, Mistaken by Own Men for Moor, But Language Saves Him"; "Howard Man Fighting Is Spanish Loyalist"; and "Harlem Ball Player Now Captain in Spain." The section ends with an article about Langston Hughes: "Afro Writer Nicked by Bullet in Spain."

The descriptive titles, some of them changed from the original by the newspaper, clearly summarize their content. Hughes does report on the black volunteers in the International Brigades, documenting a side of their history few other correspondents in Spain touched,[5] but these essays also consistently reflect his hatred of war and fascism, which preached belief in racial separation and the inferiority of darker people. Hughes encouraged black people everywhere to fight against that dogma. Hughes, like Richard Wright, felt contempt and dislike only for General Franco and his fascist government, not for the Spanish people, whose "total lack of color prejudice"[6] he praised. The Spaniards, he writes, "greet the music of Cab Calloway, Duke Ellington, and other orchestra leaders with the applause of seeing old familiars who have made good. They love Marian Anderson."[7]

Mullen includes Hughes's "Song of Spain," perhaps the most widely known poem he wrote on the theme of the Spanish Civil War.[8] Mullen also cites an interesting observation (about this poem) made by Paul Rogers, who received a copy of the manuscript from Hughes. Rogers noticed that Hughes wrongly quoted the opening lines of Cervantes' *Don Quixote*: "And I debated with myself whether to write of the error to Langston. Finally I did. He accepted with the utmost grace, and later when the poem was published, the quotation appeared in its correct form."[9] This antiwar poem, which urges workers to unite and "make no bombs" that would be used against Spain, shows Hughes's acquaintance with *Don Quixote* and Spanish culture. Hughes always loved the Spanish language and tried to read Cervantes' masterpiece in the original, "a great reading experience that possibly helped me to develop many years later in my own books a character called Simple."[10] The similarities are apparent, especially as described by John Henrik Clarke: "Simple is a man, like most men, in revolt against the world around him and those circumstances that are forever blocking the paths of his ambition. Simple is a dreamer and an optimist who is always willing to give the world a second chance."[11] That is Don Quixote exactly.

In "Song of Spain," Hughes reviews Spanish culture asking and answering the question: What is the song of Spain?

> *Flamenco* is the song of Spain:
> Gypsies, guitars, dancing
> ....
> *Toros* are the song of Spain:
> The bellowing bull, the red cape,
> ....
> *Pintura* is the song of Spain:
> Goya, Velázquez, Murillo,
> ....
> *La Maja Desnuda*'s
> The Song of Spain.
> ....
> Don Quixote: España!

But most important:

> The People are Spain.
> A worker's world
> Is the song of Spain.[12]

Mullen includes two other poems not in Berry's volume: "From Spain to Alabama" and "Letter from Spain Addressed to Alabama." "Letter from Spain" reflects a concern Claude McKay wrongly believed Hughes had ignored in his writings on Spain, namely, the North African native—the "illiterate African colonials forced to obey the commands of the fascist generals in power."[13] Hughes was saddened at the thought of Moors "just as dark as me"[14] fighting in favor of fascism; this poem and some of his prose, (for example, "Soldiers from Many Lands United in Spanish Fight") reflect his awareness that "the generals who now control North Africa and support Franco are the same generals who in the old days kept the Moors down by force, sent the Spanish army against them, and shot and starved them into submission."[15] For this reason Hughes admired "colored colonials" who joined the International Brigades and took up arms against Franco, and he was perplexed to find a "brother" fighting "against the free":

> . . . cause if a free Spain wins this war,
> The colonies, too, are free
> Then something wonderful'll happen
> To them Moors as dark as me.[16]

Mullen considers Hughes's Spanish stay his most intense and sustained relationship with the Hispanic world. During this period Hughes was extraordinarily active as a writer whose earlier attempts to decry racism and prejudice in poems from the *Crisis* and *The Weary Blues* "re-emerge here as a universalized assault on fascism and war."[17] While in Spain Hughes renewed his acquaintance with Nicolás Guillén. He also met the Spanish poets Rafael Alberti and Manuel Altolaguirre, who helped him get started on his translation of García Lorca's *Romancero gitano*, which he later published, and *Bodas de sangre*, which he did not. Hughes further honored García Lorca's memory by writing a piece for a radio broadcast in Madrid titled "Spain's Martyred Poet, García Lorca."[18] In *I Wonder as I Wander*, Hughes writes that while translating Lorca's *Gypsy Ballads*, he came across some statements from the poems as to the meaning of art. For Lorca art was life and life art, with no gulf between the artist and the people. The quote from Lorca with which he agreed was "The poem, the song, the picture is only water drawn from the well of the people, and it should be given back to them in a cup of beauty, so that they may drink, and in drinking understand themselves."[19] Just as Hughes's Jessie B. Semple ("Simple") owes something to Don Quixote, Hughes's thinking on art and life derives benefit from García Lorca, the martyred Spanish poet. Hughes also met in Spain the acclaimed poet Miguel Hernández, whom he greatly admired.[20]

Hughes was enamored of Spanish culture, having been first exposed to Spanish literature—and bullfights—in Mexico. "Nothing in the Spanish cultural tradition, except perhaps a bullfight, excited Hughes more than gypsy flamenco music."[21] R. Baxter Miller, in his reading of Hughes's autobiographies, points out the symbolic meaning of some of Hughes's experiences during the Spanish Civil War. Miller focuses, for example, on Hughes's great appreciation of Pastora Pavón, "La Niña de los Peines," the famous flamenco singer whose refusal to leave besieged Madrid signified, for the poet, human courage at its best. Hughes, who would hear La Niña sing many times, compared her flamenco to blues of the Black South because "despite the heartbreak implied, it signified the endurance of a people."[22] The spiritual intensity of La Niña, Hughes's "gypsy self," captivated the black poet; it symbolized for him the belief that great art subsumes and transcends great pain. It seemed to Hughes that her "bluesque and symbolic song"[23] resisted both war and death.

During his time in Spain, Hughes visited the sixteenth-century monastery and palace of Escorial, one of the few places not destroyed by bombs and "one of Hughes's few memories of what had once been the glory and history of Spain."[24] Hughes loved Spain and he hated to leave despite the danger, but he also loved America, even with its faults. He did not expatriate like Wright, Himes, and Baldwin nor did he take up prolonged residence in Spain as did Yerby. Hughes never did write a book about Spain, although he had hoped to publish a booklet of the 22 articles he wrote on Spain, to be called "Negroes in Spain," in which he planned to include "portraits of individual blacks on both sides of the fighting."[25] He never did.

Claude McKay's relationship with Spain is just as interesting as Langston Hughes's. McKay, who stayed outside the United States for years, spent a great deal of time in Spain in the late

1920s, especially in Barcelona. Reportedly in Spain, McKay found his religious feelings strongly awakened and he fell in love with the Catholic religion.[26] He was equally impressed with the distinctive quality of the Spanish people. In 1929 McKay wrote to William A. Bradley that

> French life is too nervous and sharp for my temperament. It may be that I exaggerate but as soon as I crossed the border (into Spain) I felt as if I had escaped from a swarm of wasps to find myself among a people who can appreciate simple dignity when they meet with it, because dignity is a fundamental of their social life. This is my fourth visit to Spain and each time my liking increases. I am afraid I shall at last grow romantic about *some* country.[27]

Spain was a revelation for McKay, and he quickly developed his preference for the people and the culture of that country and of Morocco, where he, in fact, lived from 1931 to 1934, returning thereafter to the United States. During one of his stays in Spain, McKay began work on the novel *Romance in Marseille*, which he completed in 1930.[28]

The basic reason for black expatriation was a desire "to escape from . . . the suffocating ghetto of color consciousness"[29] in the United States. McKay did not feel this suffocation in Spain. Unlike Richard Wright, who was later to look negatively at Spain's role in bringing black slaves to the New World, McKay considered Spain to be the "romantic European country, which gave the Caribbean islands their early names and terribly exciting tales of caribs and conquistadors, buccaneers, and golden galleons and sugar cane, rum, and African slaves."[30] In 1918, years before he actually went, McKay had been tantalized by the thought of a vacation in Spain when a white friend suggested and planned a trip for him:

> Yet as much as I was ready for a holiday from Harlem and though the idea was a vast surprise, I did not accept it right away. I was interested to know the details. Mr. Gray's plan was that I should be the guest of himself and his sister on a trip to Spain, where I could spend a year, or even two writing. They had lived in Spain before and thought that living there after the war would be more agreeable than in any other European country because Spain had kept out of the World War. (1970, p. 40)

As much as he had wanted that holiday in Spain, McKay did not accept. "I had my doubts that I could be comfortable, much less happy, as their guest."

McKay's passion for Spain and for North Africa led him logically, being a black poet himself, to greatly appreciate the poetry of Antar, the black Arabian poet who was born a slave and who "is as great in Arabian literature as Homer in Greek." On Antar's importance to Spain and the rest of Europe, McKay quotes W. A. Clouston, an authority on Arabian poetry: "It is far from impossible that the famous romance of Antar produced the model for the earliest of the romances of chivalry," adding that "certainly it was the Arabian poets who, upon the Arab conquest of Spain, introduced lyric feeling into the rude and barbaric accents of the Europeans." McKay then quotes some verses of Antar that include the line "My blackness has not diminished my glory," reiterating that such verses as these written more than twelve centuries ago are more modern and full of meaning for blacks than is Homer.

McKay remained abroad during most of the years "when the Negro was in vogue." He made his home, writes Addison Gayle Jr., "wherever his fancy of the moment drove him—Paris, London, Spain, Morocco. In each place, he left a poem, a memento in verse. In France, ill and despondent, he wrote the pessimistic 'The City.' In Spain, in good health and good spirits, he sang of Barcelona, recreating the spirit of his beloved Jamaica."[31] Of all of Spain, Barcelona was the most captivating to McKay. His three poems on Barcelona reflect his fascination with the color and liveliness of that city:

> Oh Barcelona, queen of Europe's cities,
> From dulcet thoughts of you my guts are twisted
> With bitter pain of longing for your sights,
> ....
> Your color flaming in the dance of life. (1970, pp. 326–27)

McKay returned often to Barcelona, and he has described some of these visits:

> I went to Barcelona with my friend the Senagalese boxer, who had a bout there. Barcelona took my sight and feelings so entirely that it was impossible for me to leave when the boxer

was returning to Marseilles. The magnificent spectacle of the sporting spirit of the Spaniards captured my senses and made me an *aficionado* of Spain. I had never been among any white people who gave such a splendid impression of sporting impartiality, and with such grand gestures. Whether it was boxing between a white and a black or a duel between man and beast in the arena or a football match between a Spanish and a foreign team, the Spaniards' main interest lay in the technical excellencies of the sport and the best opponent winning. I pursued the Spanish sporting spirit into the popular theaters, where the *flamenco* is seen and the Andalusian melodies are heard. In no other country have I seen a people's audience so exigent in demanding the best an artist can give, so ruthless in turning thumbs down on a bad artist, and so generous in applauding an excellent performance.

The three days I had intended to spend in Barcelona were increased to over three months in Spain. (1970, p. 296)

Spain appealed to him because in addition to the "sporting impartiality" of the Spanish people there was a "strong African streak in its character." This remembrance of Africa in Spain inspired him to go on to Morocco where he found "a group of pure Negroes" that reminded him even more of his native Jamaica. Because of the Moorish or African impact in Spain, McKay literally saw that country as an "antique bridge between Africa and Europe." Even when he was in Africa, McKay "hankered" after Spain. He was always quick to defend Spain, at times prophetically.

McKay wrote about a French radical friend who had once chided him about his preference for a Spain "so medieval and religion-ridden." In a response that history has proven accurate, McKay wrote the friend that he expected more radical changes in medieval Spain than in nationalistic France:

That was no prophecy. The thing was in the air; students mentioned it to you on the café terraces, waiters spoke of it in the pensions and restaurants, chauffeurs spoke of their comrades murdered in Morocco by King Alfonso, bank clerks said a change was coming soon, and even guides had something to say. That was in the winter of 1929–1930. I was in Spain early in 1930 when the dictatorship of Primo de Rivera collapsed. In the spring of 1931, I was in Spanish Morocco when King Alfonso abdicated, and in Tetuan I witnessed a wonderful demonstration of amity and fraternity between the native Moorish and civilian Spanish populations. (1970, p. 325)

Like Langston Hughes, McKay was to write more about what was to become the Spanish Civil War. Unlike Hughes, however, McKay was most concerned with the reactionary colonial policy of Spain, having witnessed firsthand the injustices of the French and Spanish colonial regimes in North Africa. In fact, in telling of an incident involving Langston Hughes, McKay underscores what he considers a shortcoming of Hughes's own writings on the Spanish Civil War:

> Returning from a recent trip abroad, where he had gone as a delegate to one of the literary pow-wows of the Popular Front, my colleague Langston Hughes brought me a letter of greeting, scrawled in bad French and English, which he had received from a young Moroccan. . . .
>
> Mr. Hughes had also visited beleaguered Madrid and wrote excellent articles about the conditions prevailing there, which was published in the Negro press. In none of those articles did I discover any significant reference to the native problem of North Africa and its relation to the Spanish Civil War. How many Americans are aware that the native North African problem is similar in some aspects to the Afro-American problem in the South? (1970, p. 285)

McKay is not altogether right about Hughes, who was aware of the problem and of "the economic and racial ties between him and his Moorish brother."[32] McKay, however, is more political-minded when he speaks of the Spanish people's opposition to the war in Morocco and the blunders of the Spanish monarchy, and he posits this theory:

> If the first Spanish Republican government had reacted intelligently to the healthy, instinctive feelings of the Spanish people and abandoned Morocco, the face of Europe would be vastly different from what it is today.
>
> Had the African cemetery been abandoned, imperialistic France and Fascist Italy would inevitably have clashed over it, but the hopeful new Spain might have been saved. . . . By holding down its Moroccan colony, the Spanish gambled dangerously with its own existence and lost . . . when the executioner of the Spanish Republic was ready, he struck from Morocco. (1970, p. 287)

While McKay comes down hard on the Spanish monarchy, the Spanish Republican government, and certainly on "the executioner" General Franco himself, he saved his sharpest words for the French because of their intervention in North Africa and for "fascist Italy," looking at both from the perspective of the North African.

Richard Wright's sharpest words are for General Franco. His views of Spain are expressed at length in *Pagan Spain*, a controversial treatise published in 1957. Wright, who died in France in 1960, knew before he went to Spain in 1954 and again in 1955 that he was heading for a fascist state, but he went anyway because he wanted to see up close the country and the people that had had a social and historical role in slavery and in bringing black people to the New World. Spain's totalitarian government at the time repelled him, and this repulsion had already led him to publish some "harsh judgments" concerning Franco in the New York *Daily Worker*. Like Langston Hughes, Wright reacted strongly against racist regimes that fascist governments represented. Unlike Hughes, he did not go to Spain during the Civil War to observe it firsthand, but he did oppose Franco and did sympathize with the Republican cause.

Wright's curiosity to see how men and women once free now lived "after the death of the hope for freedom" outweighed his reservations about going and, taking Gertrude Stein's suggestion to see for himself, he resolved to do it. Wright expected no surprises in Spain. Having lived for a time in Argentina under Perón, he said he knew what life in Spain was going to be like. His *Pagan Spain* confirms the negative impression he carried with him to that country. In fact, the book is a belated vindication of his earlier opposition to Franco's rule. Wright really went to Spain both with an intolerance for fascist governments and with a prejudice against Spaniards who "dared the ocean to get slaves and sell them . . . men who followed Columbus across the Atlantic. . . ."[33]

This prejudice intensified when, once there, Wright found himself "looking at white people who were still caught in their age-old traditions,"[34] which he considered backward.

More than anything *Pagan Spain* is a condemnation of the way the country was being run and controlled. Wright wrote of poverty and exploitation in Spain and of a church and government that did nothing to help. He especially blamed the church, the state, and the rich for keeping the ordinary people in ignorance and poverty. Yet, though he hated the degradation of human life in Spain, the longer he was there the more he began to understand that underneath the repression there was a humanity he shared, a fraternity, a Christian fellowship that cut across class and racial lines. But this fellowship did not dissuade him from seeing religion as the cause of his negative characterization of Spain. When Wright makes a Mississippi/Spain analogy, he is referring to the oppression and the death of freedom that he saw in both places—in one because of race and in the other because of religion.

Much of the negative criticism of *Pagan Spain* is based on the opinion that the book tells more about Wright than about his purported subject.[35] The accuracy and acceptability of his interpretation of Spain, namely, that the country is more pagan than Catholic or Christian, is open to question. And if one judges by negative reviews, Wright lacked the understanding of foreign society necessary for accurate description.[36] Edward Margolies[37] (1969) believes, for example, that a number of Wright's conclusions in *Pagan Spain* appear to be drawn from his own black American experience. But it is to be expected that Wright's personal experiences would influence how he perceived events and conditions in Spain and would make him more sensitive to what was happening there. His conclusions in *Pagan Spain* are, of course, influenced by his own black American experience. To deny that experience and expect it to not offer perspective on what he saw in Spain and elsewhere, for that matter, is unreasonable. Wright's perspectives and experiences are what makes his writings on Spain highly original albeit controversial.

We should read Wright's *Pagan Spain* to learn his views on Spain and to gain insight into his beliefs. The book explains why he considered Spain to be similar in so many ways to Mississippi. Because of what he saw as the degradation of human life, Spain reminded Wright of Mississippi. Like Langston Hughes, who earlier had written: "Give Franco a hood and he would be a member of the Ku Klux Klan,"[38] Wright also is reminded of the Klan in Spain. For him it is the white robes and hoods of the church brotherhoods in Seville. He takes the analogy further, considering the hooded penitents protecting the Virgin to be the Spanish equivalent or version of the Ku Klux Klan protecting the "purity of white womanhood."

What most impressed or depressed Wright was the atmosphere of death he found hanging over Spain, which the fall of the Republic represents. With that fall went Spain's "dreams of freedom."[39] Wright, in fact, did not stop there. He objected to Franco and his treatment of the Spaniards under him. And he spoke with aversion of all "arrogant Europeans" whose missionary zeal instilled in them the belief that they could behave paternalistically toward more "primitive" cultures and that they were justified in overrunning Asia, Africa, and much of America. Wright mentions Cortés's conquest of Montezuma as a drama of a European-induced confrontation of cultures. Wright even took issue with the word *negro*, which he believed Spain gave to the world for U.S. blacks.[40]

Wright, then, not only saw similarities between Mississippi and Spain, but also saw this as part of "the white shadow of the West falling across the rest of the world."[41] David Bakish's summary of Wright's Spain-as-Mississippi analogy is the best:

> Wright felt strongly that Franco's dictatorship had reimposed in Spain a form of mental enslavement not unlike that which had petrified the land during the Catholic Inquisition of 1492 and resulted in the Moors and Jews being driven out or underground. With the accession of Franco to power, no religion other than Catholicism was tolerated. . . . The result of repression, whether it is Jim Crow Mississippi or Franco Spain is, for the survivors, a living death in which existence becomes a nightmare—hopeless, neverending. . . . This trip was a dream, a horrible nightmare, a calling up of underground emotions: fear and fire lynching the mind and body. It was Mississippi all over again. In Africa, Wright had been on foreign soil and he had felt it. In Spain, he had been "at home" in the Mississippi of his youth.
>
> In a strong sense, *Pagan Spain* was really about the emotional landscape of Mississippi. It was to lead Wright to turn again directly to Mississippi in *The Long Dream* (1958). He was to see that, for him, the best way to write on universal themes, to go beyond the racial theme, was to work through his roots and the fears that had formed him.[42]

Wright and several of the early black writers who went to Europe commented on the bullfight, which Langston Hughes,

Robert Hayden, and Clarence Major first saw in Mexico. Chester Himes especially will have words about that spectacle. Richard Wright considered it "the best-known of Spain's pagan rituals,"[43] one more manifestation of the "irrational paganism" to linger on in Spain after the Inquisition. Wright asks why the human heart hungers for this blood ritual, this sacrificial killing, "this man-made agony to assuage the emotional needs of man."[44] R. Baxter Miller, touching on areas for future study, has written about Wright and the bullfight, which he considers to be a highly neglected touchstone to Richard Wright's prose: "Here Wright concerns himself with the rituals through which Man (humankind), and therefore the artist, exorcises fear through epiphany in heroic form, the impending confrontation with terror and death."[45]

THE BLACK WRITER RESIDENT IN SPAIN

Although Chester Himes expatriated to France and other parts of Europe, he did eventually settle in southern Spain where he died in 1985. Himes is best known for his stories, his novels, and his life in France. However, he did leave some record of his experiences and his search for sanctuary and escape in Spain in both volumes of his autobiography, *The Quality of Hurt* (1972) and *My Life of Absurdity* (1976).[46]

Leaving London behind, Himes and Alva, his companion at the time, set off for Spain "with our houses on our backs," looking forward "to the hot sunshine on the sandy beaches of Mallorca." On board a Spanish train en route to Barcelona, Himes describes the unforgettable first impression Spain's beauty made on him:

> We were passing along the seashore, skirting the Pyrenees, when the sun rose. The sun came out of a sea of molten gold and tinted the steep mountainside, where grapevines grew in serried rows. A Spanish peasant sitting between me and the window began to hum the high-pitched stirring melody of the corrida that goes up and up until it falls like the bull at the moment of truth; a tune filled with glory and death, ineffably stirring. That strange golden sunrise ushered in by that mounting tune, the sea and the mountain, and Alva's withdrawal, became Spain for me, hurting, bewildering, heartbreakingly beautiful.[46]

In Mallorca they set out by train for Cala San Vicente via Inca in search of a friend who was to give them help, which they needed. Himes describes with humor one of the many predicaments in which they found themselves:

> When the train stopped at Inca and most of the peasants got off, taking their livestock, we were so happy to see them go that we forgot that we should have gotten off too. So we rode on in comparative peace to La Puebla, where the line came to an end, and when we finally alighted, we were surprised to find the station deserted and no buses in sight. The snow had turned to rain and it was raining cats and dogs—cold dogs and cold cats. We tried to find someone to give us some information, but it was the luncheon hour and the ticket booth was closed. . . . "Stationmaster," I shouted. "Ticket agent!" Why is it that we always assume people will understand our language if we shout? . . . I saw we weren't getting anywhere. In desperation, I shouted, "Taxi!" Dark faces broke into sudden grins. "Taxi, sí taxi!" Taxi is taxi in any language. (I, p. 276)

The description of their arrival in Mallorca, where Himes said he often felt like a "half-ass tourist," contains some of the most engaging and readable episodes in the book. Himes's encounters abroad among new, strange, foreign customs and language strike a universal chord. He is especially good at describing situations where the newly arrived realize they are the strange ones in the eyes of the "natives," and not the other way around. Himes is at his best as a writer when he is writing about himself. He can invent no story as remarkable or as readable as his own. From his first arrival in Mallorca, we know his life there will be an adventure because of the problems of settling in and making himself understood. Resolved never to learn Spanish or any other foreign language for that matter, a rare determination for a man who chose to live much of his life in foreign countries, Himes relied on English speakers, mostly white women, to translate.

Himes does not get too involved with ideological, political, metaphorical, or philosophical expression. Nevertheless, it is easy to admire the man and his work as John Williams unabashedly does. We see this admiration expressed in his interview with "my man Himes,"[47] as he calls him. Readers, myself included, even without knowing Himes personally, can share Williams's feelings about this "fiercely independent man" who often had to live "from hand to mouth." The interview was conducted in 1968 in Alicante. Like Himes on his first trip to Spain, Williams left from London "chilly, gray, and somber" for Alicante, the eastern Spanish city, which was "clear, bright, and warm." Going down the ramp after landing, Williams was "conscious once more of all the strange sweetness that lingers in the Spanish air, as though the entire nation had been freshly dipped in sherry or cognac." Williams is as sharp in catching this "sweet smell" of Spain as he is in capturing the "masculine" or "manly" essence of Himes's life and work.

Himes did not write a book about Spain, and he wrote few stories with a Spanish setting, but he did comment often about the scenery, people, and customs of Spain, conveying in a few lines his very personal vision of what he saw and experienced. True to his down-to-earth way of seeing things and to his obsession with sex, Himes, even in his discussion of the bullfight, focuses on what he calls their aphrodisiacal effects on some women; he does not interpret bullfights as Richard Wright does, on a higher symbolic, ritualistic, or philosophical level:

> We went on a bright hot Sunday and sat in the sun, and I saw my first and last and only bullfight. I was deeply moved. . . . I was moved by the music and the toreros and the sweating spectators and the hot bright sun. . . . I have always been moved by the forced contemplation of death. Alva was caught up too. . . . I think the deaths of bulls affected her strongly . . . and that night she engineered our sexual activity to the point of exhaustion. (I, p. 326)

On Spanish women Himes has this to say: "Spanish women are extraordinarily loyal. They don't read, they don't think, they are all good Catholics, and they marry and have babies." There are many such comments. Even his compliments turn out to be insulting: "The Spanish girls were never racists; they were too ignorant to be racists. They had never learned that the black man is a harlequin. The Spanish girls didn't read, couldn't read. They had only two books, the Bible and *Don Quixote*, and both meant practically the same thing to ignorant Spaniards." On his own ignorance as a black *norteamericano* in a foreign land unable to speak Spanish, Himes writes:

The Spanish people seemed to expect me to be ignorant so they could help me. It was a damn good thing too because I needed all the help I could get. And I was grateful for it. That made me *simpático*, as they called me. From the very first I was taken up by the Spanish people because of my ignorance and my race. Perhaps the French had done the same for the same reasons but I hadn't noticed—maybe because I hadn't needed it. (I, p. 272)

The main idea Himes conveys is that among the Spanish people "I forgot that I was black with them." He also concluded that the overall view in Spain was "no one in Spain believes any Spaniard is a racist." His best words in both volumes, however, are reserved for an English couple he met in Spain, Albert and Helen Hoare. These people, he wrote, "were as free of racial prejudice as anyone I've ever met. They were the type of people I came to Spain looking for, the type of people I wanted to meet and never found before. I had been all over Europe and America looking for white people like the Hoares. We became good friends and still are."

At one low point in 1957, Himes wrote that "I hadn't gotten anything from Spain but a dose of absurd jealousy. I had accomplished nothing; I had written nothing. I hadn't learned anything except how to cook *calamares* and octopus, which I had acquired a taste for." While these comments are largely the result of a particularly unproductive six-month period, they do relate to other remarks he made to John Williams regarding U.S. black writers abroad. Although Himes would not advise them to stay in America, he sees no reason why they should *not* stay in the States and write there. "There's nothing they can learn here, that's for sure. There's nothing they can learn about their craft or anything else from going to places like Paris." Himes adds that the only reason to go to Paris is to have some freedom of movement for a limited period of time. "But they won't even get any inspiration from being in France. *I* don't think they will."

Himes said that he wrote "Spanish Gin" from recollections of a party he and Alva had attended in Puerto de Pollenca. But consistent with his own advice that the point is not to be *there* but to be *outside* the United States, he wrote little fiction based on foreign locales. Spain and the rest of Europe do not inform his fiction and rarely appear in his novels and stories. The place or locale, while providing sanctuary and escape and the freedom to write, has no role in the writing itself, which, Himes contends, must come with practice and from writing, no matter where one happens to be. John Williams was very much impressed by how Himes was able to keep up with what was going on in the United States: "Most expatriate blacks I know tend not to care. Not so Chester Himes; his information is as fresh as the morning paper." Himes's own explanation was that much of his information comes from memory, since as a U.S. black there is no way of escaping forty some odd years of experience, "so I would put it to use in writing." On this same point, Himes always thought that the major mistake in Richard Wright's life was his not sticking to the black scene in the United States. He believed that Wright wouldn't have had to live in the United States, he could simply resort to memory.

Himes sought sanctuary and escape in Spain, but again consistent with his advice to other potential black expatriates he writes:

> I wanted to get away; I wanted to leave Cleveland and Ohio and all the United States of America and go somewhere . . . black people weren't considered the shit of the earth. It took me forty years to discover that such a place does not exist. (I, p. 48)

Frank Yerby got away too and lived in Madrid for several years until his death in 1991. Yerby is perhaps the best counter to Chester Himes's assertion that experience abroad and foreign locale in no way influence a "brother's" writing. Foreign locale and experience are very influential in Yerby's work. As a writer mainly of popular fiction and historical romance, he could take his subjects from all over the world, including Spain and Latin America. Although he later admitted "that discrimination compelled his exile,"[48] Yerby abandoned America "without shrieking that bigotry had exiled him from home."[49] Yerby, whose wife is Spanish, gives his reason for living in Spain in an interview published in 1984:

> Why did you prefer to settle in Spain? For racial reasons?
> France attracted me because I was curious to know the country of some of my ancestors, on my maternal grandfather's side. . . .
> Two of my great aunts still speak Creole. My interest in France,

then, is linked to the history of my own family. But in Paris I witnessed . . . an anti-Arab racism worse even than anti-black prejudice. . . . Racism, however, had absolutely nothing to do with my decision to settle in Spain. It simply happened that during a trip to Spain I met the woman who was to later become my wife. She grew up in France. We never consciously decided to live in Madrid rather than France. At the time we thought about returning to Paris and settling there or on the coast but her parents to whom she is very attached lived in Madrid and we stayed near them.[50]

This explanation shows that his decision to settle in Madrid had absolutely nothing to do with racism or with expatriation.

Yerby lived in Spain and wrote about that country, but he was equally interested in Spanish America, and he explains why:

My interest in Spanish America stems from the fact that, as a Negro (which means I had one black grandfather) I soon decided that the United States of America came second on the list of places I don't want to live, or even visit unnecessarily, number one being the Union of South Africa, and number three Rhodesia. So, over the years I have spent a fair amount of time in Cuba, Mexico, Venezuela, Guatemala, and Colombia. . . . I suppose I do have a special fondness for the people of Spanish America, because being physically indistinguishable from most of them, I feel at home among them.[51]

Yerby has given some additional information on his background: "My mother's family is of Scottish and Irish ancestry. . . . Absolutely all the members of my mother's family were white and blond. . . . Today all my cousins on that side are legally white."[52]

Yerby's knowledge of the Spanish language and of the geography and history of Spain and Spanish America makes his work especially interesting to Hispanists. *Odor of Sanctity* (1965), for example, is a historical romance set in Moorish Spain during the medieval crusades. It is well-researched even though Yerby alleged that Dial Press, his publisher, "excises 99 and 99/100 percent of his history."[53] Yerby has argued that this novel would have been great if Dial had had the courage to publish it "the way I wrote it."[54] While Yerby blamed his publisher for cutting much of the historical material and for "demanding more sex,"[55] his work still shows knowledge not only of Spanish and Spanish American geography and history but also of some of the major Latin American literary figures from the past. These include a 17th century celebrity, Mexican poet Sor Juana Inés de la Cruz; her contemporary, Juan del Valle Caviedes of Peru; and Plácido, Cuba's 19th century romantic poet and freedom fighter.

The action in *The Golden Hawk* (1948) moves around the Caribbean, Central America, and south to Lima. Yerby gives an accurate depiction of Sor Juana and describes her writings on the rights of women, referring directly to what he calls her "immortal answer to the Bishop of Puebla,"[56] a letter in which she passionately defends these rights. Much of the travelogue background description reflects Yerby's own travels around the area. But D. Reedy was able to confirm that Yerby's characterization of Caviedes, the 17th century satirical poet, was based on a biography written by Ricardo Palma in 1873. In *Floodtide* (1950) there is the heroic story of Plácido, the black Cuban poet who wrote poetry protesting injustices of the time and who died a martyr's death, executed by the Spanish authorities. Yerby writes about the death of Plácido and his fellow conspirators of the Conspiración de la Escalera: "*Cuba libre* was conceived that day though it kicks still in the womb of tomorrow waiting to be born."[57] Reedy finds Yerby's depiction of Latin American history and events, even down to minute details of revolutionary troop movements, to be "surprisingly accurate."[58]

Hispanic characters, customs, and history appear routinely in Yerby's novels, often in works that also have U.S. settings. Yerby's "deftness"[59] with Spanish customs has been recognized as an achievement that enabled him to create characters like Kit Gerard (Cristóbal Gerardo) and his father, don Luis del Toro, in *The Golden Hawk* as well as Ross Pary in *Floodtide*. Ross Pary is Mississippi-born but his background includes study in Spain and knowledge of the Spanish language. Yerby gives some of his Hispanic characters an enlightened view on slavery and race, and he portrays pro-abolitionist sentiment. In addition, he charted the revolutionary efforts in Cuba both to free the slaves and to win independence from Spain. In one scene in *Floodtide*, however, the Cuban Conchita Izquierdo makes what turns out to be a "some of my best friends are Mulattas" speech (reminiscent

of "When I meet 'em / I treat 'em / same as if they was people").[60] She makes this speech right after giving a traditional
Latin American disclaimer: "It so happens that I have not the
blood of blacks, but only Spanish and *Indio*, a little."[61] Yerby thus
allows his Hispanic character to have it both ways on the question of race: the liberal North American way and the Latin
American practice of admitting to "black" blood only when it
does not show or when it does, to claim Indian, "a little."

I suspect that Yerby used Izquierdo to disprove the Latin
American myth of no racial prejudice. This view is consistent
with his growing reputation as a debunker of historical myth. D.
Turner, who views Yerby in this way, focuses on the author's
attacks on the American South. He points out that in *Floodtide*,
according to Yerby, Americans did not fight to rid the Western
Hemisphere of Spanish tyranny. The Spanish American War
merely climaxed a half-century of agitation by Southerners eager
for more slave-holding territory. Yerby did not stop with the
United States:

> Turning from America Yerby has debunked myths of other
> lands. A currently popular idea, best described in Charles
> Silberman's *Crisis in Black and White*, attributes the ignominious
> position of the American Negro to Anglo-Saxon inexperience
> with slavery. Briefly, the thesis is that Spaniards and
> Frenchmen, accustomed to temporary slavery, attached no
> shame to the condition. Unfamiliar with it, the Anglo-Saxons
> justified it by arguing the natural inferiority and the predestined
> enslavement of Negroes. In rebuttal, Yerby has revealed that the
> Spanish massacred their slaves (*The Golden Hawk* and
> *Floodtide*).[62]

Yerby is known as a popular novelist of entertaining, historically accurate fiction. Turner is right, however, when he urges
that Yerby ought to be known as "an entertaining debunker of
historical myth,"[63] myths that include those dealing with Spain
and Latin America. Yerby feels "at home" among the Spanish
and the Spanish American peoples, but he does not spare them
from his attacks.

Delores Kendrick, a modern-day version of the poet as traveling star, has taken Langston Hughes's lead. She has traveled
widely, and recently she spent a year in Spain teaching. Her
poetry reflects her experiences, particularly her experiences in

Barcelona. The first section of *Now Is the Thing to Praise* (1984)[64] carries the title "From Barcelona." This book, her second, contains several poems with direct reference to that city where she found "Flamenco and the Blues," Barcelona, "where / flowers drip over / sides of balconies like / honey," a "Barcelona ... / best at afternoon / when the sky is sticky / and the streets water / in the sun."

Like Claude McKay's writing on Barcelona, her poems about Barcelona contain the same praise of that city, but it is combined with her own added awareness: "We Blacks / who live / in Barcelona" who find "temporary homage," the "soul space" of racial freedom. Blackness runs throughout her poetry, from the surprise of seeing a black drummer who, as part of a Spanish ensemble, "pushed / those bongoes into / the Spanish Blues / ... keeping the faith / as only he could," to historical blackness: in the Alhambra she finds the "Black imagination" of the Emir who built it and the "Black footstep" of the black man "the Moor dancing, Black / and ripe, in bloom, / full in his juices."

Kendrick's poetry, for the most part, reflects an urge to move beyond her confines. When she writes, "I must go to another place / another country" in the poem appropriately titled "Scatterings," we know that an international vision will inform her poetry. Though her book is dedicated, in part, to the poet Robert Hayden, himself a traveler, her world consciousness reminds one reviewer of "the breadth of Langston Hughes's *The Big Sea* or Ernest Hemingway's *For Whom the Bell Tolls*."[65] Kendrick's purpose for being in Spain is different from the past masters. Hughes, McKay, Wright, Himes, and Yerby had their individual reasons for going. Kendrick has her own intensely human reasons. As her train "groans toward Barcelona," she reflects in "Un Peu de Noir" on "the fascination that makes people pick up their roots and travel,"[66] and on the "compulsive and curious" like herself who "growing older, vunerable, too alive" travel to foreign lands, even at the risk and the pain of missing "the family / the house, the familiar talk."

This personal touch relates very well to the new humanism Clyde Taylor finds at the core of what he agrees is a new black "womanist"[67] perspective. He takes this term from Alice Walker's *In Search of Our Mothers' Gardens (1983)*. I will return to this concept in the next chapter, but what best characterizes it is a "rounder perspective" of life, one that includes but goes beyond the goal of sociopolitical freedom to restore "the place of love, growth, and healing as satisfactory resolution in both life and literature."[68] Kendrick's poetry belongs to the growing body of literature seeking a new balance among the various claims made on the black woman writer.

There are differences among the U.S. black writers who have written about Spain, but there are also similarities. All of them, not just Frank Yerby, have some ties to Latin America. Delores Kendrick has seen not only "Black virgins / all over Europe"; but also "monasteries / in Spain / in Mexico / in Greece." She has been not only in Yugoslavia "where the air is warm" but also in Mexico "where gods sleep in stone." Claude McKay vacationed in Mexico as did Richard Wright, who also spent time in Argentina. Chester Himes went to Mexico to write and Langston Hughes even lived there. I will return to some of these ties briefly in the next chapter.

Himes and Yerby have been criticized for not being involved ideologically and politically, but the often-controversial, Hispanic-oriented internationalism of Hughes, Wright, and McKay is still readable today. These past masters all spoke out on matters of race, although there is no absolute uniformity even on this matter. McKay had romantic views of Spain and its historical role in the Caribbean, while Wright and Yerby believed that one of the undeniable factors against Spain was precisely its role in the slave trade. Wright thought Spaniards backward on matters of religion and politics but liberal on race. Himes settled in Spain and recognized the beauty of the country but thought most white people at home and abroad were racist. McKay and Hughes saw no prejudice in Spain and felt color did not matter there. Indeed, of the Spanish people Hughes has written, "a sweeter, kinder people I've never seen."[69]

What is obvious and understandable is that McKay, Hughes, and Wright were never reluctant to condemn the abhorrent political system that existed in Spain during their time and to sympathize with the citizens who had to live under it. The older generation of U.S. black writers identified with supporters of Republican Spain, although they had begun to discover the Third World. It will be the new generation of U.S. black writers who will look further to embrace Africa and Latin America, which emerged after World War II as part of that Third World.[70]

Notes

1. Nancy Cunard, "Three Negro Poets," *Left Review* 2 (October 1937): 530.
2. See Richard L. Jackson, *The Black Image in Latin American Literature* (Albuquerque: University of New Mexico Press, 1976), 144, footnote 17, for lengthy bibliography on blacks in the literature of Spain in the Golden Age and before.
3. See Faith Berry, *Langston Hughes Before and Beyond Harlem* (Westport, Conn.: Lawrence Hill and Co., 1983), 254, and her edition *Langston Hughes—Good Morning Revolution: Uncollected Writings of Social Protest* (Westport, Conn.: Lawrence Hill and Co., 1973), 95. Also see Edward Mullen, *Langston Hughes in the Hispanic World and Haiti* (Hamden, Conn.: Archon Books, 1977), 9; and Arnold Rampersad, *The Life of Langston Hughes*, vol. I, *1902–1941: I, Too, Sing America* (New York: Oxford University Press, 1986), 339.
4. Berry, *Langston Hughes: Good Morning Revolution*, xii.
5. Berry, *Langston Hughes Before and Beyond Harlem*, 263.
6. Mullen, 147.
7. Ibid.
8. Ibid., 36.
9. Ibid., 45.
10. Langston Hughes, *I Wonder as I Wander* (New York: Rinehart, 1956), 291.
11. John Henrik Clarke, "Langston Hughes and Jesse B. Semple," *Freedomways* 8, no. 2 (1968): 167.
12. Mullen, 162–63.
13. Ibid., 126. Reprinted from *Experiment* (Summer 1949): 276, and from *The Volunteer for Liberty* (15 November 1937), 3, respectively.
14. Mullen, 156.
15. Ibid., 128.
16. Ibid., 157.
17. Ibid., 35.
18. Berry, *Langston Hughes Before and Beyond Harlem*, 262.
19. Reprinted by Eugene C. Holmes in "Langston Hughes Philosopher-Poet," *Freedomways* 8, no. 2 (1968): 150–51, with a discussion of this quote.
20. Berry, *Langston Hughes Before and Beyond Harlem*, 252.
21. Ibid., 268.
22. R. Baxter Miller, "'For a Moment I Wondered': Theory and Symbolic Form in the Autobiographies of Langston Hughes," *The Langston Hughes Review* 3, no. 4 (1984): 4.
23. Ibid., 4.
24. Berry, 268.
25. See Rampersad, *Life of Hughes*, vol. I, 350; and Berry, *Langston Hughes Before and Beyond Harlem*, 263.
26. Jean Wagner, *Black Poets of the United States* (Urbana: University of Illinois Press, 1973), 203. Also see Tyrone Tillery, *Claude McKay: A Black Poet's Struggle for Identity* (Amherst: University of Massachusetts Press, 1993).
27. Claude McKay to William A. Bradley, 2 October 1929, Bradley-McKay correspondence, Bradley Papers, Paris, in *The Passion of Claude McKay:*

Selected Poetry and Prose, 1912–1948, ed. Wayne F. Cooper (New York: Schocken Books, 1973), 346.

28. McKay, *The Passion*, 33.
29. Ibid., 35.
30. Claude McKay, *A Long Way from Home* (New York: Harcourt Brace and World, 1970), 41. All subsequent quotations are from this edition.
31. Addison Gayle Jr., *Claude McKay: The Black Poet at War* (Detroit: Broadside Press, 1972), 41.
32. Mullen, *Langston Hughes*, 36.
33. Ellen Wright and Michel Fabre, eds., *Richard Wright Reader* (New York: Harper, 1978), 110.
34. *Richard Wright Reader*, 110.
35. John M. Reilly, ed., *Richard Wright. The Critical Reception* (New York: Burt Franklin, 1978), xxxii.
36. Reilly, xxxii.
37. Edward Margolies, *The Art of Richard Wright* (Carbondale: Southern Illinois University Press, 1969).
38. Mullen, *Langston Hughes*, 129.
39. David Bakish, *Richard Wright* (New York: Frederick Ungar Publishing Co., 1973), 81.
40. Ibid., 80.
41. Ibid.
42. Ibid., 83.
43. Ibid., 85.
44. Ibid.
45. R. Baxter Miller, "Double Mirror: George E. Kent and the Scholarly Imagination," *Studies in Black American Literature* 2 (1986): 241.
46. Chester Himes, *The Quality of Hurt: The Autobiography of Chester Himes*, vol. I (New York: Doubleday and Co., 1972); and Chester Himes, *My Life of Absurdity: The Autobiography of Chester Himes*, vol. II (New York: Doubleday and Co., 1976). All quotes are from these editions.
47. John Williams, "My Man Himes," in *Amistad* I, ed. John Williams and Charles F. Harris (New York: Vintage Books, 1970), 25–93. Also see his "Barcelona Beckons," *Emerge* (March 1992), where he advised the Olympic visitor to reflect on the African American presence in Spain.
48. Darwin T. Turner, "Frank Yerby as Debunker," in *The Black Novelist*, ed. Robert Hemenway (Columbus: Charles E. Merrill Publishing Co., 1970), 66.
49. Turner, "Frank Yerby," 64.
50. Michel Fabre, "Entretien avec Frank Yerby," *Notre librairie* 77 (November–December 1984), 102.
51. In a letter to Daniel Reedy, 15 June 1968. Cited in Daniel Reedy, "Visión del caribe en las novelas de Frank Yerby," *Homenaje a Lydia Cabrera*, ed. Reinaldo Sánchez et al. (Miami: Ediciones Universal, 1978), 239.
52. Fabre, 102.
53. Turner, "Frank Yerby," 67.
54. Ibid.
55. Ibid., 71.
56. Frank Yerby, *The Golden Hawk* (New York: Dial Press, 1948): 111.

57. Frank Yerby, *Floodtide* (New York: Dial Press, 1950): 93.
58. Reedy, 236.
59. See Carl Milton Hughes, *The Negro Novelist* (New York: Citadel Press, 1953), 156.
60. Eugene Redmond, *Drum Voices: The Mission of Afro-American Poetry* (Garden City, N.Y.: Doubleday, 1976), 321.
61. Yerby, *Floodtide*, 57.
62. Turner, 70.
63. Ibid., 71.
64. Delores Kendrick, *Now Is the Thing to Praise* (Detroit: Lotus Press, 1984). All quotations are from this edition.
65. Beth Brown, "Four From Lotus Press," *College Language Association Journal* 29 (1985): 253.
66. Brown, 253.
67. Clyde Taylor, "Black Writing as Immanent Humanism," *The Southern Review* 21, no. 3 (1985). Also see Shirley Anne Williams, "Some Implications of Womanist Theory," *Callaloo* 9, no. 2 (1986): 303–8.
68. Taylor, "Black Writing," 795.
69. From a letter to Nöel Sullivan. Cited in Rampersad, *Life of Hughes*, 350.
70. In February 1993, a conference was held in Paris and was titled "African Americans and Europe." Participants examined the lives of black expatriates. Also of interest is the journal *Letras peninsulares*, which planned a special issue titled *Spain and the Americas: Literary and Cultural Cross-Currents* (Latin American and the United States).

TWO

U.S. Black Writers and Latin America

> Mexico . . . that nourishing land of
> light and color where I was
> somehow at home.
> —Audre Lorde[1]
> The Cuban trip was a turning
> point in my life.
> —Amiri Baraka[2]

FROM SPAIN TO LATIN AMERICA

Latin America appears from the very beginning in U.S. black prose literature. Jail in Havana is one of the events included in Hammon's brief work, *A Narrative of the Uncommon Sufferings and Surprising Deliverance of Briton Hammon* . . . (1760). Cuba is central in Martin Robison Delany's novel, *Blake, or the Huts of America: A Tale of the Mississippi Valley, the Southern United States, and Cuba* (1859): "Cuba, where the novel reaches its conclusion, was the object of dreams of North American slaveholders who would extend their empire by annexing the island to the United States, and it is literally the author's example of an Afro-American society in which rebellion might occur. . . . In posing the possibility of a self-determined Black Nation in Cuba, Delany expresses what must be called utopianism."[3]

Delany's imagined utopian conspiracy was inspired by a real one in Cuba in 1844, the Conspiración de la Escalera. Some believe the conspiracy probably was led by the African Cuban Plácido and that it was designed to free the slaves and give independence to Cuba.[4] Plácido, whose real name was Gabriel de la Concepción Valdés, was a popular subject in the United States in the 19th century because of his role in that conspiracy. His heroic life, his work, and his death by execution were of interest to many, especially abolitionists. Plácido literally was a legend in his own time, partly as Cuba's best-known romantic poet, but mostly because of his suspected leadership in the movements to free the slaves and Cuba. Later, in 1868, U.S. blacks supported the Cuban War of Independence, recognizing it as an antislavery struggle. They gave speeches, wrote editorials, and formed the Cuban Anti-Slavery Committee. At the end of the 19th century, U.S. black writers became interested in the Spanish American War. Black involvement in that war prompted the creation of a valuable body of U.S. black poetry and fiction, including work by James Weldon Johnson and Paul Laurence Dunbar.[5]

Despite this beginning, many black writers today follow the more recent example of Langston Hughes, the most famous black traveler to the Hispanic world. One of the best characterizations of Hughes's globetrotting was written by Carolyn Fowler:

> As a very young man he visited Mexico and sailed as a deckhand to Africa, the Caribbean, and Europe. He washed dishes in Parisian nightclubs, was a beachcomber in Genoa, and worked at a number of menial jobs in Washington. All of these activities took place during the 1920s, while his poetry was earning him a reputation as one of the finest Black American writers of the Harlem Renaissance. During the thirties, Hughes took up writing seriously as a career, but did not stop traveling. He went to Cuba, Haiti, the Soviet Union, China, and Japan before settling down in the 1940s to a more routine existence as poet, playwright, journalist, and prose writer. His contacts were wide and varied; his style was comfortable; his curiosity about ordinary people of all cultures, especially his own, insatiable.[6]

Hughes documented much of this travel in two autobiographies, *The Big Sea* (1942) and *I Wonder as I Wander* (1956).

Hughes, like Frank Yerby, Claude McKay, Richard Wright, and Chester Himes, was known for his writings on Spain, but he also had much in common with Latin Americans. He contributed early in this century to the outreach toward Latin America that U.S. black writers continue today. Profoundly rooted in his own black experience, Langston Hughes had been exposed to foreign culture, language, and people early in his career.

Hughes had spent time in Mexico and in Cuba long before he went to Spain to cover the Spanish Civil War. He writes of his experience in Mexico in the beginning of *The Big Sea*, his autobiography of the years up to the 1930s. Hughes also published some items for children in *The Brownies Book* in 1921 and a couple of articles in *The Crisis*: "The Virgin of Guadalupe" and

"Love in Mexico." These writings on Mexico are informative and interesting culturally, as are the pages on Mexico in his autobiography.

Hughes made his first trip to Mexico with his mother when he was about five or six years old. They spent a short time there while she attempted a reconciliation with his father, who had left the United States to work abroad and was at the time the manager of an electric plant in Toluca. Hughes returned in 1919 and spent the spring with his father and again in the summer of 1920, staying until September 1921. He returned once again in 1934 after the death of his father to settle his father's affairs and to renew acquaintances.

Hughes learned Spanish and read his first Spanish literature in Mexico, and he made important contacts there with Mexican writers, artists, and literary groups, as Edward Mullen and others have documented.[7] The most significant aspect of his time in Mexico, however, was the decisive, running confrontation he had with his father; the outcome was to determine his whole future direction as a writer. Just as his writing on the Spanish Civil War revealed his consistent opposition to fascism and war, his description in *The Big Sea* of his stay in Mexico brings out how different he was to be from his father, who wanted him to abandon America and his race. Hughes was to play a tremendously important role on the world stage, and from the first, he consistently made it clear to his father that abandoning America and his race was not part of his design.

Richard Wright spent time in Mexico as well, and he used his visit there in 1940 to contrast how blacks feel about being rejected in their native land. Wright "had insisted to John Steinbeck in Mexico that he intended to return to New York via the Jim Crow country of the deep South so that his memories wouldn't grow dim."[8] He uses his story, "How Jim Crow Feels,"[9] to capture the fear experienced by blacks in the South, the insults, and the lack of respect for their human dignity they had to endure. Wright described his own feelings and observations as he traveled in 1940, crossing the south from the Mexican border to the Atlantic seaboard. Reading this story, we find it easy to understand why Wright saw Spain under Franco as "Mississippi all over again." In this story he captures the atmosphere of fear and repression that characterizes a racist/fascist state in any form. It is also easy to understand the contrast Wright felt between Mexico, where he had been vacationing in the company of friends such as John Steinbeck and Herbert Kline, and the South, where his trip home to Mississippi involved segregated coaches. Trouble, of course, started at the border crossing from Mexico.

When he took the train north from Mexico City there were in his coach American whites, Mexicans, Germans, and Spaniards, among other nationalities:

> We were merely people riding a train and there was no trouble. But when we reached the Texas border, the beginning of the Land of the Free and The Home of the Brave, the races were separated. The Whites were put into one coach and the Negro— there was only one, me—was put into another coach. Then a queer kind of separation occurred in my coach. The white American conductor motioned some Mexicans in and made them sit at the far end of my coach. According to racial tradition in America, Mexicans seemed to hover somewhere between white people and Negroes.[10]

The degradation of human life he was to see years later in Spain was similar to the situation he depicts here. In *Pagan Spain*, the issue was not race but the same small regard for humanity. In this story, as in *Pagan Spain*, he focused on how such systems work on the mind: "In reciting these incidents, I have recounted no violence, no lynchings. I have merely presented the normal routine of daily relations between Negroes and Whites."[11] Wright was fully aware that any challenge to those rigid codes of conduct would lead to violence.

In 1944, four years after his trip to Mexico, Wright corre-sponded with Antonio Frasconi. Wright could not let pass unchallenged an assumption this Uruguayan painter wanted to make, namely, that there is no injustice in North and South America. Frasconi had been advised against representing the plight of blacks in his art, since recognition of such racist/fascist practices in this hemisphere would hinder, Frasconi was advised, the antifascist cause abroad. Wright argued to the con-trary that presenting the true black experience would clarify rather than work against the antifascist cause. Wright argued that an artist knowing the facts should not hesitate to speak or act. An honest expression of, or reaction to, the problem of blacks in North and South America would help remove such "social cancers" and would "create the deepest sense of unity between the Negro in North and South America, and other oppressed men, black or white, wherever they are found on earth. . . ."[12] Wright's reply turns into a plea that the artist create, not out of fear, but from the heart. This letter has been called "a lofty statement of Wright's firm belief in what literature could and should accomplish in relation to politics."[13]

We should also recall that Wright, in *Pagan Spain*, said that he had spent a year under the police terror of Perón in Buenos Aires. Some of his experiences there, where he went in 1950 to work on the first film version of *Native Son*, are recorded by John Pyros. In tracing the events that led up to the shooting of the film in Argentina, Pyros reveals what apparently turned out to be a costly ego trip for Wright. He writes that "one of the things that persuaded Wright to enter a partnership with persons of questionable artistic and financial means was their insistence that he play the leading male role."[14] Pyros discovered that, in efforts to escape anticipated huge Argentinian taxation of foreigners, Wright did not take out a legal work permit and, as an illegally employed alien, had difficulty getting his movie out of Argentina. Wright evidently lost money on the film, which was completed in Argentina during July 1950, and it apparently "died a quiet death in mid-summer."[15]

Although Chester Himes's long residence in Europe is better known than his time in Mexico, the thought of Mexico had intrigued him early in life. He was particularly interested in Tijuana, which he saw "inhabited by Mexicans who were a mixture of Spanish, Indian, and Negro. I could envision the dark-skinned caballeros, the black-eyed señoritas, a world of gay life, and the hot southern climate. More than anything else I wanted to go to Tijuana to employ the gambling skills I had learned, play the races, and sleep with the hot-bodied señoritas."[16] Himes did make it down later to Mérida and Sisal, not to live it up but to write, and he almost died there. On his arrival in Mexico, Himes showed the racial sensitivity that characterizes him: "The Mexican customs were rough, at least on black Americans like me. They looked at my few possessions, suitcase and typewriter, and sneered when I told them that I was a writer and asked me if I had enough to live on and finally the uneducated peon let me go."[17] During his short stay in Mexico, Himes made many observations, especially on life in Sisal, the small fishing village where he had come to write:

> The natives were all descendants of the Maya Indians, somewhat attractive. . . . The people did not do anything else in that town but fish; they fished for food and for a living. . . . For alcohol I learned to drink *pisa*, a cheap version of tequila, that was made in Mérida. Sisal, the village we lived in, was named after the cactus from which tequila and rope were made; the Mexicans had enormous sisal farms, which they cultivated.[18]

Himes comments on everything in sight including native hammocks, which "the natives slept on, two, three, or four at a time, and made love on, were born on, and died on. The hammock was the most essential piece of furniture in the country."[19] In true Himes fashion, the neighbor's daughter does not escape his eyes: "She was a pretty girl, mature in appearance, but not more than twelve or thirteen in age; and several times as she was cleaning my room, I was tempted to push her over on the bed. I knew she would not have objected and the main reason for not doing so was it would interfere with my work."[20] Himes described the stroke he had in Mexico, his two-week stay in the hospital in Mérida, and the SOS letters he wrote to "everyone I knew in New York and Paris."[21] Carl Van Vechten sent him enough money to get out of the hospital and back to New York, and from there Himes returned to Europe.

Chester Himes, Langston Hughes, Claude McKay, Richard Wright, and Frank Yerby were traveling around the Hispanic world in the 1920s, 1930s, 1940s, and early 1950s. These earlier writers who spent part of their literary careers traveling to Spain and Latin America are representative of much of the U.S. black writing that appeared in this century up to the 1960s. Since then newer writers like Robert Hayden, Michael Harper, and Amiri Baraka have made some of the same journeys, as have even newer ones (Hayden first published in the 1940s) like Gayle Jones, Paule Marshall, and Al Young. The emergence of the Third World phenomenon (which includes black identification with Africa and beyond) and the widespread impact of the United States on world affairs (particularly in the Western Hemisphere) are two factors that fueled the world outlook of younger black writers, both in the United States and in Latin

America. This new outlook includes the black "womanist" perspective mentioned earlier.

THE BLACK "WOMANIST" WRITER AND BRAZIL

Since the 1960s black women writers have become increasingly dominant in American literature. In fact, the most powerful "energy" in post-Wright black writing, according to Clyde Taylor,[22] is the black "womanist" perspective. He uses Walker's term to distinguish black feminism from white feminism. Essentially the womanist perspective responds to demands made on the black woman writer by black consciousness, feminism, and the Third World. Writing about her own life, June Jordan brought this perspective into sharp focus:

> You begin with your family and the kids on the block, and next you open your eyes to what you call your people and that leads you into Black English into Angola . . . leads you back to your own bed where you lie by yourself, wondering if you deserve to be peaceful or trusted or desired . . . or left to the freedom of your own faltering heart.[23]

I mentioned briefly the search for balance among claims on the black woman writer in our earlier discussion of Delores Kendrick in Spain. Other black women writers have brought their black consciousness to bear on Latin America and the Third World, especially on Brazil. Among them are Ntozake Shange, Paule Marshall, Toni Cade Bambara, and Gayle Jones.

Raised in a family grounded in Third World concerns, Ntozake Shange writes that "we used to go hear Latin music, jazz, and symphonies, to see ballets. . . . I was always aware that there were different kinds of black people all over the world because my father had friends from virtually all of the colonized French-, Spanish-, and English-speaking countries. So I knew I wasn't on this planet by myself. I had some connection with other people."[24] Shange's international compassion for others is clearly evident in *A Daughter's Geography* (1983), a collection of poems dedicated to male and female heroes of worldwide aesthetic and political revolution. Her geography is a "map of the world's oppression."[25] In "Bocas: A Daughter's Geography," she describes the conflicts in Mozambique, Angola, Salvador, and

Johannesburg. In addition, she writes about "the darkest soul of the Diaspora: Nicaragua, Costa Rica, Cuba, Puerto Rico . . . Panama."[26]

Shange's poem "Tween Itaparica and Itapuna" is a meditation on Brazilian history and the slave trade that nourished it:

> itaparica is an island / near salvador
> where my mother sat on a cannon
> that usedta guard slave ships comin to the new world
> ....
> itapua with a church on the highest hill
> like land houses in curaçao
> the safest place for slave owners
> on crests of waves of slaves
> who cd not move without being seen.[27]

French, Spanish, and Portuguese influences abound in Shange's poetry as she sings in a "New World Coro," which moves through male-female relationships to the struggle beyond, to larger conflicts that have enslaved both. "New World Coro," the last poem in the section titled "Bocas: A Daughter's Geography," repeats the following verses from the first poem, also called "Bocas: A Daughter's Geography":

> we have a daughter / mozambique
> we have a son / angola
> ....
> salvador and johannesburg / cannot speak
> the same language
> but we fight the same old men / in the new world[28]

The implication here is clear: the fight is the same in the New World as in Africa because, as she writes in "Hijo de las Americas," nothing can be taken for granted[29] anywhere. Shange has been to Cuba several times and was one of the leaders in the struggle against apartheid in South Africa. Shange's *A Daughter's Geography* is her international book, or at least part of it is. This book truly reflects the widening focus of black writers today.

Paule Marshall also has traveled to Latin America "gathering wisdom and imparting it in her works."[30] Her long story called simply "Brazil" from *Soul Clap Hands and Sing* (1961) reflects the time she spent there. Marshall's story takes place in Brazil and the protagonist, "the Great Caliban," is Brazilian; but the account of this old man and his search for self could be about anyone, anywhere. So while "Brazil" does have universal appeal, the story makes Marshall's knowledge about Brazil clear. It is reflected in her understanding of Portuguese, of the Latin lover/macho image, of the Brazilian musical atmosphere heavily laden with "the erotic beat of a samba,"[31] and of the *favela*, Brazil's slums. Her description leaves an indelible impression:

> Later, as Caliban climbed the first slope leading to the *favela*, his shoes became covered with red dust and clay. He could see just above him the beginning of the slums—a vast, squalid rookery for the poor of Rio clinging to the hill above Copacabana, a nest of shacks built with the refuse of the city: the discarded crates and boxes, bits of galvanized iron and tin, old worm-eaten boards and shingles—and all of this piled in confused, listing tiers along the hillside, the wood bleached gray by the sun. The *favela* was another city above. . . . It was an affront—for that squalor rising above Rio implied that Rio herself was only a pretense; it was a threat—for it seemed that at any moment the *favela* would collapse and hurtle down, burying the city below. (1968, p. 419)

Also, in this tale of advancing age and diminishing effectiveness on stage, Marshall manages in one paragraph to sum up, on the one hand, the racist aspect and the ignorance of the "ugly American" and, on the other, the Brazilian ethnic mix:

> In the beginning when Caliban's dark face had appeared around Miranda's white thigh, they had tensed, momentarily outraged and alarmed until, with smiles that kept slipping out of place, they had reminded each other that this was Brazil after all, where white was never wholly, no matter how pure it looked. They had begun laughing then in loud self-conscious gusts, turning to each other for cues and reassurance, whispering, "I don't know why I'm laughing. I don't understand a word of Spanish. Or is this the place where they speak Portuguese?" (1968, p. 404)

Marshall knows Brazil well, and she knows human nature. The strength of her story about the entertainer Heitor Baptist Guimares, "the Great Caliban," lies in her fine portrayal of his suffering as he experiences both an identity and a midlife crisis.

She is adept at depicting the flashes of youthful intensity and the decrepitness that characterize this old man. Marshall gets inside the character's mind and reflects his awareness and emotions and his realization that his talent has slipped away. Marshall's concept of community moves from her roots in Barbados to include Brazil, but her stage is really the entire world and especially "all the places where a stolen people were taken and where they carved for themselves a new world."[32]

Toni Cade Bambara, like Shange, has been to Cuba and like Paule Marshall she set one of her stories, "Corcovado," in the *favelas* of a Brazilian city. She put South American characters in "The Sea Birds Are Still Alive," and she wrote a story on wife-killing called "Minor Incident of Movement," which she says is based on a news item in Rio's *Jornal*.[33] Bambara describes the writing of *The Salt Eaters* (1980), her first novel, as bizarre. She was writing, she said, "and the next thing I know, my characters are talking in tongues: the street signs are changing on me. The terrain shifts and I'm in Brazil somewhere speaking Portuguese. I should mention that I've not been to Brazil yet, and I do not speak Portuguese."[34]

Toni Cade Bambara, Paule Marshall, and Ntozake Shange all depict Brazil, but no one does it more frequently than Gayle Jones. Jones earned a doctorate in arts from Brown University, where she was Michael Harper's student ("probably the best student I ever had").[35] She credits him with helping her develop the themes she brings out in her first novel, *Corregidora* (1975). Like Langston Hughes, Jones is familiar with *Don Quixote*, Cervantes' classic novel. She considers it one of her favorite books and includes it among her first influences.[36] When she reads the novel, Jones connects it with the picaresque African American slave narrative.[37]

Gayle Jones is well grounded in Latin American literature and history. In response to the question, "Have the Spanish novelists influenced your notions of fiction?" she made the following statement:

When you say Spanish novelists, I have to clarify and say Spanish American or Latin American novelists. (There's one Spanish novelist I like very much—that's Cervantes—but I haven't read many other Spanish novelists.) But the Latin American novelists— they're the ones. How have they influenced my notions of fiction?

Well, the two that I think of right off are Carlos Fuentes and Gabriel García Márquez. . . . Their influence has to do with the use of language, the kinds of imagery, the relationship between past and present. . . . They're technically innovative, but the technical innovation isn't devoid of its human implications. . . . Latin American writers as well as . . . black writers and native American writers . . . are always responsible. The human implications, the moral, social implications are always there. So I feel a kinship with Latin American writers. . . . They've helped to reinforce my own traditions. And I trust them. . . . The past two years . . . with the exception of Chaucer and Cervantes I've only read Latin American writers.[38]

Jones's interest in African Brazilian history led her to write *Corregidora* (1975) and other works like *Song for Annino* (1981). The latter tells the story of a slave revolt and a love relationship between a black man and a black woman in colonial Brazil. Jones, a leader among U.S. black writers who combine scholarly work with the creative act, returns to the Brazilian theme again and again. Often she develops short works into longer ones. Excerpts from *Song for Annino*, which took several years to complete, had appeared in 1976 as "Work in Progress" in *Obsidian*[39] and in 1979 as "Almeyda" in *Chant of Saints*.[40] "Ensinança"[41] is another story based on the black experience in Brazil.

While these stories are significant examples of her artistic treatment of black Brazilian history, *Corregidora* is her best-known work and is one of the best descriptions of black consciousness expressed in dialect. Ursa Corregidora, the protagonist, has been described as "the last female descendant of a brutal, sex-mad, incestuous Portuguese master who fathered slaves on his own daughters and granddaughters."[42] More than anything else, this is a novel of black female memory. Jones remembers the past and re-creates it, focusing in flashback form on generations of black women and the abuse they suffered from the early Portuguese slavetraders to today. She cannot forget:

"Forget what they went through."
"I cannot forget."
"Forget what you been through."
"I can't forget."
"Forget the past."
"I can't."[43]

Jones pictures the first generation of Portuguese in America as pimps and whoremongers with black slave women as their victims. *Corregidora* describes the perversity and immorality of whites as well as the sexist and racist exploitation and oppression of black women. She shows that these practices of the past continue today. By working the 200-year-old story of Palmares into the narrative, the novel captures the absolute and total disregard for black humanity, male and female, that existed during slavery. Palmares, the rebel slave community of colonial Brazil, continues to be a symbol of black dignity and the struggle for freedom even today.

Jones described what she had in mind for this novel and her technique for achieving it:

> I think that in the Corregidora story I was concerned with getting across a sense of an intimate history, and to contrast it with the broad, impersonal telling of the Corregidora story. Thus one reason for Ursa's telling her story and her mother's story is to contrast them with the "epic" almost impersonal history of Corregidora.[44]

True to the black womanist perspective, Gayle Jones is interested in the intimate self, not just the self in conflict with external institutions. Her work reflects what she sees as the difference between black women writers, especially of slave narratives, and men. That is, she concentrates on intimate relationships and personal history, not social grievances and the social implications of revolt.

Some fiction by black women writers deals with abuse black women suffer at the hands of their men. Jones's novel *Corregidora* seems to suggest that nothing black men do is as bad as what Corregidora did to the slave women. Corregidora is portrayed as the ultimate brutalizer of black women. Ursa, the pregnant protagonist, suffers abuse at the hands of her jealous husband, but this is not new for black women. While the movie version of Alice Walker's *The Color Purple* might not represent the typical black male, Ursa in *Corregidora* could be said to represent the black female abused throughout history. Mel Watkins[45] recently wrote that black women writers for the most part have concluded that sexism is more oppressive than racism. Gayle Jones, by moving back and forth from Ursa's own time with her black abusive husband to the incest, rape, and sexual violence suffered by slave women before her, makes it clear to the reader that they are equally abhorrent.

In *Song for Annino*, a long narrative poem, Gayle Jones takes us inside Palmares again, this time to tell a tender story of hope, a love story of a black man and woman during colonial times. In "Middle Passage," Robert Hayden (1975, p. 121) defines the Middle Passage as a "voyage whose chartings are unlove," using the term *unlove* to denote a total absence of love or compassion. Jones describes this unlove in her first novel *Corregidora*; in *Song for Annino* she tells us a love story. The tale of sexual exploitation in *Corregidora* and the story of black love in *Song for Annino* are both told by a female protagonist. Almeyda is the voice in the narrative poem. We see through her eyes. We hear her private conversations with herself and with others. And we feel the slaves' desire for freedom. Slave revolt frames the work, but Jones also manages to probe the psychology of her characters and the human relationships that motivate them in their slave stronghold. Jones tries to capture the feelings of the people inside Palmares before its final destruction. Similarly, in *Corregidora*, she contrasts the personal story of her female protagonist with the broad impersonal tale of the Portuguese slave master and the social types he represents.

Song for Annino gives an account of the slaves' escape from Palmares, of Almeyda's mutilation at the hands of Portuguese soldiers, and of her memories of better times with Annino. Times were hard, but through flashback Almeyda recalls the "good place" that was Palmares. She remembers the kindness and the love Annino had for her that extended beyond the merely physical. In a larger sense, *Song for Annino* is a spiritual journey through memory over time, a remembering beyond Palmares that establishes a place for blacks in the world. In this sense, *Song for Annino* is a story of hope and freedom, of perseverance, and of the will to survive. Through remembering one cannot just survive destruction but "survive it loving." In the end *Song for Annino*, perhaps more than anything else, is a song of heroism and of an enduring and sustaining love that transcends actions, death, and hardship.

MEXICAN INTERLUDES

Audre Lorde, who died in St. Croix in November 1992, recognized as did Gayle Jones and Alice Walker that black women writers explore human concerns somewhat differently than do men. Lorde, named the poet laureate of New York State in 1991, launched what she calls "a new feminist outlook"[46] (Walker's womanist perspective) for black women on the whole process. This new outlook, she says, is the origin of *The Cancer Journals* (1980). Refusing to define *feminist* in its archaic European sense, she advises black women not to be afraid to feel and not to be afraid to write about their feelings. This she does herself in *The Cancer Journals*, a three-part prose monologue about her own experience with mastectomy. In chapter 2 of this work, Lorde describes "a discrete episode, a Black Lesbian experience" (the subtitle of that part) that took place in Mexico years earlier. Lorde, on the whole, is thoroughly political in her work, but that episode was as important to her poetic and her personal awareness as any other. In fact, the same can be said about her entire Mexican experience, which she described at length again in *Zami: A New Spelling of My Name*,[47] her "biomythography," to use her term for it.

Lorde's trip to Mexico, which she had long awaited and planned, came at the right time for her. Returning to New York after her father's death, Mexico became her chief goal. The idea of Mexico "shone like a beacon that I could count on, keeping me steady." Her departure to Mexico was like an escape from New York, leaving behind problems of personal relationships, family tragedy, and political disappointment, namely the electrocution of Ethel and Julius Rosenberg, for whose freedom she had worked. Lorde personalizes Mexico, converting the country into a wish fulfillment that even she could not explain:

> I don't know why I was seized with such a desire to go to Mexico. Ever since I could remember, Mexico had been the accessible land of color and fantasy and delight, full of sun, music, and song. And from civics and geography in grade school, I knew it was attached to where I lived and that intrigued me. That meant if need be, I could always walk there. (1982, p. 147)

Mexico City was "a sea of strange sounds and smells and experiences that I swam into with delight daily ... moving through streets filled with people with brown faces had a profound and exhilarating effect upon me, unlike any other experience I had ever known." Defining her exhilaration more precisely, Lorde explains the comfort she felt being in Mexico:

Friendly strangers, passing smiles. Admiring and questioning glances, the sense of being somewhere I wanted to be and had chosen. Being noticed, and accepted without being known, gave me a social contour and surety as I moved through the city sightseeing, and I felt bold and adventurous and special. (1982, p. 154)

The friendliness of the people in the street who "smiled without knowing me" together with an ever-present festive feeling of color and light added to her delight in being in Mexico, where she felt herself "unfolding like some large flower." The liberating effect of Mexico changed old habits:

It was in Mexico City those first few weeks that I started to break my life-long habit of looking down at my feet as I walked along the street. There was always so much to see and so many interesting and open faces to read that I practiced holding my head up as I walked, and the sun felt hot and good on my face. Wherever I went, there were brown faces of every hue meeting mine, and seeing my own color reflected upon the streets in such great numbers was an affirmation for me that was brand new and very exciting. I had never felt visible before, nor even known I lacked it. (1982, p. 156)

Lorde eventually settled in the American colony of Cuernavaca with Eudora, a newspaper woman who had lost her job in Chicago over a byline on the Scottsboro case and who, like Lorde herself, had lost a breast to cancer surgery. Lorde learned much from Eudora about love, both of women and of Mexico, Eudora's adopted land.

Eudora helped her feel at home in Mexico. It was Eudora "who showed me the way to the Mexico I had come looking for . . . in this land of color and dark people who said *negro* and meant something beautiful." In Mexico, Audre Lorde felt at home, validated, and visible. Her stay there gave her promise and hope and put her "actively into a context that felt like progress." Mexico to Lorde was a "wakening." In short, "It was in Mexico that I stopped feeling invisible." Lorde also wrote about Mexico, in her early poem "Oaxaca," where the "land moves slowly under the carving drag of wood."[48]

Langston Hughes had his Mexican interlude in the 1920s and 1930s, Richard Wright in the 1940s, and Chester Himes in the 1950s. Later black writers like Audre Lorde continued to trek south of the border, and what some of them write clearly reflects their experiences in what Langston Hughes called a "beautiful neighbor country." Henry Dumas, for example, who could write "with a verbal intensity, in the manner of Nicolás Guillén, the Afro-Cuban poet,"[49] in "Ngoma" chose instead to cast a poetic glance in the direction of Mexico to invoke an air of anticipation and arrival. In his poem "Mexico Through a Clear Window," he wrote: "I want you . . . to leap high in the sky / with me until I see / yellow trees and the blue gulf." The Pulitzer Prize–winning poet Yusef Komunyakaa, whose remembrances are captured in "Mexico Memorabilia," transfers "black blues" south of the border to characterize Mexican sorrow, or "lamentations of Ixtilton."[50] Further, in an allusion to the African-related Olmec civilization Komunyakaa writes:

> The cabeza colosal
> Chants an African
> arpeggio
> Puts a spell on people
> and dung drops from startled mouths. (1975, p. 79)

Komunyakaa, who was a student at the University of Colorado when he published this poem, has managed to incorporate black cultural signposts, adapting them to Mexico's own history but with a current social comment.

Clarence Major's poem "Is Natural, Takes Me In" includes the following verses:

> my sense
> of my self a
> black self
> unshocking to
> Mexican eyes[51]

These lines contain the key, the reason why some blacks, certainly Audre Lorde, felt comfortable in Mexico. In two other poems, "In Chapala, Jal" and "Guadalajara," Major writes about his Mexican experience that, however unshocking his blackness was to Mexican eyes, included some unpleasantries like "a red mud / colored 30 pesos per day hotel room, . . ." and "sick looking dogs" that drag themselves along the "filthy streets" of

Tizapan, and "everywhere the horror of so many / Texas license plates / I want to blow this town baby / in the morning we go back to Guadalajara." Major finds Guadalajara to be a "beautiful city" but marred by the presence of "just as many Arkansas and Texas eyes as in the shitty town Chapala." And in sharp contrast to "unshocking to Mexican eyes," Major refers to the owners of the Arkansas and Texas eyes:

> The dead skin of their boneskull
> cracks as they perceive
> us Africa & Europe in the
> Mexican rain married without
> raincoats
> after 6 splendid weeks
> ....
> still in my sanity. (1976, p. 86)

In a conversation about *No* (1973), his second book of fiction, Major says that the bullfight scene in it "came out of an idea I had. I've never had a dream like that and naturally I've never jumped in a bullring and challenged a bull. But in Mexico I saw a boy in a bullring."[52] He goes on to explain how the boy got his stomach ripped open and suggests that incident probably inspired his own fictional account of an unauthorized person going into the bullring. Moses, Major's character in that novel, explains the meaning of his daring confrontation with the bulls: "I felt that, if I could touch the bull's head, and survive such a feat, life, from this perhaps unworthy moment, would be invested with essence. . . . I touched his head and in a strange and beautiful way that single act became for me a living symbol of my own human freedom." Major also talks about *All Night Visitors* (1969) and about a long section he wrote in Mexico "at top speed" called "Scat" that ran nonstop for sixty pages but was cut.

Al Young, like Clarence Major, has been to Mexico and Spain as well. In fact, since Spanish was his major, he could be considered a specialist in Hispanism. His work, both his prose and his poetry, shows his experience in the Hispanic world. I particularly like his "arrival" poems, especially those about big Hispanic cities. In these poems he intertwines personal reminiscences with exposure to new places, customs, politics, and people. His poem, "I arrive in Madrid," comments on Spain's political system and links his experiences to memories of his mother:

> So this is dictatorship
> a watery Monday morning
> smell of the Atlantic
> .... salty
> like the taste of my mother's tears
>
> ....
> . . . Spain was the name of some country
> she knew from the words of some popular song
> publicized over the radio,[53]

And "Malagueña Salerosa" contains these words:

> I always loved that Mariachi song,
> learned it on the Three Gold Star Bus
> runs out of ratty Tijuana on out
> thru dusty Sonora where they stop you
> for no reason to search your bags
>
> ....
> on up to Michoacán my green Indian dream
> to the top of it all—Mexico D.F. (1965, p. 58)

While the poet goes along "exploring time" in search of adventure, romance, tenderness, and love, he does not fail to note "a poverty even wine cannot shut out" or to feel that "the wretched of the earth are my brothers." Nor does he fail to poeticize the practical side of foreign travel: "For me / There is language and Spanish to cope with," or "midtown Madrid / Sept. 1963 / young and dumb and lonesome / a long way from home . . . / right up the street from where Quixote's Cervantes once died," or "me so sad for my only California."

Young's sojourns do bring the reader down to earth as he goes "tripping up calle Shakespeare, / arm in arm with joyous Doris . . ." when he describes "these fields of Jalisco / the flowery dungsmell / sweet organic smell of burro and milkcow." Again the natural odor of dung and body sweat is central to "Ponce de León / A Morning Walk," one of Young's best "Hispanic" poems. In this poem Young captures "One morning's moment in this / ageless / stone thoroughfare named after just one / dead Spaniard who wanted to live forever." The poem reflects all the hustle and bustle, sound, poverty, color, and smell that attack the senses in an atmosphere "where cosmetic fragrances mingle / with scents of ripe and overripe fruits / and vegetables, where the smell of breakfast / and dinner are almost the same."

Mexico to Al Young is not all dungsmell. In "Moon Watching by Lake Chapala" (prose he included among his poems), he has written: "It can be beautiful sitting by oneself all alone except for the world . . . at some remove, in spirit at least, from where they are busy building bombs and preparing concentration camps to put my people into." Mexico can be serene. The poet writes, "I am still free to be in love with . . . lights in the skies of high spring." Mexico "can be moon can be madness can be Maya," but despite the loneliness ("no one to drop in on, no one to drop in on me"), Young preferred his Mexican interlude to New York, San Francisco, and points in between littered with "not-together Bloods strung out on dreams."

Al Young has said that "for me it's touch that matters most,"[54] and touching other human beings is his strength—that is what he does. Young reaches out and touches the reader who sees Mexico in his poems in both new and sometimes familiar ways. Through his writings on Spain and Mexico, Young takes his place among the "original men and women striving to express and give shape to the unthinkable variety of feelings and thoughts in the black communities, which we weren't allowed to share in the 1960s say, when Black anger was all the rage and media made a killing."[55] Young's poetry is a poetry of "remembered places" like "Avenida Cinco de Mayo / Guadalajara Guadalaja." But sometimes a poem is not enough to "contain what I need to say. Sometimes the saying takes the form of an extended solo in prose, a short story, a novel."[56]

In his novel, *Who Is Angelina?* (1975), Young does explore problems that are often raised in his poetry such as identity, need, and loneliness. These problems are worked out, in part, during the protagonist's stay in Mexico. Angelina's itinerary calls for a sojourn to Mexico in search of the truth about herself. Her stay in Mexico provides some clues. Angelina knows what her "roots" are, but she is uncertain where that knowledge is taking her: "Everybody nowadays is busy digging for roots. Well, I know my roots. I know them well, and it doesn't make a damn bit of difference when it comes to making sense of who I am and why I make the kinds of mistakes I do."[57] Young has his protagonist trying desperately to understand her own feelings. The novel could be considered a reaction to the ideological rhetoric of the 1960s, when blacks were expected to constantly defend and define a black position.

In Mexico, Angelina does not have to constantly define herself as black; there she can pass as Latin and so escape the burden of having to deal with skin color. Young uses Mexico as an unpressured setting for working out Angelina's identity problem, a place where her character would not have to deal with the additional stress of race, and where she, like everyone she met, could be seen as an individual. To Young, the mixed culture of the Hispanic world represents an opening to the world and to the possibility of growth for the individual, because it is a setting free from ethnic humiliation. Young seems to be saying in this novel that people should know where their roots are, but that then they should go on from there to enrich and to realize themselves in the world. The novel implies that Mexico is a good place to start. Angelina's fictional existence in Mexico, in part, parallels Audre Lorde's real life: both found the soul space there necessary for comfortable acceptance of themselves as visible human beings.

The journey, as process of self-discovery, is important also in the poetry of Jay Wright, a 1986 MacArthur Foundation "search for geniuses" award winner. The poet as traveler characterizes several of his poems on physical travel to Mexican cities. "Jalapeña Gypsies" and "Morning, Leaving Calle Gigantes" are two examples. The poet is physically in Guadalajara, but there is also a spiritual journey, as self-knowledge and self-discovery are the result of those trips. But Wright goes beyond this process in his works; he also takes the reader on a journey through the culture and history of Africa, the Caribbean, North America, South America, and Europe.[58] Robert Stepto discusses the importance of journeys in Wright's art while raising at the same time what he calls "insidious culturally prescribed questions." Wright's multicultural poetry itself suggests:

> Is this poet black? Is this poet Catholic? (If he is a black Catholic, why?) Why does this poet go to South America? Are Ocumare and Cumana in *black* South America (somebody better check). Does this black poet consider South America home; if so, why? Why is there some Spanish in those lines? (How many black people "around here" know Spanish?)[59]

Wright, who has described himself as "black and bilingual" in "Bosques de Chapultepec,"[60] not only knows Spanish but also has read Spanish and Spanish American literature, among many others. This literature provides him with source material. "For me," he has said, "multiculturalism is the fundamental process of human history . . . no black African American can have escaped grounding in other cultures."[61] Wright admits he is a "bookish" poet, and it is not surprising to find the landscape of Mexico and South America and some of the indigenous cosmologies of those areas informing his poetry. As Stepto has noted, there is a good deal of Spanish incorporated in his poetry, and some of the references to foreign language and culture are clarified by the poet himself in footnotes. This use of diverse sources in his work partly accounts for his reputation as a "difficult poet," a learned poet, a discursive poet, a brilliantly intellectual poet."[62] Wright's own assessment of what he does is worth quoting: "A young man, hearing me read some of my poems, said that I seemed to be trying to weave together a lot of different things. My answer was that they are already woven; I'm just trying to uncover the weave."[63]

Born in Albuquerque, New Mexico, this black, bilingual poet from the Southwest has also been called, correctly, a "truly New World poet."[64] His knowledge of Spanish enabled him early on to build this reputation through what Langston Hughes called "a curious creative process—variations on themes from other poets, but rather good."[65] Hughes was referring to some poems the young Wright had sent for an anthology Hughes and Arna Bontemps were planning. The poems arrived too late for consideration but probably included Wright's now well-known poem "The Neighborhood House." This poem uses, as a point of departure, three poems by the African Cuban poet Nicolás Guillén: "Casa de vecindad," "Deportes," and "El apellido." From these three poems written in Spanish, Wright weaves a four-part poem of his own in English. He manages to capture the essence of Guillén (to "uncover the weave" that was "already woven") while projecting his own interpretation of the black New World experience:

So many people lie in this alley
we call it the neighborhood house.
....
the roofs are lined with young black boys,
threatening indifferently to jump.

It looks bombed-out here.
Bricks jut up like stubbled old men
....
a youth............................
. . . stands in this filthy garden
....
Tense drums beat in his eyes:
Yelofe, Bakongo, Banguila, Kumbá, Kongué.
....
I have a name,
an interminable name,
made from interminable names
....
and I live in the neighborhood house.
....
A house nurturing epic poets
who may sing no more. . . . [66]

Wright's message essentially is that young blacks seemingly without a future do have one, and a past and an identity too, which can enable them to rise above the despair and rubble of this "bombed out" and "filthy garden" of a neighborhood. They can do this despite the violence and indifference that surrounds them. From this alley called "the neighborhood house," even epic poets can be born. Though not as overtly political as Guillén, Jay Wright draws on Guillén for inspiration as part of his cross-cultural approach to poetry. When we read lines such as "I forget my name; / I forget my father's and mother's name,"[67] we again think of Guillén. Wright's poetry explores a "larger world," an "enhanced world" as he puts it, in which New World black culture, poetry, and consciousness play a large part.

Michael Harper has done something very similar, but he used New World paintings as a catalyst. Part of his interview with John Obrien follows:

Interviewer: A number of the poems in *Dear John, Dear Coltrane* concern Mexico. Did you spend much time there? How did it influence you? Did it affect your style?

Harper: Yes, I've been in Mexico. I spent a summer there. I used to live in Los Angeles and would commute down to Ensenada and places south of there. On this particular occasion, I spent a summer there with my wife and oldest son. I'm not sure whether it affected my style or not. What it did do was make me understand how to write about painting.[68]

Harper's poem, "Zócalo," on a painting by Diego Rivera, clearly demonstrates what he learned:

> We stand pinned
> to the electric mural
> of Mexican history
> and listen to a paid guide
> explain fresco technique
> and the vision of Diego Rivera:
> Cortés crippled with disease,
>
> ....
> Hidalgo forced into Independence
> . . . near him Montezuma. . .
> the mistake of his people:
>
> ....
> To your left Rockefeller
> Morgan, the atomic bomb,
> Wall Street, the pipeline to the Vatican;
> below, the Mexican people. . . .[69]

The poem like the mural deals as much with present-day Mexico as it does with history. In it Harper captures the essence of the Mexican muralist's view of the history of his country. He explains the message of the painting through the voice of the Mexican guide whose words, a pointed protest against America's might, end the poem: "take the painting, absorb it— / then give us back our land." Harper, intensely observant, was able to absorb and understand what he saw and then was able to reduce centuries of abuse, hypocrisy, and hope to a few well-chosen characterizations: Cortés, "crippled with disease;" Montezuma, the "mistake of his people;" Wall Street, the "pipeline to the Vatican." Harper's reputation as "an interpreter of the past, a historical poet,"[70] explains his attraction to the Mexican mural-as-history. In "Zócalo" Harper understands the present as an extension of the past, as it is reflected in Rivera's painting. The angle or perspective Harper takes in his presentation of that historical continuum illustrates what the poet himself considers being "historically responsible." A painting can be a conversation with the past. A poem can be too.

Harper remembers other things about Mexico, and he writes about them in "Remember Mexico":

> Villages of high quality
> merchandise—hand-tooled leather,
> ....
> the peasants clean
> tanned and bilingual:
> ....
> I think of Montezuma's
> unspeakable rites
> ....
> and Indian, and Indian
> farther up the mountainside.[71]

There is none of Al Young's dungsmell here. Rather, in this appropriately titled poem Michael Harper has sketched an almost idyllic setting. This poem, like "Zócalo," is very special because it portrays Mexicans, like other people in his poetry, as persons whose lives have an integrity and dignity won from having had to deal with things "meant to annihilate them."[72] Harper writes about people "who have been tested . . . people—black, white, or whatever—who have experienced hardship and loss and who have come through it."[73] This is a theme that interested Rivera also, and it is portrayed in the murals he painted. Michael Harper came away from Mexico with an understanding of more than just how to write about painting. His visits to Mexico and to Europe broadened his scope and interest in poetry and in the culture of other countries. And his travels had the added advantage of making him look more closely at the wealth of material in his own life.[74]

Perhaps the best-known group of poems on Mexico are those of Robert Hayden. He has given the title "An Inference of Mexico" to a set of eight poems, which he numbers as Nicolás Guillén did his set of eight in *Motivos de son* (1930). Hayden's poems, published in his *Selected Poems* (1966),[75] are (1) "Day of the Dead" (Tehuantepec), (2) "Mountains," (3) "Veracruz," (4) "Idol" (Coatlicue, Aztec goddess), (5) "Sub Specie Aeternitatis," (6) "Market," (7) "Kid" (Cuernavaca), and (8) "La corrida." In a conversation with Paul McClusky, Hayden provided extensive commentary on some of these poems and on his stay in Mexico.[76] The conversation is rich with insights into the poet, his art, his choice of form and, indeed the whole creative process.

The conversation is divided into five sections, each one dealing with major segments of the poet's career. Part 5, appropriately called "An Interlude in Mexico," concerns us here. Hayden considered his "interlude" in Mexico to be an important stage in his career, and thanks to a Ford Foundation grant, he was able to spend a year (during 1954 and 1955) traveling, studying, and writing. McClusky first asks Hayden what, as an artist and poet, he expected to accomplish there? Did he go to Mexico "consciously looking for poems"?

> **Hayden**: I suppose every poet, every artist, when he visits another country, hopes to replenish his resources, hopes to find material his imagination can make use of. . . . When I went to Mexico, I hoped to be stimulated to write, yes. . . . But I went to Mexico primarily because I wanted to experience another culture. I was a Spanish major in college, and I've always been intensely interested in Latin America, in everything Spanish. (1972, p. 195)

Hayden comments in detail about the background of the poem "Sub Specie Aeternitatis." It begins: "High amid / gothic rocks the altar stands / that honored once / a tippling fiercely joyous god / . . . ." The title, Hayden explains, "means 'under the aspect of eternity.' " He goes on to describe how the idea for the poem came to him after visiting a convent in Tepotzlán, a little Mexican town where the old gods and the ancient beliefs and customs still exist.

Hayden's idea of "the past within the present" in this poem stems from his own strong sense of history and his feeling for irony and contrast. In Mexico, he says, the impact of the past is everywhere dramatically apparent. This impact accounts "for some pretty startling contrasts":

> You will see Indian vendors in regional dress selling birds in the Paseo de la Reforma, Mexico City's most elegant boulevard. Modern buildings, almost futuristic in design, will have mosaic murals—fantastic, kaleidscopic—depicting scenes from Mexican history or simply blazing with Aztec symbols, Aztec iconography. The national cathedral is built on the site of an Aztec temple—actually over the ruins of it. There are the great pyramids of the sun and the moon built centuries ago. And the faces of the people often remind you of old Aztec masks. The

Mexican past seemed remarkably viable to me, gave Mexico its
special kind of ambience. (1972, p. 198)

At McClusky's urging, Hayden (pp. 199–200) talked at length
about "Market," another "Mexico" poem. The interviewer calls
this poem Hayden's "thinnest," in reference to how the poem
appears on the printed page. In the poem, "Ragged boys / lift
sweets" and haggle for "acid-green / and bloody gelatins" while
"*Turistas* pass" striding "on the hard good legs / money has
made them" amid "starveling dogs" and entreaties of "*Por caridad, por caridad*" from a "twist foot" beggar. This whole scene is
presided over by a "Fire King's / flashing mask of tin."

Both Hayden and McClusky agree that the poem, ostensibly a
picturesque description of a marketplace and the people seen
there, is more than that. While the poem vividly describes the
activity, color, exotic atmosphere, and squalor, Hayden
acknowledges he was after more than the merely picturesque:

> The market scene focuses impressions, certain feelings I had
> about Mexico—the harshness of existence for the poor; the indif-
> ference, or seeming indifference, to human misery I so often
> encountered there; the cruelty and beauty inherited from the past.
> The beggar in the poem unifies these, pulls the whole poem
> together so that it's a little drama, not simply description.

And he adds:

> I was thinking mostly of the large indoor market in Mexico City I
> went to a few times. But I also used imagery remembered from
> other markets I visited in Toluca, Puebla, Pátzcuaro. The things I
> describe might have been found in any of them. The crippled beg-
> gar, the boys, the dogs came readily to mind, since they are so
> much a part of any market scene in Mexico. (p. 201)

Hayden mentions that in the poem the beggars in the streets
speak Spanish, which suggests a lack of communication between
them and the affluent tourists.[77] He also refers to the symbolic tin
mask that appears in the last four lines of the poem, which, he
says,"can be interpreted as representing the dead, yet living past
of the Mexican Indian and the powerlessness of the old gods to
help him" (pp. 201–2).

McClusky and Hayden discuss "Kid," a third poem from the

Mexican collection. It tells the story of a child found with "home-less dogs / that worry sidewalk cafés / where gringos in dollar bills / deplore and sip . . ." (p. 202). Hayden explains that the child is a little boy he had observed in Cuernavaca, a tourist town with homeless kids left to fend for themselves. At this point the conversation turns toward a discussion of the artist and the temptation to argue for social, racial, and political causes, and toward the foreigner as gringo or outsider. Hayden declares that he is not "above the battle," but that he joins the fray as a poet, not as a spokesman for a cause. Because he speaks Spanish, he had no communication problems in Mexico, but he does recount how he learned from the Mexican people things he did not learn in college.

Hayden, with his knowledge of Spanish, his interest in all things Spanish, and his desire to learn about another culture, contrasts sharply with Chester Himes. Hayden went to Mexico perhaps in search of a little "soul space," but also to find new sources of inspiration. His academic background combined with his powers of observation enabled him to comprehend and express the spirit of Mexican culture. In the poem "Veracruz," Hayden writes: "Leap now / and cease from error / Escape." Fred Fetrow[78] considers the poem the least typical and most telling of the Mexican poems. Hayden had intended to go to Mexico "to loaf and invite the soul." But here, Fetrow believes, Hayden "bares" rather than invites the soul, turning more inward than outward.

Hayden, McClusky, and Fetrow do not mention "La corrida," but in this poem the poet combines the bullfight with his meditation on life and death. The poem dramatizes this meditation in the final two verses: "Die for us that death / may call us back to life. Olé!"[79] Using these words as a point of departure, Michael Harper has written that Hayden's poems "elegize and insist on man as an art form to be beautified: his concretized craftsman binds form in content that signifies the way."[80] In this poem the bullfight is portrayed as a "strict Christian allegory: the bull is death; the matador is Christ, who dies, but does not truly die, to conquer death for mankind."[81] The three-point focus in this poem covers all three players in the drama of death and life: first the bull, then the bullfight, and last the spectators themselves who, in Hayden's poem, turn the spectacle into a religious experience.

Hayden's Mexican poems reflect the man as well as what he observed there. This reflection is true not only in "Veracruz" and "La corrida," but also in "El Cristo." In this poem, Hayden discovers in a Mexican mannequin "an embodiment of the spiritual belief that suffering in the name of God is a supreme form of happiness."[82] Hayden's Mexican poems give the reader a good sense of the culture and the history of the place. There are Mexican customs and evocations of myth and ritual. He contrasts the magnificence of nature with the reality of children in need ("ragged boys"). He shows the poverty of the Mexican poor and their contempt for American tourists. William Hansell gives us a good summary of these poems:

> The "inference" of these combined poems may be that Mexico, for Hayden, represents a stage of spiritual development firmly in possession of the idea of a divinity, but still too much dominated by superstition, too much influenced by the primitive concept of gods as malign and cruel powers who demand bloody propitiation. Even the emphasis in "La corrida" on the bullfight-as-Mass, the ritual reenactment of Christ's crucifixion, suggests that violence excessively pervades this concept of divinity. . . . A further possible implication of the poems, taken as a unit, is that primitive faith in gods that demand absolute subservience is superior to the spiritual condition of the tourists. . . .[83]

These "inference of Mexico" poems tell us much about Mexico, and many of them can be read on a symbolic level as well, certainly those that refer in one way or another to death ("Day of the Dead," "Idol," "La corrida," "El Cristo," "Veracruz") and to the Mexican fascination with it. John Hatcher believes Hayden sees Mexican struggles as a reflection of his own.[84] Yet, a mark of Hayden's art, the poet himself believes, is his ability to keep a distance between his personal self and his literature. In an interview with John O'Brien, Hayden discusses Michael Harper's contrasting style: "I greatly admire the way Michael Harper, for example, makes poems out of personal experience. . . ."[85] In his own work, Hayden says, he uses a literary *persona*. Perhaps this approach accounts for the direct absence of blackness in his Mexican poems. But Hatcher has shown an integral relationship between Hayden's examination of Mexican culture and African American culture. Both cultures, as seen through the poet's eye, represent people "struggling for vitality and transcendence."[86] Also, as Vera Kutzinski[87] has shown, Hayden's poem titled "For a Young Artist" is linked to the black American canon.

"For a Young Artist" is the poet's tribute to Gabriel García Márquez. Márquez's short story titled "A Very Old Man with Enormous Wings" forms the basis for the poem. Michael Harper considers the poem to be the signature piece of Hayden's collection called *Angle of Ascent* (1975). Hayden believes artists should take note of this poem about a naked "angel"[88] who is found in a pigsty, who refuses to cover his nakedness, and who spends his nights continuously trying to rise up from his "seemingly bestial circumstance, the world of the pigsty." Kutzinski[89] sees black mythology and African tradition in this poem. She discusses Hayden's realization that certain texts in Latin American literature are vehicles for specific black American myths and allegories. She says this realization opens new possibilities for studying processes of canon-formation in American literature(s). The relationship between the poem and García Márquez's story, she concludes, is representative of a larger pattern of cross-cultural interpenetration in modern literature.[90]

Many U.S. black writers such as Robert Hayden and Michael Harper remember Mexico in their work because they returned from that country enriched. But not all the U.S. black writers who went to Mexico had pleasant experiences. Lindsay Patterson, for example, went to Mexico to write a novel but did not succeed, not even with Langston Hughes's blessing and encouragement. Patterson writes: "In October I decided to go to Mexico and work on another novel. Mr. Hughes hailed the decision by advising me to take more clothes than books. 'If you're well dressed,' he said, 'someone will always buy you a meal.' But Mexico turned out disastrous for me. I had completed only two short stories before I was stricken with a very painful and long illness. There was always a card or letter from Mr. Hughes, inquiring how I was and giving me encouragement."[91]

Charles Wright, author of *The Wig* (1966), *The Messenger* (1963), and *Absolutely Nothing to Get Alarmed About* (1973), is another U.S. black author who spent time in Mexico, but he often thought, "Oh, God, let me out of this place!"[92] Wright spent the summer of 1972 in Veracruz, and the change of locale "seemed to have rescued him from the terror of New York."[93] Wright talks about his experience in Mexico in an interview with John O'Brien, conducted partly by telephone while he was still in Mexico:

> **Interviewer**: This question may call forth an obvious answer because when we met last year in New York, you talked about wanting to leave the city, and both of your novels concern characters who are trying to escape there, but why did you go to Veracruz?
>
> **Wright**: Years ago Katherine Anne Porter was here in Veracruz. When I was younger, I was sort of hung up on Katherine Anne's work and I decided to come here. But, of course, things have changed for me after nine years. It's no longer a Graham Greene setting as it was then. I don't know whether you have read too much of Katherine Anne's work, but she was not totally happy in this particular city. The same can be said for me also.[94]

For Charles Wright, as for Chester Himes, a change of locale provided an escape and a certain distance from the United States, although the United States remained clear in his mind and appeared in his writing. Veracruz provided Wright with sanctuary and an escape from New York, and even though he was not happy there, Wright saw it as a better alternative to living in New York.

Blacks felt at home in Mexico, accepted and certainly not invisible. Whether traveling, vacationing, or studying, or just attempting to escape, most of the experiences they had there were positive ones that nourished and reaffirmed their humanity. Unlike earlier black writings on the Spanish Civil War, there is little of the overtly political in this Mexican writing. There is a good deal of productive soul searching and personal discovery as well as identification with the Mexican poor, but perhaps as Amiri Baraka wrote in 1960:

> We go to Mexico for a vacation. The place is a haven for bearded young men of my generation to go and make their "scene," but not one in a hundred will come back realizing that there are students there getting murdered and beaten because they are protesting against the fraudulent one-party regime that controls the country, which is backed to the hilt by our "well-meaning" government.[95]

Some U.S. black writers, conversely, went to Cuba, not for a vacation but to look for alternatives, notably Baraka himself in July 1960 and Lance Jeffers in 1976.

THE IMPACT OF CUBA AND CHILE

Even before traveling to Cuba, Baraka in 1959 had been fascinated by the headlines from Cuba and had wanted to publish a pamphlet in honor of Fidel Castro. The Cuban experience was one cause and, in the view of some critics, the main cause of Baraka's transformation from aesthetic to political protester. Baraka viewed that experience as the turning point of his life. He talks of the beginning of his conversion:

> I met Pablo Armando Fernández, the poet, and people at La Casa de Cuba, an arts center. We also visited ministries and got lectured to about what Cuba was trying to do. . . . I met intellectuals from all over Latin America, including a young woman, Rubi Bentancourt, from Yucatán, and Jaime Shelly, a poet from Mexico. These young people assaulted my pronouncements about not being political. It was the first time I'd been taken on so thoroughly and forcefully and by people my own age. . . . For twelve or fourteen hours on the train I was assailed for my bourgeois individualism. . . .[96]

Baraka met the great African Cuban poet Nicolás Guillén, who, he said, "asked me straight out where was Langston, and did I think Langston had gotten more conservative."[97] He met and talked with Fidel Castro and heard him speak "for perhaps two hours nonstop, relating the entire history of the revolution to the *campesinos*, soldiers, intellectuals, and foreign visitors. . . . It was a rare moment in one's life; and if the harangues of Rubi and Jaime and the others weren't enough, this final stroke was. . . . I carried so much back with me that I was never the same again. The dynamic of the revolution had touched me. . . . When I returned, I was shaken more deeply than even I realized. . . . It was not enough just to write, to feel, to think. One must act."[98]

Baraka acted but he also wrote a great deal about his Cuban experience, beginning with his essay "Cuba Libre,"[99] which won an award after being published in *The Evergreen Review*. Baraka said the award was the most money he had ever gotten for any of his writing. Following a brief preface, the essay is divided into two parts: "What I Brought to the Revolution" and "What I Brought Back Here." What he brought to the Revolution essentially was a determination to act. The essay is a detailed account first of his skepticism and then the beginning of the transformation that moved Baraka from black nationalism to socialist revolution, from the attitude "I'm a poet . . . what can I do?" to one that sought "a real alternative to America."

During his trip and shortly afterwards, Baraka also wrote poems about his Cuban experience. "Betancourt" and "The Disguise" reflect the great impression the young intellectuals he met in Cuba made on him. The poems are responses to conversations he had with Rubi Betancourt. Baraka even wrote an essay on Nicolás Guillén, one of several first developed as lectures in university courses he taught at Yale and George Washington and that he still teaches at State University at New York at Stony Brook. "It is obvious to me now," he writes, "that such essays as these [the others deal with Langston Hughes, Sembene Ousmane, Richard Wright, and Aimé Césaire] focusing on the great Pan-African writers are badly needed, since not only are black writers ignored by the racist U.S. academic establishment, but certainly Marxist criticism is important to correct the largely bourgeois-oriented criticism and 'analysis' of black literature that does exist."[100]

Baraka acknowledges that Guillén was heavily influenced by Langston Hughes and the Harlem Renaissance. He reviews the course of Guillén's career in poetry through all its stages, from his early Modernist time in the 1920s through the late 1960s, and he laments that Guillén, in his view one of the most popular writers in Latin America, was not as well known in the United States as he should have been. To Baraka, Guillén is "one of the great writers of the world," certainly "one of the best known writers in Spanish internationally."[101] To Baraka, the reason Guillén at the time was so little known in the United States is simple: "He is a poet of the people, he is an openly political poet, and lastly he is a Communist. One other reason, of course, is that Guillén is an Afro-Cuban."[102] While Baraka understands that Guillén's work is concerned with blackness and revolution, Baraka, like Guillén himself, does not see the Cuban as a poet of negritude in the manner of Senghor and Césaire. Rather, Baraka considers Guillén to be a true internationalist fighting for the liberation of humanity.

The Cuban experience was just as important to Lance Jeffers as it was to Baraka. In 1976 Jeffers went to Cuba with Robert Chrisman (who was later to meet and recognize the importance of Guillén) and members of *The Black Scholar* editorial staff. In response to a question posed by Doris Laryea about how his experience in Cuba affected him as a black man and as a writer, Jeffers replied:

> The Cuban experience was one of the most moving experiences I've ever had. It's the experience I had in Europe in 1944 and 1945 intensified—the experience of being able to forget about race. Except that in Cuba the emphasis on smashing ideas of race was intentional. Writing *The Flesh of the Young Men Is Burning*—which was about my Cuban experience—I cried continually, because in Cuba I was treated nonracially. There was none of this business of continually being reminded of your caste, which happens constantly in North Carolina and every part of America. In Cuba you were a human being every second of every hour. Foreigner ever, nigger never. It was a beautiful country psychologically.[103]

His Cuban experience accounts, perhaps, for what he admits is a progression in his work away from concentrating on the racial experience—not away from race, but to a broader conception of race, of the human experience in every black person.[104] Jeffers was profoundly touched by his treatment in Cuba. He singles out Eliseo Diego, the Cuban poet who translated two of Jeffers's poems into Spanish ("Trellis" and "When I Know the Power of My Black Hand") and published them in *Union, The Journal of Cuban Writers and Artists*. To Jeffers, his reception in Cuba with the group from *The Black Scholar* "was the kind of perfect warmth I received from poor black folk in San Francisco."[105]

The reception they received contrasted sharply with John Clytus's account[106] of his own (he felt none of that warmth) and with the experiences of Robert Williams, Eldridge Cleaver, and Stokely Carmichael. Since the Cuban Revolution, such criticism has been leveled at Cuba by blacks who accuse Castro of perpetuating a racist fraud. Castro labels as counterrevolutionary anyone who wishes to identify with blackness as Williams, Cleaver, and Carmichael did when they were there.

Robert Chrisman, publisher of *The Black Scholar*, and Robert Allen, the editor, wrote about their second visit to Cuba in 1978.

Their report appeared in 1980 in a special issue of the journal. Of particular interest is Robert Chrisman's report containing conversations he had with Nicolás Guillén. Chrisman recognizes Guillén's importance as Cuba's national poet and the significance of his early poetry of the 1930s. This poetry affirmed black pride and dignity in the language and meters of blacks. It "permanently changed the face of Cuban poetry."[107] The period has special significance for U.S. blacks, Chrisman reminds us, because Langston Hughes and Guillén formed a close friendship then that lasted until Hughes's death in 1967. "Did Langston ever see the Cuban Revolution?" Chrisman asked.

"No," was Guillén's response, "he died. It was the worst thing he could have done."[108]

Following an exchange of poetry reading, Guillén gave Chrisman a handful of photocopies:

> These are some letters Langston and I exchanged. Nobody from the States has published them. Langston was the first man to translate me in the U.S. Feel free to use them any way you want. Don't worry about Langston's Spanish. It was always a bit, here he paused, "tentative."[109]

Chrisman has since published these letters and I will return to them in the next chapter's more detailed discussion. The next chapter will show how Guillén, who has had an impact on black consciousness in the United States since the 1960s, was influenced by Hughes to write black poetry.

Since the 1960s, Guillén and Nancy Morejón, his protégé, have become, through translations of their work, better known in the United States and the rest of the world. Their poetry and support for the Cuban Revolution have made them as worthy of emulation, certainly among the literati seeking to link blackness, Third World causes, and feminist issues, as Che Guevara and Fidel Castro were earlier. Baraka's move from black nationalism to socialist revolution was a change in ideology like that of Nicolás Guillén. Other U.S. blacks less ideologically inclined, like Jay Wright, also drew on Guillén for inspiration. Yvonne Gullon Barrett,[110] in fact, sees spiritual ties between Guillén's earlier work and the black arts movement in the United States, considering his poem titled "Negro bembón" ("Big-Lipped Black") to be an early "Black Is Beautiful" statement.

Eugene Redmond has also placed Guillén into proper context for understanding his importance to blacks in the United States:

> During the sixties and into the seventies, literally hundreds of black poets started writing and publishing. . . . And the atmosphere was enhanced by a number of African thinkers, artists, poets, and novelists who arrived in America to teach, lecture, perform, and travel. The importance of this interaction among Blacks cannot be overemphasized. . . . Black writing received a significant boost when, in 1971, Senghor and Afro-Cuban poet Nicolás Guillén were nominated for the Nobel Prize for literature. . . .[111]

Guillén was nominated for the Nobel Prize, from 1971 on, until his death in 1989. Let Baraka have the last word on this nomination, and why, in his judgment Guillén never got it:

> His work is obscured only by the bourgeoisie in their attempts to keep Guillén's example and message and great work from the masses inside the capitalist countries. (The bourgeoisie would celebrate instead, with the Nobel Prize, an obscure surrealist like Alexandre in Spain—who did not even have to leave Spain during Franco's time, he was so weird.)[112]

Pablo Neruda, the Chilean poet who did receive the Nobel Prize, is mentioned by Baraka. Guillén, he writes, "wrote poems about the tragedy of Spain, as the Spanish fascists killed García Lorca—just as in the seventies the Chilean junta murdered the great Pablo Neruda."[113] Neruda's death, like García Lorca's, did not go unnoticed by U.S. black writers. Quincy Troupe, who has collaborated heavily in publications on the Third World, has written the poem titled "'These Crossings, These Words,"[114] for Pablo Neruda, a poem Baraka knew.

U.S. black writers have their foreign black heroes—Fanon, Nkruma, Lumumba, Mandela among them—but they also continue to acknowledge world-class figures from Latin America like Pablo Neruda and, of course, Che Guevara, the subject of a play by Lennox Raphael[115] and a long poem "For Che" by Conyus.[116] Today, with so many war zones worldwide, black writers' interests in politics, peace, and the survival of humanity cover the globe. Works international in scope, like June Jordan's *Living Room* (1985), Ai's *Sin* (1986), and Jayne Cortez's *Coagulations and Selected Poems* (1984), dramatize this widening concern. Even the Spanish Civil War, once considered the last great cause, is still evoked by Cyrus Cassells.

Cassells has written a long poem, "To the Cypress Again and Again,"[117] dedicated to the Catalan poet Salvador Espiu, in which he writes of "Catalonia. Exile. Theft. Horror of Franco" and asks "Damn it, what was I reaching for? / Something more than Cervantes' language." Cassells ("The name could be Mallorcan") also has written a poem in homage to Picasso: "These Are Not Brushstrokes" after a viewing of Guernica in Madrid. Cuba appears in Ai's "Cuba 1962" from her *Cruelty* (1976) and in Jayne Cortez's "When I look at Wilfredo Lam's painting."[118] Jay Wright continues to infuse his new work with Mexican and Latin American history, legend, and language. Some examples are "Guadalupe-Tonanzin," "Tlazoltéotl," and "Guadalajara,"[119] as well as *Boleros* and his play, *Daughters of the Water* (see note 67).

Cuba's Nicolás Guillén, who inspired some of Jay Wright's earlier poems as well as some of his most recent work, continues to grow in reputation in the United States because of ideology and also in recognition of his earlier poems of "Africanness." J. Bekunuru Kubayanda[120] did not see much of this "Africanness" in Guillén since 1959 and the triumph of the Cuban Revolution, but he did recognize Guillén's influence on Portuguese African negritude thinkers, and within Latin America, on Nicomedes Santa Cruz in Peru, and on Nancy Morejón in Cuba. I will return to these two writers in later chapters, but first let us look at the influence of U.S. black writers—especially Langston Hughes— on their Latin American black counterparts.

Notes

1. Audre Lorde, *Zami: A New Spelling of My Name* (New York: Crossing Press, 1982), 171.
2. Amiri Baraka, *The Autobiography of Leroi Jones* (New York: Freundlich Books, 1984), 163.
3. See John M. Reilly's study of these novels and others in "History Making Literature," in *Studies in Black American Literature II: Belief Versus Theory in Black American Literary Criticism*, ed. Joe Weixlmann and Chester J. Fontenot (Greenwood, Fla.: Penkevill Publishing Co., 1986), 85–120. Also see German J. Bienvenu, "The People of Delany's *Blake*," *College Language Association Journal* 36, no. 4 (1993): 406–29.
4. See Robert Chrisman, "Langston Hughes: Six Letters to Nicolás

Guillén," trans; Carmen Alegría, *The Black Scholar* 16, no. 4 (1985): 54. Plácido is a central character in the Cuban part of the novel, and Blake, in fact, is made to be Plácido's cousin. Blake himself is revealed to be a native Cuban, born Carolus Henrico Blacus. See Eric J. Sunquist, *To Wake the Nations: Race in the Making of American Literature* (Cambridge: Harvard University Press, 1993), 199.

5. See James Robert Payne, "Afro-American Literature of the Spanish-American War," *Melus* 10, no. 3 (1983): 19–32.
6. Carolyn Fowler, "The Shared Vision of Langston Hughes and Jacques Roumain," *Black American Literature Forum* 15, no. 3 (1981): 84.
7. Edward Mullen, *Langston Hughes in the Hispanic World and Haiti* (Hamden, Conn.: Archon Books, 1977), 9–46.
8. Edward Margolies, *The Art of Richard Wright* (Carbondale: Southern Illinois University Press, 1969), 43.
9. Richard Wright, "How Jim Crow Feels," *True: The Man's Magazine* (November 1946): 25–27, 154–56.
10. Ibid., 26.
11. Ibid., 156.
12. Ellen Wright and Michel Fabre, eds., *Richard Wright Reader* (New York: Harper and Row, 1978), 71.
13. *Richard Wright Reader*, 50.
14. John Pyros, "Richard Wright: A Black Novelist's Experience in Film," *Negro American Literature Forum* 9, no. 2 (1975): 53.
15. Ibid., 54.
16. Chester Himes, *The Quality of Hurt: The Autobiography of Chester Himes I* (New York: Doubleday, 1972), 48.
17. Ibid., 255.
18. Ibid., 257.
19. Ibid., 260.
20. Ibid., 258.
21. Ibid., 261.
22. Clyde Taylor, "Black Writing as Immanent Humanism," *The Southern Review* 21, no. 3 (1985): 790–800.
23. June Jordan, *Civil Wars* (Boston: Beacon Press, 1981), xi.
24. Claudia Tate, ed., *Black Women Writers at Work* (New York: Continuum, 1983), 157.
25. Beth Brown, "Book Review," *College Language Association Journal* 28 (1984): 379.
26. Ibid., 378. Cuba holds a "special place in her heart." See Donna Williams Vance, "Ntozake Shange Finds the Poetry in Sisterhood," *USA Today*, 6 December 1994, 50, where she quotes from *Liliane*, Shange's latest work: "No COLORED ONLY in Cuba. That's why my dreams went there."
27. Ntozake Shange, *A Daughter's Geography* (New York: St. Martin's Press, 1983), 25.
28. Ibid., 52.
29. Ibid., 48.
30. Eugenia Collier, "The Closing of the Circle: Movement from Division to Wholeness in Paule Marshall's Fiction," in *Black Women Writers (1950–1980)*, ed. Mari Evans (Garden City, N.Y.: Anchor Books, 1984), 315. Also see Dorothy Hamer Denniston, *The Fiction of Paule Marshall*

(Knoxville: University of Tennessee Press, 1995).

31. Paule Marshall, "Brazil," in *Dark Symphony*, ed. James A. Emanuel and Theodore L. Gross (New York: Collier-MacMillan, 1968), 402.

32. Collier, "Closing Circle," 314.

33. *Black Women Writers (1950–1980)*, 44.

34. *Black Women Writers at Work*, 31.

35. Sandra Reeves, "Following the Poet: Glimpses of Michael S. Harper," *The Brown Alumni Monthly* 76 (1975): 14.

36. Unlike Nikki Giovanni who finds the book foolish and clumsily written. See Nikki Giovanni, *Gemini* (New York: Penguin Books, 1971), 94.

37. *Black Women Writers at Work*, 94.

38. Michael S. Harper and Robert Stepto, eds., *Chant of Saints* (Urbana: University of Illinois Press, 1979), 365.

39. *Obsidian* 2, no. 3 (1976): 38–46.

40. *Chants of Saints*, 349–51. Also see "From the Machete Woman. A Novel," *Callaloo* 17, no. 2 (1994): 399–404.

41. *Confirmation: An Anthology of African American Women*, ed. Amiri Baraka and Amina Baraka (New York: Quill, 1983), 174–76.

42. Arthur P. Davis, "Novels of the New Black Renaissance (1960–1977): A Thematic Survey," *College Language Association Journal* 21, no. 4 (1978): 486.

43. Gayle Jones, *Corregidora* (New York: Random House, 1975): 99.

44. *Black Women Writers at Work*, 92.

45. Mel Watkins, "Sexism, Racism, and Black Women Writers," *New York Times Book Review*, 15 June 1986, 34–37.

46. Tate, *Black Women Writers at Work*, 92.

47. Audre Lorde, *Zami: A New Spelling of My Name* (Trumansburg, N.Y.: The Crossing Press, 1982). All quotes are from this edition.

48. Eugene Redmond, *Drum Voices: The Mission of Afro-American Poetry* (Garden City, N.Y.: Doubleday and Co., 1976), 338.

49. Jay Wright, Introduction to *Play Ebony Play Ivory: Poetry by Henry Dumas* (New York: Random House, 1974), xxi.

50. *Obsidian* 1, no. 2 (1975): 79. Komunyakaa has published several books since this poem, including his latest *Neon Vernacular: New and Selected Poems* (Middletown, Ct.: Wesleyan/University Press of New England, 1993).

51. *Natural Process: An Anthology of New Black Poetry*, ed. Ted Wilentz and Tom Weatherly (New York: Hill and Wang, 1976), 85.

52. Jerome Klinkowitz, "Clarence Major: An Interview with a Post-Contemporary Author," *Black American Literature Forum* 12, no. 1 (1978): 32.

53. Al Young, *The Song Turning Back into Itself* (New York: Holt, Rinehart, and Winston, 1965), 58.

54. Abraham Chapman, ed., *New Black Voices: An Anthology of Contemporary Afro-American Literature* (New York: New American Library, 1972), 553.

55. Ibid., 554,

56. Ibid., 553.

57. Al Young, *Who Is Angelina*? (New York: Holt, Rinehart, and Winston, 1975).

58. Gerard Barrax, "The Early Poetry of Jay Wright," *Callaloo* 6, no. 3 (1983): 99.

59. Robert Stepto, "The Aching Prodigal: Jay Wright's Dutiful Poet," *Callaloo* 6, no. 3 (1983): 78.

60. Jay Wright, *The Home Coming Singer* (New York: Corinth Books, 1971), 44.
61. Charles Rowell, "The Unraveling of the Egg: An Interview with Jay Wright," *Callaloo* 6, no. 3 (1983): 14.
62. Barrax, 86.
63. Rowell, 12.
64. Robert Stepto, "The Aching Prodigal: Jay Wright's Dutiful Poet," *Callaloo* 6, no. 3 (1983), 76.
65. *Arna Bontemps–Langston Hughes Letters, 1925–1967*, ed. Charles A. Nichols (New York: Dodd, Mead and Co., 1980), 479.
66. Chapman, 360–61.
67. Jay Wright, *The Double Invention of Komo* (Austin: University of Texas Press, 1980), 108. Jay Wright has also translated Guillén's poetry. See the two poems titled "The Cane Field" and "Cities" in *Freedomways* 2, no. 3 (1962): 261–62. Also see his play titled *Daughters of the Water*, in *Callaloo* 10, no. 2 (1987): 215–81, which again draws on Guillén. His latest work includes the book *Boleros* (Princeton, N.J.: Princeton University Press, 1990) and several poems on Latin America in *Callaloo* 17, no. 2 (1994): 451–58.
68. John O'Brien, *Interviews with Black Writers* (New York: Liveright, 1973), 103.
69. Chapman, 258–59.
70. Richard Jackson, *Acts of Mind: Conversations with Contemporary Poets* (University Ala.: University of Alabama Press, 1983), 183.
71. Michael S. Harper, *Dear John, Dear Coltrane* (Pittsburgh: University of Pittsburgh Press, 1970), 42–43.
72. Reeves, 9.
73. Ibid., 10.
74. Ibid.
75. Robert Hayden, *Selected Poems* (New York: October House, 1966), 25–36.
76. Robert Hayden, "Robert Hayden: The Poet and His Art: A Conversation with Paul McClusky," in *How I Write/1* (New York: Harcourt Brace and Jovanovich, 1972), 133–213. Partly reprinted in Robert Hayden, *Collected Prose*, ed. Frederick Glayshen (Ann Arbor: University of Michigan Press, 1984), 188–98.
77. For a rather tenuous literary-psychoanalytic interpretation of this poem, see Richard O. Lewis, "A Literary Psychoanalytic Interpretation of Robert Hayden's 'Market,'" *Negro American Literature Forum* 9, no. 1 (1975): 21–24.
78. Fred M. Fetrow, *Robert Hayden* (Boston: Twayne, 1984), 88.
79. Hayden, *Selected Poems* 36.
80. Michael S. Harper, "Review of Robert Hayden, *Angle of Ascent*," *Obsidian* 2, no. 3 (1976): 90.
81. William H. Hansell, "The Spiritual Unity of Robert Hayden's *Angle of Ascent*," *Black American Literature Forum* 13 (1979): 27.
82. Ibid., 25.
83. Ibid., 27.
84. John Hatcher, *From the Auroral Darkness. The Life and Poetry of Robert Hayden* (Oxford: George Ronald, 1984), 135.
85. O'Brien, 116.
86. Hatcher, 134.
87. Vera Kutzinski, "The Logic of Wings: Gabriel García Márquez and Afro-

American Literature," *Latin American Literary Review* 13 (1985): 135–46.

88. Harper, 90.
89. Kutzinski, 143.
90. Kutzinski, 143.
91. Lindsay Patterson, "Langston Hughes—An Inspirer of Young Writers," *Freedomways* 8 (1968): 180.
92. O'Brien, 249.
93. Ibid., 246.
94. Ibid.
95. Amiri Baraka (LeRoi Jones) *Home: Social Essays* (New York: William Morrow and Co., 1966), 39.
96. Amiri Baraka, *The Autobiography of LeRoi Jones* (New York: Freundlich Books, 1984), 164.
97. Ibid., 104.
98. Ibid., 166.
99. Jones, 11–62.
100. Amiri Baraka, *Daggers and Javelins: Essays, 1974–1979* (New York: William Morrow and Co., 1984b), 12.
101. *Daggers and Javelins*, 182.
102. Ibid.
103. Doris Laryea, "A Black Poet's Vision: An Interview with Lance Jeffers," *College Language Association Journal* 26 (1983): 430.
104. Laryea, 431.
105. Ibid., 428.
106. John Clytus, *Black Man in Red Cuba* (Miami: University of Miami Press, 1970).
107. Robert Chrisman, "Impressions of Cuba: Revolutionaries and Poets," *The Black Scholar* 11 (1980): 15.
108. Ibid., 16.
109. Ibid., 18.
110. Yvonne Guillon Barrett, "Nicolás Guillén y el movimiento de arte negro," *Iris* 3 (1982): 47–55.
111. Redmond, 306.
112. *Daggers and Javelins*, 188.
113. Ibid., 186.
114. Quince Troupe, "These Crossings, These Words," *Callaloo* 1, no. 3 (1978): 87.
115. *Natural Process*, 110.
116. Ibid., 7–10.
117. Cyrus Cassells, "To the Cypress Again and Again," *Callaloo* 9, no. 1 (1986): 20–23. Also see his new poems "Night Mist" and especially "Lament for Lorca," *Callaloo* 10, no. 3 (1987): 375–84.
118. Jayne Cortez, "When I Look at Wilfredo Lam's Paintings," *Callaloo* 9, no. 1 (1986): 26, and other poems that refer to Chano Pozo's music.
119. Jay Wright, *Callaloo* 9, no. 1 (1986): 130–37, 138–39, 140–41. Vera Kutzinski studies Wright's new world poetry in her book titled *Against the American Grain: Myth and History in William Carlos Williams, Jay Wright, and Nicolás Guillén* (Baltimore: Johns Hopkins University Press, 1987).
120. See his book titled *The Poet's Africa: Africanness in the Poetry of Nicolás Guillén and Aimé Césaire* (Westport, Conn.: Greenwood Press, 1990).

THREE

The Influence of U.S. Black Writers

> I identify with the United States through
> Langston Hughes. Even now
> when I think of that country
> I see it through his eyes,
> even after his death.
> —Manuel Zapata Olivella[1]
> Haley finally told me to stop talking
> about it and just do it.
> —Roman Foster[2]

THE SLAVE NARRATIVES

We begin the question of influence with the *Autobiografía* of Juan Francisco Manzano (1797–1854), the only known Cuban narrative written by a slave. Edward Mullen, I believe, was the first to point out a number of "striking similarities"[3] between the Manzano work and the North American slave narrative. He illustrates the similarities by focusing on parallels between the Cuban work and the *Life and Times of Frederick Douglass*:

> In the first place, both books are buttressed by considerable supporting materials (prefaces, letters, appendices), which no doubt reflect the intervention of abolitionists in their printing. Both appear to be informed by a similar alienating vision of society, and rather closely parallel each other in terms of their structure (organizational pattern). Both begin with the narrator's account of his genealogy, and move on to describe a "loss of innocence" when the narrators are catapulted from the protected world of childhood to experience the full rigors of slavery. There is, too, a similar realization of the alternatives to slavery, which leads to a dramatic escape. It is not only the presence of similar stylistic devices, recurrent imagery, and a careful selection of events to maintain a narrative momentum, which ultimately links these works; but also—perhaps more importantly—both narratives project a similar portrait of psychological and physical torment firmly rooted in the alien-exile theme, which has characterized much of black literature from the early times to the present.[4]

Richard Madden brought the manuscript version of Manzano's autobiography to England, translated it, and published it in 1840. Important American slave narratives had also appeared in British editions; even prominent authors of slave narratives like Frederick Douglass had spent extensive periods in England. Such facts as these led Mullen to conclude possible mutual influence: "Bearing in mind that Madden was an ardent abolitionist and was no doubt thoroughly familiar with the North American slave narrative, it would not seem unreasonable to assume that he discussed this popular and highly influential form with Domingo del Monte and other members of his *tertulia*."[5]

Del Monte was the wealthy Cuban patron who had helped Manzano obtain his freedom in 1836 and had encouraged him to write his autobiography, which Manzano completed in 1839. But was Manzano "influenced" by North American slave narratives? I think not. Even though there are similarities, we need not seek literary models for Manzano's quest for freedom. The trauma of slavery and the psychological and physical torment associated with it suffice. Besides, Frederick Douglass's *Narrative of the Life of Frederick Douglass: An American Slave*, only the first volume of his story, was not published until 1845. Manzano finished his in 1839 at the latest. Manzano's *Autobiografía* can be viewed in the broader perspective of black American literature as a tradition. U.S. black influence in Latin America starts with Langston Hughes; few black American writers have matched Hughes's "gigantic international reputation."[6]

THE EXAMPLE OF LANGSTON HUGHES

When Hughes died in 1967, writers in Latin America who had known him personally issued statements of grief as did others who had known only his work. Through personal contacts and through his literature in translation, Hughes had long been considered a link between North and South America. He was a dedicated translator and had, as we have seen, an authentic affinity with the language, literature, and customs of Spain and Spanish America. He translated book-length works not only of García Lorca and Nicolás Guillén but also of Gabriela Mistral. His contacts with Hispanic associates on both sides of the Atlantic were life-long as he enjoyed friendships that dated back to his on-the-spot coverage of the

Spanish Civil War, to his trips to Cuba, and even further back to a childhood and youth spent partly in Mexico, where he first learned the Spanish language and read his first Spanish literature.

Much of the recent criticism in the relatively new field of Hispanic black studies focused on the friendship Hughes and Nicolás Guillén maintained over the years, with attention given not so much to influence but rather to their differences and their similarities. These two giants first met in February 1930, later traveled together in Spain, and kept in touch partly through correspondence. Some of the correspondence has recently been published.[7] The first letter (dated July 15, 1930) contains advice from Hughes, the "seasoned" celebrity, to Guillén on how to handle the pressures of sudden success brought about by the publication in 1930 of *Motivos de Son* (*Sound Motifs*), Guillén's first black poems. Hughes, whose *The Weary Blues* dates from 1926, was already famous when they met and that first meeting, I believe, helped turn Guillén away from the Hispanic Modernism of Rubén Darío, the estheticist, toward Afro-Hispanic blackness.

When Guillén, "already accomplished but still searching for his authentic voice,"[8] first met Hughes, the black American author was considered "the greatest Negro poet in the United States of America—indeed, the greatest Negro poet in the world."[9] Arnold Rampersad, who writes convincingly about Hughes's immediate impact on Cuba's future national poet, had access to a brief diary Hughes kept of his visit to Cuba. In it Hughes indicated how, after hearing Guillén's poems, he went to bed thinking about how they might be improved. Hughes's important recommendation for Guillén was that "he should make the rhythms of the Afro-Cuban *son*, the authentic music of the black masses, central to his poetry, as Hughes himself had done with blues and jazz."[10] The month after Hughes's departure, Guillén published his *Motivos de son*, considered to be "the best kind of Negro poetry"[11] Cuba had ever had.

Nicolás Guillén, then, introduced his *son* poems shortly after meeting Langston Hughes, who had already tried blues and jazz forms in literature. Verses such as the following by Guillén rely on the repetition of popular forms and recall Langston Hughes's blues forms:

> Soy como un árbol florido,
> que ayer flores no tenía;

soy como un árbol florido
que ayer flores no tenía:
a leer me enseñó el pueblo,
    caramba,
aunque el pueblo,
leer tampoco sabía.[12]

(I am like a tree in bloom,
that before had gone to seed;
I am like a tree in bloom,
that before had gone to seed:
I have learned from the people,
    caramba
even though the people
did not know how to read.)

"The Backlash Blues" is an example of the style of Langston Hughes:

Mister Backlash, Mister Backlash,
Just who do you think I am /
Tell me, Mister Backlash,
Who do you think I am /
You raise my taxes, freeze my wages,
Send my son to Vietnam.[13]

Both Hughes and Guillén went to Spain to oppose fascism during the Spanish Civil War. They shared the same vision of war, one that considered uppermost the tragedy of the individual soldier. Hughes's poem titled "Without Benefit of Declaration"

Listen here, kid
It's been said
Tomorrow you'll be dead
Out there where
The rain is lead[14]

foreshadows Guillén's poem titled "Dead Soldier," which reads as translated by Hughes himself:

What bullet killed him?
Nobody knows.
....

Rat-ta-tat-tat!
THERE GOES THE DEAD SOLDIER
....
A SOLDIER AIN'T NOTHING.
Rat-ta-tat-tat!
THERE'RE PLENTY OF SOLDIERS.[15]

Langston Hughes's numerous writings about the war in Spain also included the text of a speech, "Too Much of Race." Hughes made the speech to the 1937 Second International Writers Congress in Paris as a delegate from the United States. He used the Scottsboro injustice to illustrate fascism in action in the United States.[16] Guillén and other Hispanic black authors shared Hughes's hatred of fascism, his antiwar sentiments, and his support for Loyalist Spain; the Scottsboro case was perhaps the affront they all felt most sharply. It helped alert blacks in the New World to the kind of racial injustice they needed to guard against. The warning was passed on to Regino Pedroso in Cuba, who urged blacks in "Hermano negro" to "listen to what's going on in Scottsboro. . . ,"[17] and to Marcelino Arozarena, who, in harmony with his Afro-Cuban compatriot, suggested that blacks "think about Scottsboro and not about Ogún."[18] Both of these writers were fully aware, as was Langston Hughes, of the far-reaching negative implications the Scottsboro case held for black people.

Langston Hughes was well known in South America, and he was aware of the impact he had there. About the sales potential and translation possibilities of his work, Hughes wrote, "Many of my poems and several of my short stories have appeared in various countries down there, and I am in two Latin American anthologies of verse."[19] One of the anthologies he refers to probably was Ildefonso Pereda Valdés's *Antología de la poesía negra americana* (*Anthology of Black Poetry in America*) first published in 1936 by Ediciones Ercilla in Santiago, Chile, and reprinted in 1953 in Montevideo, Uruguay, by Biblioteca Uruguaya de Autores. The other anthology must have been Emilio Ballagas's *Mapa de la poesía negra americana* (*The Best of Black Poetry in America*), published in 1946 by Editorial Pleamar in Buenos Aires, Argentina.

Some of Hughes's poems and short stories were included in anthologies and newspapers in Mexico, Cuba, Puerto Rico, Chile, Argentina, and Uruguay. Some of his longer works were translated into Spanish and published in Argentina and Chile as well. His work continues to appear in English and in Spanish translation in many Latin American anthologies. In one of them, *Black Poetry of the Americas (A Bilingual Anthology)*, edited by Hortensia Ruiz del Vizo, he is referred to as "the most internationally known American poet."[20]

Many of the anthologies of black verse in Latin America focus on black poetry important during the late 1920s, 1930s, and 1940s, particularly in Cuba and Puerto Rico.[21] Hughes had some impact on this movement, which was, in a sense, the Harlem Renaissance of Latin America, a time when the black entered literature both as subject and as author. The heightened awareness of blacks and blackness had an influence in much of Latin America that continues to this day. Langston Hughes was the best known of the Harlem Renaissance writers, and the ethnic significance of his person and his writings provided a formative example for black writers throughout the hemisphere.

Langston Hughes's reputation in Latin America grew "by leaps and bounds."[22] Perhaps in part because of his work on the Scottsboro case, his name appeared often in the black press in Uruguay during the 1930s and 1940s. He had a symbolic significance for the black diaspora in Uruguay. Many blacks there saw themselves as part of a wider black world, and they derived inspiration from Hughes, whom they saw as a role model. In fact, black literary celebrities such as Langston Hughes and Cuba's Nicolás Guillén were probably as widely read in Uruguay as in their home countries.

Though Hughes never traveled to Uruguay, he did correspond with writers there. He wrote to Pilar Barrios, the acknowledged dean of black letters in Uruguay. Barrios had sent Hughes a copy of *Piel negra (Black Skin)*, his first book of poetry. The book included a poem the Uruguayan poet had written about Hughes called "Voces" ("Voices"), in which Barrios writes of his admiration for Hughes. It is not surprising to find such phrases as "tireless fighter" and "world traveler," which, as Marvin Lewis has written, "aptly describe the Black American poet who fought for respect and human rights in both the New and Old World."[23]

> Id, luchador incansable,
> generoso trotamundos
> de la tierra

y de las mares,

.............................[24]

(Go, tireless fighter,
generous world traveler
of the earth
and of the seas

...........................)

Lewis who did this translation, believes that Barrios perhaps was inspired by some of Hughes's more militant writings, "those from a Marxist perspective that concerned social class and economics and appeared in *New Masses* and *The Negro Worker* in the 1930s."[25] These kinds of political writings reflected what Faith Berry called Hughes's deep sense of social consciousness that, she says, he possessed from 1925 on, even though not all of his poetry revealed it.[26] Berry has shown that although best known for blues and jazz poems, Hughes was more than a good black poet. Her work has helped set the record straight on Langston Hughes, the "black radical poet."

That same phrase, *black radical poet*, can be applied to several Hispanic black poets of revolution in Latin America. Berry's *Good Morning Revolution* (1973), a collection of Hughes's social protest writings, and her biographical study, *Langston Hughes: Before and After the Harlem Renaissance* (1983), have underscored the fact that Langston Hughes's overall image is very close to that of Nelson Estupiñán Bass, Ecuador's black poet and novelist of revolution; of Nicomedes Santa Cruz, the Peruvian black; and, of course, of Nicolás Guillén.[27] Berry writes that "Langston Hughes was best known as a folk poet, pursuing the theme 'I, too, sing America' " But that image, she adds, "is only part of his legacy, since during his lifetime Langston Hughes wrote some of the most revolutionary works by any American writer of his generation."[28] This radical aspect of his vision did not come late in his life, though some of his revolutionary pieces were written as late as 1957. Langston Hughes simply chose not to publicize this aspect of his work, and his audience chose to ignore it. Langston Hughes never joined the Communist Party, but he did visit the Soviet Union and returned "speaking with favor of it."[29]

Hughes's radical image helped account for his popularity outside the black diaspora in South America. We should remember that he was revered by nonblacks like José Antonio Fernández de

Castro, who "lionized" him in Mexico and Cuba and kept his name before the public by writing articles about him and translating his poetry into Spanish. Hughes felt a strong affinity with Latin Americans and they with him. Remembering Langston Hughes, a Mexican author wrote: "There have been very few foreign poets for whom we have felt as much affinity as we feel for Langston. . . . Few poets from other countries have earned as much admiration and affection from us as he has."[30]

Such comments raise the question: Why is Hughes so fondly remembered and so widely admired by blacks and nonblacks in Latin America? In the late 1920s and early 1930s, when he first came to the attention of writers in Latin America, Langston Hughes was seen as the "quintessential black poet: jovial, spontaneous, and possessed of an innate sense of natural rhythm."[31] White writers in the 1930s even in Latin America sought what Mullen calls that "natural spontaneity" in blacks and believed they found it in Langston Hughes. Although he was seen as part of a romanticized vision of blacks popular at the time, Hughes was also considered in the 1930s to be a poet *engagé* and spokesman for proletarian causes. Langston Hughes's "left" side did not go unnoticed in Latin America, where he was recognized not only as a black bard but also a poet of all people.

In 1936 sensing Hughes's wider concern for the exploited of all colors, the Uruguayan writer and critic Ildefonso Pereda Valdés already had noted two distinct tendencies in Hughes's poetry. One was characterized by the racial poems on black themes and the other was represented by poems on revolution and social reform.[32] In 1938 Pereda Valdés wrote a book, a collection of essays called *Línea de color* (*Color Line*), which he dedicated to Langston Hughes. Hughes, who maintained a correspondence with Pereda Valdés, sent him biographical information to be used especially for *Línea de color*. Pereda Valdés incorporated this information into his book, but the book also includes a separate article on Langston Hughes called "Langston Hughes, un poeta de la raza negra"[33] ("Langston Hughes, Poet of the Black Race"). It was written by Pereda Valdés before he received the biographical data. This article is one of the earliest assessments made in Hispanic America of Hughes's work aside from those that appeared in Mexico and Cuba in the early 1930s.

It is clear from Pereda Valdés's article that he considered Hughes a model poet. In his study, he stated the view that

Langston Hughes was not only a black poet but also a universal poet who sang of the human problems, social misery, and revolution he had seen in his travels around the world. Already by 1938 Langston Hughes, according to Pereda Valdés, had changed from a race poet to a universal poet of all oppressed people. It is likely that this side of Langston Hughes had some influence on another objective of the black press in Uruguay—support for the underdog regardless of color. Even when writing about Nicolás Guillén[34] and the "promise" he had shown of becoming the poet of revolution that he did become in Cuba, Pereda Valdés pointed to Langston Hughes as the model, as the one who had shown the example that, in Valdés's estimation, all black wriiters should follow.

In the 1930s Hughes was identified with the left in Mexico; in the 1960s he became the idol of a new generation of socially committed poets in that country. Mullen quite rightly believes it ironic that Hughes's earliest literary contacts in Mexico had been clearly apolitical, because "he was eventually to become inextricably identified with the left in that country."[35] Mullen also hinted at the real cause of Langston Hughes's enduring reputation in Latin America when he indicated that Hughes's denunciation of the tragedy of Spain was contemporary with and parallel to the activities of the foremost poets of the Hispanic world.

I use the word *hinted* because Latin American writers and intellectuals there, I believe, saw Hughes in the same vein and tradition as they saw their own great poets. Hughes wrote racial material, but his work on capitalist exploitation, unemployment, and poverty also reflected the kinds of social protest themes Latin Americans had grown accustomed to hearing from writers such as Pablo Neruda, César Vallejo, and Nicolás Guillén—generally considered three of the best poets of our time. These giants have been very critical of the United States. Latin Americans recognized in Hughes a poet who wrote of the experiences all blacks share, but we should not underestimate the importance of Hughes's own criticism of U.S. society in the eyes of Latin Americans making similar criticisms. That Hughes was doing the same thing their own local national heroes were doing might have contributed to Hughes's "enormous popularity in those lands whose national poets have been vehemently anti-American."[36]

Not all Latin American writers, of course, write in the tradition of social protest, but many of the best are or were "among the foremost exponents of Marxism in their respective countries."[37] Langston Hughes's appeal in Latin America, in short, goes beyond the black diaspora, because his revolutionary message is so similar to that expressed in the literature of its own outstanding writers. Unlike Pablo Neruda, César Vallejo, and Nicolás Guillén, Langston Hughes never became a member of the Communist Party, but his poetry, like theirs, ultimately came to merge political activism and poetic vision in his search for human justice.

Langston Hughes himself recognized the leftist leaning of many Latin American writers. In fact, that leaning guided his own selection of writers to include in a Mexican-Cuban anthology of short stories in English translation—never published in book form—that he and his Cuban friend José Antonio Fernández de Castro began putting together in 1935 during a stay in Mexico. "We have done thirty-four so far," he wrote at the time, "and I think we will have a swell collection. All stories of contemporary authors: the revolutions and uprisings, sugar cane, Negroes, Indians, corrupt generals, American imperialists—mostly all left stories because practically all the writers down there are left these days. . . ."[38]

Hughes had influenced the poetry of one of these leftist writers, Nicolás Guillén, who published his first volume of black poems in 1930 shortly after they first met. Hughes's impact on Guillén is well known; less well known is his impact on the African Colombian Manuel Zapata Olivella. Zapata Olivella is perhaps the most outstanding black novelist writing in Spanish today. I have discussed elsewhere[39] Zapata Olivella's account of his relationship with his American idol, whom he met in New York in the 1940s. He described this meeting in *He visto la noche* (*I Have Seen the Night*), a little book he wrote in 1946 and first published in 1953. Years later, after Hughes's death, Zapata Olivella in an interview with Yvonne Captain-Hidalgo reminisces about that meeting:

Yvonne Captain-Hidalgo: In *He visto la noche* you talk about Langston Hughes. Could you comment on your relationship with him?

Manuel Zapata Olivella: The human quality of L.H. came through exactly as one would expect from reading his poems. When I arrived in New York, the only thing I knew about him was some of his poems.

Yvonne Captain-Hidalgo: Do you remember some of them?

Manuel Zapata Olivella: Of course I hadn't read many. Perhaps the one that most influenced me in the sense that it made me feel like a brother to him even long before I met him was "I, Too, Sing America." I had also read his novel *Not Without Laughter*. I even carried around in my backpack a copy of his book *The Big Sea*. At any rate these were the first things, I knew about the poet. Obsessed with the possibility of meeting him, I looked him up when I got to New York. I was hungry when I arrived and badly dressed. In a great spirit of brotherhood he took me in as if he were an old friend of mine. . . . When I was getting ready to leave, he asked me if I had a place to stay and I shook my head no. He then gave me his own bed. I did not know it at the time, but the next day I realized he had slept on a sofa and given me his own bed. After I left his house, I saw him two or three more times. . . . When winter approached, I got ready to return to Mexico. We said goodby, but over the years we corresponded. Not a lot but every time he published a book, he would send me a copy with a dedication. I sent him copies of mine. I did not see him for twenty-five years. His death, which I learned about through the papers affected me deeply. . . .[40]

Langston Hughes also appears as a character in *Changó, el gran putas. Shango, The Holy Fucker* (1983) is Zapata Olivella's own translation of his big epic on the black diaspora in the New World. Zapata Olivella's work, which I will discuss in the next chapter, is undoubtedly the most ambitious black novel ever written in Spanish. Hughes appears in this work as a character at times reciting his poetry and at times in mythic association with other black heroes and role models, some of them Harlem Renaissance figures. In this novel, Zapata Olivella relives and recreates some of the conversations held with Langston Hughes while in New York. By integrating Hughes's poetry and person into this novel, Zapata Olivella pays the ultimate homage to black history and to Hughes's role in it. Poets of African descent in Latin America for a long time have hailed Langston Hughes in song and verse. Now, Manuel Zapata Olivella, the African Colombian novelist, has done it in prose as well. Even Zapata Olivella's travels are, in a sense, a tribute to Langston Hughes. One could say that in the "traveling" sense, Zapata Olivella is the Langston Hughes of Latin America. Zapata Olivella had other influences.[41] There were other travelers who inspired him. But like all of them, and certainly like Hughes, Zapata Olivella saw travel as a way to acquire knowledge of the world. Zapata Olivella walked over a good part of it.

Black writers in Haiti and Brazil also looked to the example of Langston Hughes for inspiration. In the 1930s and 1940s Hughes's work appeared in journals in Haiti "where Blacks felt solidarity with him and knew by heart his poetry in transla-tion."[42] Hughes said that "the first book about me in any lan-guage"[43] was published in Haiti. This book, *Langston Hughes: un chant nouveau* by Réné Piquion, appeared in 1940. In Brazil, Hughes was a model of inspiration to Abdias do Nascimento and to the Experimental Black Theater he founded in 1944. Nascimento lectured on Hughes's work in 1947, and when in 1949 he sought out black dramas to add to his company's reper-toire, he found Hughes's play *Mulatto*. Nascimento had con-cluded that traditional Brazilian theater stereotyped blacks. Since his own group lacked Brazilian plays that reflected his way of thinking, he looked outside Brazil and obtained Eugene O'Neill's permission to stage *The Emperor Jones* in 1945. Langston Hughes also gave the Experimental Black Theater permission to put on his play that, Nascimento tells us,[44] had Aurea Campos in the role of Cora, the tragic mother of the lynched Mulatto. He tells us that the black theater group stirred up other blacks and that another group in Sao Paulo formed its own Experimental Black Theater, which also presented Hughes's play *Mulatto* among its repertoire.[45] According to James Emmanuel, Hughes's drama opened in Buenos Aires, as well, in 1959.[46]

Nascimento's choice of this play is intriguing. His attraction to it could have resulted from his interest in using the work as a symbolic reflection of the mixed nature of Brazil. Nascimento wanted the dramas he chose to function as psychodramas, and he constantly rejected the notion that Brazil was a "white" coun-try. In fact, the whole program of the experimental Black Theater group was to combat or "to expose the fraud of Brazilian white-ness,"[47] which had even some light-skinned mulattos in that country declaring themselves white. Langston Hughes's early poetry contributed to the literary beginnings of *négritude*. The Experimental Black Theater group for many years was consid-ered the cultural headquarters of *négritude* in Brazil.[48] It is fitting that Hughes's drama *Mulatto* should play some role in the devel-opment of a black cultural movement in that country.

Nascimento moved to the United States in 1968. In 1967 he had reiterated his admiration for Langston Hughes whom Nascimento includes among a "black constellation of model men."[49] When Nascimento speaks of the "harvest of heritage"[50] passed on by great black figures, he recognizes the role model blacks like Hughes in the United States provide for other blacks the world over and for others as well. This heritage is continued, for example, in the work of the contemporary black Brazilian poet Solano Trindade, who died in 1974. Trindade's poem "Sou negro" ("I Am a Black") recalls such familiar Langston Hughes poems as "Negro" and "The Negro Speaks of Rivers," especially when the Brazilian writes:

> I am Black.
> My ancestors were burned
> by an African sun.
> My soul received the
> baptism of the drums
> ....[51]

The Brazilian critic Cassiano Nunes[52] compares Trindade with Langston Hughes and suggests that Trindade was greatly influenced by his U.S. black model. Trindade's poem, like Hughes's, is about racial identity and positive affirmation of blackness. In his poem "I Am a Black" Trindade becomes the voice "of all black Brazilians and in so doing takes on the same collective identity as does Langston Hughes in his similarly titled poem."[53] It has been said that Trindade's poem marked the turning point in modern Afro-Brazilian poetry, because it ends on a "note of racial protest and deep cultural pride."[54] The bold affirmation of Trindade in his 1958 poem and the "potent assertiveness"[55] of "Ser negro" ("To Be Black") by Abelardo Rodriguez, an African Brazilian poet who began publishing in the late 1970s, signified the "harvest of black heritage" Nascimento forecast, which is coming to fruition in Brazil.

Langston Hughes was a model for Latin American black writers, but beyond that he was considered a great humanitarian whose words often transcended race.[56] Latin Americans saw him not only as a proud voice of blacks but also as a voice of all the oppressed everywhere. Latin Americans also knew of his devotion to translation projects from the Spanish. For in addition to his

book-length translations of work by García Lorca, Nicolás Guillén, and Gabriela Mistral, Hughes frequently supplied periodicals with translations of the work of important Latin American writers who he felt deserved attention from English readers.[57] Faith Berry[58] put his translations into perspective when she intimated that if understanding another person's language is the first step toward understanding the person, then these translations would seem to be Hughes's modest offering toward better world understanding. Through his translation work; through his symbolic link, friendship, and radical image; and through his example, Langston Hughes enhanced his standing in Latin America inside the African diaspora and outside as well.[59]

HARLEM AND THE JAZZ AGE: BLACK MODERNISM AS MODEL AND THREAT

Manuel Zapata Olivella met Langston Hughes in Harlem and recorded his reactions to Hughes and to the place as well. Other black Hispanic writers, among them Nicolás Guillén and Jorge Artel, saw and knew Harlem firsthand through personal visits. Guillén was one of the first black Hispanic writers to write about Harlem, warning Cubans in the late 1920s to avoid going the way of Harlem, which he saw as a separate city within a city. Zapata Olivella and Guillén saw misery in Harlem, but they also saw the power, beauty, and vitality of the artistic products it exported to the world. At a time when parts of white America "were hungry for black art and culture,"[60] the energies of Harlem went beyond the U.S. borders and carried, it has been said, "effective voltage to the Caribbean, Africa, and South America"[61] and beyond.

Clearly this vitality had a positive impact on Hispanic black writers and affected nonblack authors as well. As examples are Rubén Darío, the leading Modernist poet, and César Vallejo, the leading Vanguardist poet, who had occasions while in Paris as foreign journalists to observe U.S. blacks and black artists in action. And they did not like what they saw. Darío felt apprehensive toward blacks from the United States, regarding them as bold and aggressive menaces[62] and Vallejo at times had reservations.[63] Both seemed to see these artistic energies as threatening. Vallejo in particular thought those blacks aggressively seeking the new were in bad taste. Both of them, pace-setters themselves,

ironically seemed to fear the radical, daring, and aggressive nature of what came to be known as the "New Negro."

Vicente Huidobro, the Creationist poet of Chile, however, saw black art metaphorically as a harbinger of the future. Rubén Darío and Vallejo did not realize it but the audacious nature reflected in black art was an indication or manifestation of a black modernism that rivaled in artistic inventiveness their own propensity for daring innovation. The last thing these Latin American writers considered black art to be was "old fashioned"[64]—Houston Baker's recent assessment of the prevailing white opinion of the time. Baker is right in his view that modernism is not the invention of white people alone. Black art in the United States early in this century clearly represented for Latin American writers something new and bold in expression and in attitude. Some took the black sounds and expressive movement of this "modernism" positively and others cautiously, if not negatively.

Huidobro, like García Lorca in the 1930s, clearly saw the positive side of black art in all its "terribleness" and he had the foresight to take it as a model, arguing that—despite their long history of slavery—blacks were much less slaves than whites, at least where art was concerned.[65] Their postslavery aggressiveness in the arts led Huidobro to say of black art that "it is not an art of slaves,"[66] indirectly criticizing what he saw as a lack of freedom in artistic expression. Whites were depicted in a Guillén poem of 1929 as seeking this freedom "in Harlem and Havana," in "jazz and *son*,"[67] at a time when blacks not only were in vogue but also were very bold about it. Huidobro admired very much the artistic liberty U.S. blacks took in creating their original dance and music, which was the trademark of African art as well.

Huidobro has told us that he was collecting black art even before it became fashionable to do so. And Vallejo had moved to Europe, where in the 1920s and 1930s he was able to see much of this art up close from his base in Paris. Vallejo, however, might not have been witnessing the real thing. Huidobro recognized that in Paris, especially in the black Revues put on at the big theaters, entrepreneurs turned black art into a grotesque distortion, forcing the public to swallow in the name of "Black Art" something ridiculous and trivial, put on by Europeans who had no idea what black art really was or meant. Huidobro's point was that when black art reached Paris, it had been taken out of the hands of knowledgeable people, connoisseurs who truly admired, loved, and understood it. Black art fell prey, he thought, to "the ridiculous Parisian craze for imitation."[68]

Clearly not all Europeans were guilty of misinterpretation. There were those like Picasso, Stravinski, and Apollinaire who, like Huidobro himself, embraced black art for its nontraditional nature. Perhaps when he spoke of imitation, he had in mind the entertainment scene in the 1920s. Also known as the Jazz Age, the 1920s produced such well-known entertainments as Al Jolson's 1927 movie titled "The Jazz Singer." By the mid-1920s, Paris, like New York, "was being swept by an artistic enthusiasm for all things 'primitive' and exotic, particularly African,"[69] including black music, with jazz at its core, and black dance. Josephine Baker, at one time considered perhaps the most "primitive" black entertainer of all, started her reign in Paris in the 1920s. "Jazz Cleopatra," as La Baker is called in a book by Phyllis Rose,[70] came to symbolize more than anyone else not only the "exoticism" of Africa but also "the vitality of the American jazz age"[71] in the 1920s. She and Langston Hughes were two of the best-known figures from what can be called Black Renaissance I (the "Turbulent Sixties" will produce Black Renaissance II); they both went on to become known globally.

Vallejo was confronted with this "New Negro" in Paris. A Peruvian expatriate, he lived in Paris writing prose "from Europe,"[72] in the mid- to late-1920s and the early 1930s. He came face to face with the new black consciousness being exported from the United States to Europe and the world. His reaction, to judge from his writing, was surprisingly conservative considering his own radical art. He felt the whole of Western art was threatened by this revolutionary show of black emotion run amuck, which is what he considered black art to be. Vallejo formulated his vision of blacks largely on what he saw in Paris, but he did have some existing prejudices, perhaps influenced by José Carlos Mariátegui, his mentor and countryman. It is well known that Mariátegui viewed blacks as savages. Similarly, Vallejo considered black music and especially black dance to be savage. Vallejo also thought black expressive art too modern and, what is more, too representative of a rising tide of color he saw sweeping the world, or at least making inroads in the West at the beginning of the twentieth century, certainly in his native Peru and in his adopted city, Paris. This tide came from Africa and America and from the Orient as well.

Vallejo was aware of the positive influence blacks had in the music of Stravinski and Satie, for example, and he knew of the impact of black art on Picasso. He acknowledged the work of Langston Hughes as early as 1929, but the black dance of Josephine Baker, which he thought came right out of the jungle, caught his attention and led him to use the radical and expressive image it represented as a negative symbol for all he opposed. Huidobro saw black art as a metaphor for the new; Vallejo actually did also, but he, unlike Huidobro, did not see this new as anything good. Vallejo, in fact, saw blacks as a negative metaphor in triplicate: (1) as representative of the new, revolutionary, and unorthodox, in effect, of a wild and unintellectual wave he hoped would not reign in the future; (2) as part of what he saw as a global problem, namely the division of the world into whites and people of color, his hope being that Latin America would line up racially with Europe and the "white" West; and (3) as part of what is bad in Peru, along with the presence of Chinese and Japanese, his preference here being for more immigration from Europe.

Vallejo for all his humanity certainly was no admirer of blacks, whom he considered unintelligent and devoid of culture; nor did he appreciate black music, which he thought noisy; nor black dance, which he considered to be a savage, crude, and grotesque caricature. More than anything else, references to jazz predominate in those prose writings of Vallejo that convey his reservations about what black art was giving to the world early in this century. What is most depressing is that Vallejo had more reservations about blacks than he had even about the KKK in America or Europe, although he labeled the KKK in Europe as "much more vicious than the one in the United States."[73] Vallejo reports on "vicious" KKK activities perfunctorily or dispassionately at least three times in his prose, with no apparent indignation. Amiri Baraka once said, "Harlem is vicious modernism. . . . Can you stand such beauty?"[74] César Vallejo, Latin America's leading Vanguardist poet, apparently could not. Furthermore, he seemed to view the Jazz Age and Harlem's vicious modernism with more alarm and as more of a menace and a threat than the KKK's activities.

FROM WRIGHT TO REVOLUTION

Langston Hughes was the most famous of the Harlem Renaissance writers whose influence was felt in Latin America. Other influential U.S. black writers include Richard Wright in the 1940s and James Baldwin in the 1950s. Additional influences were felt in Latin America: during the 1960s, the New Black Renaissance (or Black Renaissance II) and its Civil Rights/Black Power/Black Arts Movement; in the 1970s, Alex Haley's *Roots*. These and other high points in U.S. black literature had repercussions in Latin America. Black writers in Cuba particularly are familiar with the works of many U.S. black writers—James Baldwin, Sonia Sanchez, Amiri Baraka, and Lance Jeffers, among others—and they are concerned "for the future and preservation of black writers in the United States."[75] Guillén and the Caribbean poets did not impress the Afro-Colombian writer Jorge Artel, for example, as much as the work of U.S. black writers such as Paul Lawrence Dunbar and Langston Hughes in whose writings, Artel would say, "the true image of the race and its unmistakable voice"[76] can be found.

Adalberto Ortiz does not hesitate to place the negritude of *Juyungo* (1943), his African Ecuadorian classic, alongside Richard Wright's *Native Son* (1940) and the works of James Baldwin and Langston Hughes.[77] One can, in fact, easily compare the dignity of Richard Wright's "sheer brute man, just as he is"[78] (Bigger) of *Native Son* to Ortiz's Ascensión Lastre of *Juyungo*. Ascensión has that same dignity. Both black characters rely on rebelliousness as a way out even when none exists. Both must meet life "head on," and because of their individual actions, they stand out as unforgettable literary creations. Ortiz also likes to underscore the impact of George Jackson and Angela Davis when he discusses the role economic factors play as obstacles to black liberation. Such factors as well as race, Ortiz believes, affect the social situation of blacks in Ecuador. Ortiz also refers to George Jackson to support his belief that racism is a product of slavery.[79] Even though he ranks *Juyungo* right up there with *Native Son*, it should be noted that Ortiz does not acknowledge any specific influence from U.S. black writers on his work. He does, however, prefer U.S. black music—jazz, blues, spirituals—over black Ecuadorian music.[80]

We should mention the inspiration Ortiz received from the 1936 Emilio Ballagas anthology, the *Antología de la poesía negra americana*, which Ortiz discovered in 1937. This volume, he has

said, was what caused him to start writing black literature. As
Florence White was one of the first to point out, " One cannot
help but notice the strong similarities shared by Ortiz with
Guillén, de Lima, and especially, Countee Cullen."[81] All three
are represented in the Ballagas anthology in Spanish translation.
So many other U.S. black poets are there that Ballagas himself
admits that "with the exception of Cuba and Brazil, black poetry
in the rest of the continent pales in comparison to the United
States."[82] Cullen's poem "Heritage," which begins "What is
Africa to me; / Copper sun or scarlet sea," recalls some of
Ortiz's own black poems such as "Contribución," which begins
with the words "Africa, Africa, Africa / great land of green and
sun. . . ." Some of Ortiz's poems have become staples in anthologies of black poetry in the Americas since 1945, when he published his first black poetry in *Tierra, son y tambor* (*Earth, Sound,
and Drum*).

I remember hearing Ortiz give a lecture in Washington, D.C.,
at Howard a few years ago in which he extolled the rhythmic
virtues of Vachel Lindsay's "The Congo" (1914), especially the
lines "Then I saw the Congo, creeping through the black / cutting through the jungle with a golden track. . . ." The poem has
been translated and published in Spanish. Arthur P. Davis has
said that U.S. black writers have been influenced by white poets
like Vachel Lindsay.[83] Though never acknowledging influence
from U.S. black writers, Ortiz, like other Latin American black
writers, does admit to influence from several other U.S. sources,
from Europe, and from local authors. The "Oidos y ojos de la
selva" sections of *Juyungo*, for example, were inspired in part by
John Dos Passos's novel *42nd Parallel* (1930), especially the chapter "The Cinematographic Eye." Ortiz also has mentioned the
influence of Erskine Caldwell and John Steinbeck on his prose
and Ezra Pound on his poetry.[84]

Both Antonio Preciado and Manuel Zapata Olivella acknowledge the influence of Langston Hughes. Preciado has mentioned,
in addition to Hughes, the influence of Guillén, Césaire, Fanon,
Vallejo, and Neruda. Zapata Olivella points to the impact of
Mariano Azuela, and he could easily include the work of Martín
Luis Guzmán, one of his mentors in Mexico. Zapata Olivella has
also spoken of the influence of the Mexican muralists and other
Mexican associates he knew during his three-year stay in Mexico
(1943–1946), before he went north to the United States.[85]

In an interview with Ian Smart, Quince Duncan said, regarding influences on his work, "Strangely enough the strongest influence came from the North American writers. I could mention James Baldwin and another one—and this always surprises people—William Faulkner."[86] Duncan also mentions John Steinbeck, and he thinks that among the Spanish American writers, Vargas Llosa exerted the strongest influence on him.

Black writers in Latin America have been influenced not only by U.S. literary figures but also by events in the United States. What were some of the events or factors that helped shape post-1960 black literature in the United States and, indirectly, in Latin America? According to Davis:

> One of the most turbulent periods in the Negro's history, the '60s and early '70s witnessed the sit-ins, the kneel-ins, the pray-ins, and other defiant practices on the part of Negroes; the dangerous and effective voter-crusade marches in the South; the rise to national attention of the Black Power movement; the rise to prominence of two martyr-leaders, Martin Luther King Jr. and Malcolm X; the bitter reaction to the tragedy in Vietnam; the rise to power of the Black Panthers; the rejection of Christianity by many Negroes; the riots, burnings, and lootings in the inner cities of America; and many acts of militancy and rejection on the part of Negroes—acts which told America in strong terms that Negroes were fed up with promises, that they wanted equality NOW.[87]

The history of what has been called "The Second American Revolution" was recently told in the acclaimed documentary film titled "Eyes on the Prize: America's Civil Rights Years, 1954–1965,"[88] produced by Henry Hampton for Blackside Inc. This six-part program begins in the mid-1950s with the lynching of Emmett Till; it reviews others killed in the struggle—James Chaney, Medgar Evers, Andrew Goodman, Viola Liuzzo, Michael Schwerner, among others—and moves on to Martin Luther King Jr. and other black leaders. It continues with the Montgomery, Alabama, bus boycott; to the integration of Central High School in Little Rock, Arkansas; to James Meredith's enrollment at the University of Mississippi; to the sit-ins and freedom rides; to the church bombings in Birmingham; to the formation of the Student Nonviolent Coordinating Committee and the Mississippi Freedom Democratic Party; to the Selma marches; and of course to the 1963 March on Washington, the Civil Rights Act of 1964, and the Voting Rights Act of 1965.

Much of this black American history, like earlier racist episodes in the United States, found its way into Latin American literature. In the United States, the turbulence of the 1960s and early 1970s was reflected in the tone and in the political nature of black literature of the time. The Black Aesthetic or the Black Arts Movement, led for the most part by Amiri Baraka, insisted on a black focus in creative and critical literature. The Black Arts Movement (BAM), the "storm center"[89] of the New Black Renaissance in the 1960s, like the Harlem Renaissance of the 1920s, affected not only Latin America; it also "influenced a whole generation of artists in Europe and among the Euro-Americans. The emphasis was on a people-shaped, high-oral, intensely direct statement. The BAM said the function of art is to teach and educate and move and unify and organize people, not to mystify them or offer dazzling support of the *status quo*!"[90]

Manuel Zapata Olivella's earlier novel, *Chambacú, corral de negros* (*Chambacú, Black Slum*), made just such an "intensely direct statement," one that even included depiction of a black male/white female relationship. Such a radical theme almost always constituted a prominent challenge to racism, the 1950s and 1960s included. This 1963 novel has been described as "the first Afro-Hispanic novel to call for revolution as a solution to the plight of the oppressed."[91] Since *Chambacú* is similar in theme to 1960s novels such as Sam Greenlee's *The Spook Who Sat by the Door* and John Williams's *The Man Who Cried I Am* and Ronald Fair's *Many Thousand Gone*, Michael Brookshaw has said pointedly that Zapata Olivella was influenced by 1960s U.S. novels of protest and revolution. I am not so sure. Zapata Olivella was more influenced, I believe, by the turbulent events of the 1960s and by the blazing headlines they produced worldwide than by any particular U.S. black writer influenced by those same events.

I have always thought that *Chambacú, corral de negros*, particularly the 1963 version published in Cuba, which depicts civil disobedience and organized resistance to white oppression, drew on those headlines. Also, Zapata Olivella knew the United States very well, having written already in *He visto la noche* about his experiences in the 1940s and about the "roots" of black protest he had observed in person long before Greenlee, Williams, and Fair started publishing. At any rate, just as the novels of these three writers are considered landmarks of black protest fiction, *Chambacú, corral de negros* can also be placed, quite rightly, "in the vanguard of militant Afro-Hispanic fiction."[92] *Changó, el gran putas*, Zapata Olivella's greatest novel, will come to fruition twenty years later in 1983 and will re-create the black struggle that took place in the United States in the 1960s and before. The novel will also remind the reader of the thoughts of W. E. B. Du Bois.

FROM BLACK POWER AND THE TURBULENT SIXTIES TO *ROOTS*

The 1960s was a time of great social and political upheaval and was "without a doubt the most profound and meaningful period of this century for black Americans."[93] The 1960s and the early 1970s witnessed many defiant practices and "genuine heroism by thousands of Blacks."[94] Those years, which gave birth to the Civil Rights Movement, also created the Black Power Movement. The Black Power slogan got attention and headlines. The rationale of Black Power, however, was not violence and black supremacy, though it was perceived in that light. Its aim was simply to build pride and a positive sense of identity and self-sufficiency among blacks and to put control of their destiny in their own hands. The Civil Rights Movement achieved that goal to some extent but as Adam Clayton Powell said in 1966: "Civil rights are man-made. Human rights are God-given."[95] In what was, perhaps, the first use of the words *black power*, Powell then said that to demand those God-given rights is to seek *black power*. The Black Power concept, as Adam Clayton Powell understood it, is more applicable to Latin America than to the Civil Rights Movement in the United States, because in theory Latin American blacks have always had civil rights (even in slavery times, some would argue) in the sense that there is no segregation by law. Human rights, or the God-given rights, are what blacks and black writers have been seeking in ever-increasing numbers in Latin America.

In 1980, the effect of the "Turbulent Sixties" in the United States on black consciousness in Latin America was a topic of discussion.[96] The historian Marvin Harris predicted that a Black Power Movement in Latin America would emerge certainly in Brazil. Harris was not far off the mark, because a couple of such movements reportedly were begun in Brazil. One had started, in fact, in the 1970s using protest and pressure tactics patterned after, or at least similar to, those that had already emerged in North America. The other sprang up in the 1980s when black youths turned their backs on Brazilian music to initiate a black soul movement. It involved identifying with U.S. blacks by imitating U.S. black "soul music," dances, fashion, and hair styles and by referring to themselves as "black."[97] There clearly are expanded efforts in Brazil to raise black consciousness through organizations, through publication, and through contacts with black leaders in the United States. African Brazilian literature, written by and for blacks, has been on the rise since the late 1970s and early 1980s, partly a byproduct of political liberalization but also a result of the growing racial consciousness.[98]

One reason for this growing racial consciousness is that racism continues in Brazil 100 years after slavery was abolished. A recent report in the Montreal *Gazette* on racism in Brazil confirms this developing sense of black consciousness. The report by William Ruiz[99] of *Southam News* referred to united black movements that were established in Brazil in the 1980s and that were designed to combat racial prejudice. The organizers of these movements believe that racial prejudice persists despite being officially outlawed. There are new Black Power movements emerging in Brazil, but what is happening today among the new generation is not all that new; because black consciousness has a history in Latin America particularly in Brazil. In fact the slogan "Black Is Beautiful" had already been proclaimed by some black Brazilians, especially in the 1940s and 1950s, most notably by Abdias do Nascimento and the sociologist Guerreiro Ramos. Nascimento, despite his admiration for Langston Hughes, recently declared that black Brazilians had no need to imitate the Black Power Movement in the United States because blacks in Brazil "have a long history of struggle, beginning 20 years before Africans ever set foot on U.S. soil, with the founding of the Quilombo of Palmares in 1595."[100]

Nascimento's argument is that black movements in Brazil borrow nothing from the United States, but rather address the specific needs of Brazilian blacks. In part, this argument is true not only for Brazil but also for other parts of Latin America. For instance, the "bloody events" in 1844 and 1912 in Cuba grew out of the racial struggles of their time and place. But recently we are witnessing an increase in aggressive declaration of black consciousnes even in places such as Costa Rica. The "Turbulent Sixties" provided a special catalyst that encouraged black writers in Latin America to take control, certainly of their own image. The African Peruvian poet Nicomedes Santa Cruz goes so far as to say that before the U.S. black liberation movement of the 1960s, no black person in Latin America accepted being called black.[101]

There was another report, this one in the *New York Times*, about the post-1960s black consciousness in South America. James Brooke, the author of the report, quotes one of his Peruvian informants who said that when he was growing up in the 1960s, Martin Luther King Jr., Angela Davis, and Nelson Mandela affected him profoundly.[102] Brooke writes of other blacks all over Spanish-speaking South America who are asserting their African identity. He mentions the Francisco Congo Black Movement in Lima, the Afro-Ecuadorean Institute in Ecuador, and the Cimarrón Group in Colombia. He also mentions *Mundo Afro*, a black journal in Uruguay.

The 1960s Black Power cry "Black Is Beautiful," as Manuel Zapata Olivella wrote, "shook the very foundations of those who had not yet come to terms with their blackness,"[103] forcing them to examine their own situations in their own countries. Zapata Olivella has given an account of how he confronted and came to understand his own racial identity in a series of recent publications, most notably in *Lève toi, mulâtre* (1987) (*Mulatto Arise*), his autobiography. In this work he recognizes that negritude burst forth in 1932 in Paris, but that its origins can be traced back to the Harlem Renaissance and before, to the Haitian Revolution, and even further back to Palmares in Brazil—a source of pride to Nascimento. But the 1960s and highly publicized figures of that time such as Martin Luther King Jr., Angela Davis, and George Jackson gave special impetus and inspiration to the new generation in Latin America and to Zapata Olivella's old guard as well.

Earlier I said that the principal aim of Black Power was to build pride and a positive sense of identity among blacks and to put some control over their destiny into their own hands. Zapata Olivella opens his autobiography with the questions: "What is my race?" "What is my culture?" and "What is my destiny?" He then goes on to answer these questions, which have concerned him since his early 1920s when he first realized his "hybrid nature." As he comes to terms with his race, his ancestry, and with himself, Zapata Olivella makes it clear from the outset that in his search for self-identity he will not conceive of Latin America as a mirror image of Europe. *Lève toi, mulâtre* is, in fact, a personalized history of Latin America. Part 1, "My Ancestors," is a tale of race mixture that can be multiplied many times over, but in Zapata Olivella's tale he emphasizes that blackness can be beautiful even in *mestizo* Latin America.

Zapata Olivella is especially proud of his sister Delia, who studied dance with Katherine Dunham in New York and who eventually formed her own group. She is "the blackest of us all,"[104] he writes, in every way, especially in her rebellious nature. Already in the 1940s she was declaring, as Abdias do Nascimento had done in Brazil, that "Black Is Beautiful." The re-emergence of this slogan in the United States during the 1960s reminded him of his own evolution toward an understanding of what he considers most important in human life — our understanding of "who we are." He continues his autobiography with a review of the events of the Turbulent Sixties punctuated by the Black Power salute at the Olympics in Mexico City and the assassinations of Martin Luther King Jr. and Malcolm X. He concludes by recounting new initiatives toward liberation during the 1970s and 1980s. He gives a general account of these events in Africa and America and a detailed account of events in Colombia.

These new initiatives include the completion of his own novel *Changó, el gran putas* (1983), which he had begun writing in the mid-1960s. It is a huge work, and the last 300 pages are devoted to the black struggle in the United States. That is appropriate because the novel, I believe, like his *Chambacú*, was inspired by events there during the 1960s. Since the 1960s black writers all over Latin America have been confronting and attempting to understand their identity, either in autobiographical statements or in creative literature. Black protagonists such as José Pastrana, in Nelson Estupiñán Bass's Afro-Ecuadorian novel *El último río* (*Pastrana's Last River* 1967), and Charles McForbes, in Quince Duncan's Afro-Costa Rican novel *Los cuatro espejos* (*The Four Mirrors* 1976), live similar experiences as those described by Manuel Zapata Olivella in Colombia. We should remember also that Nicolás Guillén wrote some of his most important poems on U.S. blacks after the 1960s, among them his tributes to Angela Davis and to Martin Luther King Jr. Nancy Morejón, arguably the most important of the new generation of Latin American black writers, has written a poem that she gives an English title "Freedom Now." She dedicated this poem to the black struggle in the United States. In short, much of the new black literary activity was clearly helped along by events of the Turbulent Sixties in the United States.

Finally, there can be little doubt that the Turbulent Sixties in the United States left a mark on African Brazilian literature as well, especially on black writers such as Eduardo de Oliveira and Oliveira Silveira. There is some doubt though that Hughes or any other U.S. black writer influenced African Brazilian literature directly.[105] "The black Civil Rights Movement in the United States, the emergence of African nationalism, and the increasing publicity given to the brutalities of the apartheid system in South Africa enabled Oliveira to raise his voice in solidarity,"[106] writes David Brookshaw. He also tells us that Silveira, who began writing in the early 1960s, was clearly influenced by the same events.[107]

Solano Trindade was also aware of U.S. blacks' struggle for justice, which he illustrates in his poem "Conversa com Luci," dedicated to "Miss Lucy," who "after much trial and travail had won an important court case in her quest to be admitted to the University of Alabama in Tuscaloosa in 1956."[108] This poem is reminiscent of Guillén's on Angela Davis. Brookshaw even believes that Amiri Baraka, one of the major figures identified with the "Turbulent Sixties," influenced Abdias do Nascimento.[109] Some of Brookshaw's insights, like this one, are impressive and valuable. We also learn from Brookshaw that the early twentieth-century mulatto writer Manuel Querino was a fervent admirer of Booker T. Washington.[110]

The Turbulent Sixties gave blacks in the United States and in Latin America the courage to protest. In the 1970s, Alex Haley's *Roots* (1976) gave blacks in the United States the momentum and the motivation to research their history and their African identity. Haley's work represented what some believe was "the greatest incident"[111] since the Civil Rights Movement of the 1960s. The intense search for roots and identity[112] that the book inspired in the United States undoubtedly encouraged similar searches in Latin America. African Central American authors of

West Indian descent like Quince Duncan, Carlos Guillermo Wilson, and Eulalia Bernard were involved in this search. Comparison of parts of their work with Haley's novel is inevitable. Elsewhere I have called Wilson's novel *Chombo* (1981) a Panamanian *Roots*,[113] based as it is on conversations Wilson remembered from childhood. His autobiographical protagonist, who had read *Roots*, blends these memories in with things he himself had seen. Cubena, as Wilson prefers to be called, is fond of the Marcus Garvey quote: "We must realize that upon ourselves depend our destiny, our future. We must carve out that future, that destiny," which he uses to begin his latest novel, *Los nietos de Felicidad Dolores* (*The Grandchildren of Felicidad Dolores*, 1990).

The book is set partly in the United States, and many of the black Panamanian characters attribute their success to the Black Power Movement and to the passive resistance efforts led by Martin Luther King Jr. Both Manuel Zapata Olivella and Carlos Guillermo Wilson have celebrated their own past in their literature, paying homage in the process to those who were influential in their development and their present success. Their works are the ultimate products of the post-*Roots* era, when black writers in Latin America not only have read Haley's novel but also have produced their own versions of it.

The Central American writers are considered by Ian Smart[114] to be the most important black writers in contemporary Spanish America. They invoke Africa but they also seek to define a West Indian aesthetic designed to proclaim their roots and their place in their New World societies. The result of Haley's achievement "is an enduring account of a race of people preserved for untold generations."[115] In this sense his impact, especially in Central America, goes beyond the literary search. One of the opening quotes for this chapter comes from the filmmaker Roman Foster, who wanted to tell the history of the one hundred thousand blacks "who built the Panama Canal, three thousand of whom died in the process from yellow fever, malaria, landslides, and dynamite blasts."[116] With Haley's encouragement, Foster set out to bring their story to the world before the last survivor died, thus doing through film—ensuring the survival of West Indian cultural heritage—what Central American writers of West Indian origin are doing in literature. I will return to some of these writers in a later chapter.

Notes

1. Yvonne Captain-Hidalgo, "Conversacíon con el doctor Manuel Zapata Olivella, Bogotá, 1980; 1983," *Afro-Hispanic Review* 4, no. 1 (1985): 26.
2. Patrick A. Ettrick and Roman Foster, "The Making of 'Diggers,'"*Panama Chronicle* (New York), (Winter 1984): 9.
3. Edward Mullen, ed., *The Life and Poems of a Cuban Slave, Juan Francisco Manzano, 1797–1854* (Hamden, Conn.: Archon Books, 1981), 24.
4. Ibid., 25.
5. Ibid.
6. "Notes and Reports," *The Langston Hughes Review* 5 (1986): 47.
7. Robert Chrisman, ed., "Langston Hughes: Six Letters to Nicolás Guillén," trans. Carmen Alegría, *The Black Scholar* 16, no. 4 (1985): 54–60.
8. Arnold Rampersad, *The Life of Langston Hughes, 1902–1941:* vol. I,: *I, Too, Sing America* (New York: Oxford University Press, 1986).
9. Ibid., 178.
10. Ibid., 179.
11. Ibid., 181.
12. Nicolás Guillén, *Obra poética*, vol. I (Havana: Editorial de Arte y Literatura, 1974): 164.
13. Langston Hughes, *The Panther and the Lash* (New York: A. A. Knopf, 1967), 80.
14. Ibid., 54.
15. *The Langston Hughes Reader* (New York: George Braziller, 1958): 141–42.
16. Langston Hughes, *Good Morning Revolution: Uncollected Social Protest Writings by Langston Hughes*, ed. Faith Berry (New York: Lawrence Hill and Co., 1973), 97.
17. Regino Pedroso, *Poemas* (Havana: Ediciones Unión, 1966), 100.
18. Marcelino Arozarena, *Canción negra sin color* (Havana: Ediciones Unión, 1966), 19.
19. Included in Donald Dickerson, *A Bio-Bibliography of Langston Hughes, 1902–1967* (Hamden, Conn.: Shoe String Press, 1967), 118.
20. Hortensia Ruiz del Vizo, *Black Poetry of the Americas (A Bilingual Anthology)* (Miami: Ediciones Universal, 1972), 162.
21. See Richard L. Jackson, "The *Afrocriollo* Movement Revisited," *Afro-Hispanic Review* 3 (1984): 5–9.
22. Faith Berry, *Langston Hughes: Before and Beyond Harlem* (Westport, Conn.: Lawrence Hill and Co., 1983), 321.
23. Marvin Lewis, *Afro-Hispanic Poetry, 1940–1980: From Slavery to Negritude in South American Verse* (Columbia: University of Missouri Press, 1983), 46.
24. Pilar Barrios, *Piel negra* (Montevideo: Nuestra Raza, 1947), 38.
25. Lewis, 44.
26. Berry, 59.
27. See Richard L. Jackson, "The Shared Vision of Langston Hughes and Black Hispanic Writers," *Black American Literature Forum* 15, no. 1 (1981): 89–92.
28. Hughes, *Good Morning Revolution*, xi.
29. Ibid., 139.
30. Germán Pardo García, "Honrando la memoria de Langston Hughes," *Nivel* 65 (15 February 1963): 1.

31. Edward Mullen, *Langston Hughes in the Hispanic World and Haiti* (Hamden, Conn.: Archon Books, 1977), 22.
32. Ildefonso Pereda Valdés, *Antología de la poesía negra americana* (Santiago: Ediciones Ercilla, 1936), 31.
33. Ildefonso Pereda Valdés, *Línea de color* (Santiago: Ediciones Ercilla, 1938), 79–87.
34. See Ildefonso Pereda Valdés, "Nicolás Guillén y el ritmo del son," *Línea de color*, 151.
35. Mullen, *Langston Hughes*, 25.
36. Ibid., 38.
37. José A. Balseiro, "Some Political Trends in the Literature of Hispanic America," in *The Americas Look at Each Other: Essays on the Culture and Life of the Americas* (Coral Gables: University of Miami Press, 1969), 88.
38. Langston Hughes to Marie and Doug Short, 20 May 1935. Reprinted in Berry, *Langston Hughes: Before and Beyond Harlem*, 231.
39. Richard L. Jackson, *Black Literature and Humanism in Latin America* (Athens: University of Georgia Press, 1988).
40. Yvonne Captain-Hidalgo, "Conversacíon con el doctor Manuel Zapata Olivella, *Bogotá*, 1980; 1983," *Afro-Hispanic Review* 4, no. 1 (1985): 26.
41. Captain-Hidalgo, 28.
42. Janheinz Jahn, *A History of Neo-African Literature*, trans. Oliver Coburn and Ursula Lehrburger (London: Faber and Faber, 1968), 217.
43. According to Mercer Cook, "Some Literary Contacts: African, West Indian, Afro-American," in *The Black Writer in Africa and the Americas*, ed. Lloyd W. Brown (Los Angeles: Hennessey and Ingalls, 1973), 130.
44. Abdias do Nascimento, "The Negro Theater in Brazil," *African Forum* 2 (1967): 51.
45. Ibid., 51.
46. James Emanuel, *Langston Hughes* (New York: Twayne Publishers, 1967), 44.
47. Abdias do Nascimento, ed., *Dramas para negros e prologo para brancos* (Rio de Janeiro: TEN, 1964), 21.
48. Frederic M. Litto, "Some Notes on Brazil's Black Theater," in *The Black Writer in Africa and the Americas*, ed. Lloyd W. Brown, (Los Angeles: Hennessey and Ingalls, 1973), 215.
49. Nascimento, "The Negro Theater," 48.
50. Ibid., 48.
51. Translated by Jane M. McDivitt and Phyllis Reisman. Reprinted in Jane M. McDivitt, "Contemporary Afro-Brazilian Protest Poetry," *Caribe* (April 1980): 10.
52. Cassiano Nunes, "A poesia negra no modernismo brasileiro," *Cultura* (1972): 120. Cited in Jane M. McDivitt, "Contemporary," 10.
53. McDivitt, "Contemporary," 10.
54. Ibid.
55. Ibid.
56. Berry, 325.
57. Dickerson, *Bio-Bibliography of Hughes*, 107.
58. Berry, 108.

59. In addition to the volumes by Berry, Mullen, and Rampersad, see the entire issue of *Black American Literature Forum* 15, no. 3 (1981) and *The Langston Hughes Review* 5, no. 1 (1986), both devoted to Langston Hughes's international reputation.

60. Peter Watrous, "Harlem of the '20s Echoes in America Today," *New York Times*, 22 January 1989, NR H5.

61. Langston Hughes cited in Houston A. Baker Jr., *Modernism and the Harlem Renaissance* (Chicago: University of Chicago Press, 1987), 115. Also see Guido A. Podestá, "An Ethnographic Reproach to the Theory of the Avant-Garde: Modernity and Modernism in Latin America and the Harlem Renaissance," *Modern Language Notes—Hispanic Issue* 106, no. 2 (1991): 395–422.

62. See Richard L. Jackson, "La presencia negra en la obra de Rubén Darío," *Revista iberoamericana* 33, no. 64 (1967): 395–417; and Richard L. Jackson, *The Black Image in Latin American Literature* (Albuquerque: University of New Mexico Press, 1976), 76–77.

63. See several prose items in César Vallejo, *Crónicas. Tomo I: 1915–1926* (Mexico: UNAM: 1984); and in César Vallejo, *Desde Europa. Crónicas y artículos (1923–1938)*, ed. Jorge Puccinelli (Lima: Ediciones Fuente de Cultura Peruana, 1987).

64. Baker, xiv.

65. This view of Huidobro's can be seen both in his poem "Ecuatorial" (1918) and in his article "El Arte Negro," both available in *Obras completas de Vicente Huidobro*, vol. I (Santiago: Zig-Zag, 1963), 295, 733–35, respectively.

66. Huidobro, 733.

67. Nicolás Guillén, *Obra poética, 1920–1972*, vol. I, ed. Angel Augier (Havana: Editorial de Arte y Literatura, 1974), 120.

68. Huidobro, 735.

69. Adam Lively, "Singing Stereotypes," *Times Literary Supplement* (13–19 January 1984), 30.

70. Phyllis Rose, *Jazz Cleopatra: Josephine Baker in Her Time* (New York: Doubleday, 1989).

71. Michiko Kakutani, "La Baker, the Twentieth Century's Empress Josephine," *New York Times*, Word and Image Sec., 13 October 1989.

72. See note 63.

73. César Vallejo, *Crónicas* 23.

74. Baker, *Modernism*, 1.

75. Robert Chrisman, "Impressions of Cuba: Revolutionaries and Poets," *The Black Scholar* 11, no. 3 (1980): 19.

76. Laurence Prescott, "Jorge Artel frente a Nicolás Guillén: Dos poetas mulatos ante la poesía hispanoamericana," in *Ensayistas de literatura colombiana*, ed. Raymond Williams (Bogotá: Plaza y Janés, 1984), 132.

77. Michael Walker, "The Black Social Identity in Selected Novels of Nelson Estupiñán Bass and Adalberto Ortiz," (Ph.D. diss., University of California, Riverside, 1977), 162.

78. Anne Cauley, "A Definition of Freedom in the Fiction of Richard Wright," *College Language Association Journal* 19, no. 3 (1976): 332.

79. Walker, "Black Social Identity," 189.
80. Antonio Planells, "Adalberto Ortiz: el hombre y la creación literaria," *Afro-Hispanic Review* 4, no. 2 (1985): 32.
81. Florence White, "*Poesía negra* in the Works of Jorge de Lima, Nicolás Guillén and Jacques Roumain, 1927–1947," (Ph.D. diss., University of Wisconsin, 1952), 85.
82. Emilio Ballagas, ed., *Antología de la poesía negra americana* (Madrid: Aguilar, 1935), 14.
83. Arthur P. Davis, *From the Dark Tower: Afro-American Writers, 1900 to 1960* (Washington, D.C.: Howard University Press, 1974): 5.
84. Planells, 31.
85. Yvonne Captain-Hidalgo, "Conversacíon con el doctor Manuel Zapata Olivella, Bogotá, 1980; 1983," *Afro-Hispanic Review* 4, no. 1 (1985): 31.
86. Ian Smart, "The Literary World of Quince Duncan: An Interview," *College Language Association Journal* 28, no. 3 (1985): 281.
87. See Arthur P. Davis, "Novels of the New Black Renaissance, 1960–1977: A Thematic Survey," *College Language Association Journal* 21, no. 4 (1978): 458.
88. See a companion book by Juan Williams, *Eyes on the Prize: America's Civil Rights Years, 1954–1965*, (New York: Viking, 1987).
89. Dellita Martin Ogunsola, "In Our Own Black Images: Afro-American Literature in the 1980s," *Melus* 8, no. 2 (1981): 65.
90. Amiri Baraka, "Afro-American Literature and Class Struggle," in *Daggers and Javelins: Essays, 1974–79*, (New York: William Morrow and Co., 1984), 317.
91. Michael Brookshaw, "Protest, Militancy, and Revolution: The Evolution of the Afro-Hispanic Novel of the Diaspora," (Ph.D. diss., University of Illinois, 1983), 327.
92. Ibid., 328.
93. Francis Ward and Val Gray, "The Black Artist—His Role in the Struggle," *The Black Scholar* 5, no. 2 (1971): 23.
94. Tom Morganthau et al., "Decade Shock," *Newsweek*, (5 September, 1988): 15.
95. In Chuck Stone, "The National Conference on Black Power," in *The Black Power Revolt*, ed. Floyd B. Barbour (New York: Collier Books, 1968), 225.
96. See Richard L. Jackson, *Black Writers in Latin America* (Albuquerque: University of New Mexico Press, 1979), 195.
97. See James H. Kennedy, "Political Liberalization, Black Consciousness, and Recent Afro-Brazilian Literature," *Phylon* 48, no. 3 (1986): 204–5. In fact, many more black organizations have emerged "to champion the causes of Brazil's disadvantaged African descendants." See Lori S. Robinson, "The Two Faces of Brazil," *Emerge* (October 1994): 38. Black activists in Brazil told her that the Civil Rights and Black Power Movements were significant inspirations. Rap today also provides Brazilian blacks with a U.S. style art of protest. See Katherine Ellison, "Rap Finds a Proud Niche: Musical Form Has Become Brazilian Blacks, Art of Protest," *Gazette* (Montreal), 14 July 1994, B5.
98. Kennedy, "Political Liberalization."
99. William Ruiz, "100 Years After Slavery Abolished, Racism Continues in Brazil," *Gazette*, Montreal, 3 August, 1989, A2.

100. In Elisa Larkin Nascimento, *Pan-Africanism and South America: Emergence of a Black Rebellion* (Buffalo: Afrodiaspora, 1980), 2.
101. In *Negritude et Amerique Latine* (Dakar: Les Nouvelles Editions Africaines, 1978), 174.
102. James Brooke, "Blacks of South America Fight 'a Terrible Silence,'" *New York Times International*, 28 September 1989, A4. Also see Brooke's more recent report: "The New Beat of Black Brazil Sets the Pace for Self-Affirmation," *New York Times*, 11 April 1993, E7. Brooke discusses that Brazilians have a new interest in black North America, in Martin Luther King Jr., in the Black Panthers, and in Malcolm X. He quotes Brazilian blacks who say the North American black community should know more about blacks and black culture in Brazil.
103. Manuel Zapata Olivella, "Negritud, indianidad y mestizaje en Latino America," *Présence africaine* 145 (1988), 65.
104. Manuel Zapata Olivella, *Lève toi, mulâtre* (Paris: Payot, 1987), 293. Published in Spanish as ¡*Levántate mulato!* (Bogotá: Rei Andes, 1990).
105. Dellita Martin Ogunsola, "Langston Hughes and the Musico-Poetry of the African Diaspora," *The Langston Hughes Review* 5, no. 1 (1986): 9–10.
106. David Brookshaw, *Race and Color in Brazilian Literature* (Metuchen, N.J.: The Scarecrow Press, 1986), 227.
107. Ibid., 236.
108. Zelbert Moore, "Solano Trindade Remembered, 1908–1974," *Luso-Brazilian Review* 16, no. 2 (1979): 234–35.
109. David Brookshaw, 308.
110. Ibid., 55.
111. Helen Chavis Othow, "Roots and the Heroic Search for Identity," *College Language Association Journal* 26, no. 2 (1983): 318.
112. O. R. Dathorne, *Dark Ancestor. The Literature of the Black Man in the Caribbean* (Baton Rouge: Louisiana State University Press, 1981), 254.
113. Jackson, *Black Literature and Humanism*, 73.
114. Smart, 283.
115. Margaret Styles Ambrose, "*Roots*: A Southern Symposium," *Callaloo* 2 (1978): 126.
116. Patrick A. Ettrick and Roman Foster, "The Making of 'Diggers,'" *Panama Chronicle* (New York), (Winter 1984): 9.

FOUR

Hispanic Black Writers and the United States

> The worst thing American blacks have
> is American whites. But actually,
> that is not true. There are
> many whites who are
> friends of blacks.
> —Nicolás Guillén[1]

RACISM AND BLACK AMERICA

The issue of racism and the status of black Americans in the United States have had a strong impact on African Hispanic writers. Renée Larrier[2] has done a very fine study of poems written about this issue in French and in Spanish. She begins her study with the Caribbean poets, discussing the political and social background in the Caribbean that helped shape the poets' outlooks. She focuses specifically on the pervasive presence of the United States in the area. Noting that worldwide black consciousness was high and that concern for U.S. blacks was strong, she reviews specific incidents in the United States that, over the years, have fueled protest from abroad.

U.S. troops from the South brought their racist attitudes, habits, and policies with them into countries such as Cuba, imposing their style of segregation and discrimination. Caribbean poets experienced this climate of imported racial bias at home, and through the media they also kept abreast of Jim Crow practices in the United States. Cable and radio carried reports of beatings, lynchings, and bombings in the South, and Cuban newspapers and the world press kept their readers informed about the civil rights struggle in the United States. Larrier cites specific newspapers that carried coverage of events such as the 1963 March on Washington, the integration attempts in Alabama as well as Governor Wallace's resistance, the bombing of the Birmingham church in which four young girls were killed, and the desegregation of schools in Little Rock, Arkansas. Larrier also mentions personal testimony as another source of information and inspiration for black Hispanic writers. One example is the speech given in Havana by Paul Robeson's wife describing her status in the United States. Nicolás Guillén, in particular, did not miss an opportunity to question people about his black brothers. He used interviews with writers such as Waldo Frank (a practice he had started years before with Langston Hughes himself when the latter came to the island for the first time) to inquire about particular friends and to get opinions about the race problem in general.

Black writers in Latin America had heard and read about racism in the United States and some of them, like Guillén himself, had experienced it firsthand on trips to the United States. Perhaps as much as anything else, Guillén's own journey in 1937 (between Mexico and New York) solidified his disgust with the United States. Thirty years after writing it, Guillén includes the text of his comments about a 1952 stopover in New York en route to Moscow: "It was not the first time I had set foot on North American land. In 1937 I had passed rapidly through the States on the way to Canada in a train trip from Mexico. . . . It was a slow and monotonous trip."[3] When Guillén saw Harlem, he felt a familiarity with the famous black district because he had read so much about it and because many Cuban and American friends had told him about it. A marked curiosity led Guillén to get to know this black city within a city: "I wanted to see with my own eyes a half million people separated from the rest of the population as if they were suffering from some terrible contagious disease. . . . Harlem left me with a feeling of anguish not easily forgotten, even though a long time has passed since I was there."[4]

Guillén saw Harlem close up, but long before he saw it with his own eyes, he had written an article about Harlem, which even preceded his first black poetry. In this 1929 short essay, titled "Camino de Harlem,"[5] he admonished Cubans to avoid going the way of Harlem, that is, avoid imposing segregation and discrimination that inevitably would lead to the creation of a city within a city. Guillén saw Harlem as the result of two societies in conflict and urged Cubans to work against the creation of such a "black district" in Cuba. Guillén as journalist wrote other articles about the "cancer of racism"[6] in the United States in which he continued to argue against the creation of "separate" even if equal facilities.

Larrier divides the poems she discusses into three categories: those dealing with the Scottsboro case, those on the South in general, and those on black heroes. On the Scottsboro case she cites the active role Cubans took in the worldwide outcry after the arrest, trial, and conviction of the eight boys for the alleged rape of two white prostitutes in a railroad car. She cites poems from the 1930s, among them, Regino Pedroso's "Hermano negro" ("Black Brother"): "Escucha allá en Scottsboro, en Scottsboro, en Scottsboro" ("Listen to what is going on there, in Scottsboro, in Scottsboro, in Scottsboro"), which probably inspired Ana González's "Romance negro del negro" ("A Black Ballad") and Marcelino Arozarena's "Evohé": "Piensa un poco en Scottsboro y no en Ogún" ("Think a little bit about Scottsboro and not about Ogún").

The next category, the South, is a large one that she divides into two subcategories: those poems that treat lynchings and Jim Crow, and those that were inspired by the desegregation efforts of the 1950s and 1960s. Guillén's poems "Lynch" and "KKK" characterize the first subcategory; his Alabama poems—together with Nancy Morejón's "Freedom Now," "Gobernador" ("Governor") with its obvious reference to George Wallace, and "Escolares" ("Students")—characterize the second. All of these poems are extremely critical of racism and the treatment of U.S. blacks. For the Caribbean poets, Alabama became a symbol of the worst in the United States because of the ferocity with which officials in that state fought integration. Guillén addressed white resistance in Arkansas in the poem "Little Rock." Larrier believes the definitive and most militant poem in this group is "Está bien" ("All Right"), from *Tengo* (*I Have*, 1964), in which Guillén says that marches, demonstrations, court suits, clenched fists, and sermons are "all right" as means to an end—integration.

Because many of the U.S. black figures from the civil rights movement had died by the time this poetry was written, the poems lauding these latter-day heroes are almost always elegies: Guillén's "Elegía a Emmett Till" (1955), poems on assassinated civil rights leaders in the 1960s like Medgar Evers, Malcolm X, and Martin Luther King Jr. Perhaps the best known in the group are Guillén's "¿Qué color?" on Martin Luther King Jr., the "noble pastor," and the poem "Angela Davis" on the female activist Guillén greatly admired. This poem had been discussed in 1973 by Miriam DeCosta,[7] who also provided a full

translation. Guillén's poem sees Davis as an "inexhaustible force" capable of enduring the burnings and lynchings and the Ku Klux Klan, anything her "executioners" can throw at her. De Costa's article refers to the Scottsboro incident and the murder of Emmett Till, as well as to Guillén's poems "Little Rock" ("in that faubus world / beneath the hard faubus-sky of gangrene . . ."), and "A Black Sings in New York" (his"hymn" against Jim Crow). Surprisingly, however, in her article designed for black American readers, DeCosta makes no reference to "¿Qué color?" (Guillén's poem on the greatest of U.S. black heroes, Dr. Martin Luther King Jr.).

Blacks in the United States are seen by Guillén and by other African Hispanic writers as heroes who have been victims of oppression in American society. U.S. blacks have also been shown as martyrs and as symbols of resistance, model figures in the fight against racism in this hemisphere. Amiri Baraka has commented on this "interesting aspect" of Guillén's work, namely, "his attention not only to the face of United States imperialism in the Caribbean and Latin America, but also to its vicious oppression of the Afro-American people in the U.S.A., particularly in the black-belt South."[8] The two fundamental preoccupations in Guillén's work have always been, first, the presence and impact of United States imperialism in Cuba, the West Indies, and Latin America, and, second, the treatment of blacks in the United States itself. Baraka recognized that Guillén was always "full of fight," spending his time celebrating and defending the Revolution but pointing out at the same time the injustice that was still going on inside the United States and the rest of the world.

Joseph Pereira explains why Guillén continued to attack racism in the United States even after 1959: "His attack against racism in the United States is a continuation of his attack against the imperialism that has been intimately linked to it, which Guillén attacked in his earlier poetry."[9] Pereira posits that by keeping United States racism on the front burner, Guillén guarded against its ever reappearing in Cuba. Pereira makes another interesting point: Guillén used racism in the United States "to criticize those Cubans who leave Cuba";[10] he criticized them in his prose and in his poetry. In the 1960s, Guillén was still writing articles about racism in the United States, reminding blacks who leave Cuba for the United States that they will never

find, certainly not in the South, the kind of brotherhood they had left behind in Cuba. This brotherhood was just not possible historically and traditionally in the United States, particularly in view of the tremendous social upheaval the country was then undergoing at battlegrounds like Watts in Los Angeles and in what Guillén called "the Harlem ghetto." He considered Harlem to be like a pot heating up from below and about to boil over.

The world press at the time had told of the climate of terror and armed struggle. Why should blacks want to leave Cuba, Guillén asked, to go into such an atmosphere of blood and death? Guillén's prose and poetry often mutually complement, and on this subject he wrote the poem, "¡Ay, qué tristeza que tengo!": "Un negro en Miami / no tiene casa donde vivir: / un negro en Miami / no tiene mesa donde comer . . . / Ay, qué tristeza que tengo / . . . viendo correr a este negro / sin que lo persiga nadie."[11] ("Ay, how sad I am!": "A black in Miami / has no place to live: / a black in Miami / has no food to eat . . . / Ay, how sad I am / . . . seeing the black run / when no one is chasing him." One of the most inclusive, though prosaic, summaries of Guillén's Yankee bashing is found in Harvey Johnson's survey article:

He finds nothing good in the United States, symbolized by Little Rock, the Ku Klux Klan, Jim Crow, battleships in Cuban waters, drunken marines, imperialism, neocolonialism, materialism, and rapacious capitalism. Furthermore, the U.S. places obstacles to the growth of a national consciousness in Cuba and the development of its culture and ideology. He disparages the United States for the practice of racial discrimination and denigrates Presidents Truman, Eisenhower, Kennedy, and Nixon; Governor Faubus; and Senator McCarthy. He condemns the United States because of its constant involvement in the affairs of Cuba and other Spanish American nations. He denounces North Americans for exploitation of the resources and inhabitants of the islands of the Caribbean, Central America, Venezuela, and other small countries. He shows contempt for Cubans who, in pursuit of the dollar, sell themselves to Yankee capitalists and censures, albeit somewhat sadly, those who emigrated after Castro's victory. He pities the Puerto Ricans who live under the menace of losing their native language and ancestral tradition. He makes a plea for an end of United States hegemony in Latin America.[12]

Perhaps no Latin American writer kept an eye focused on the United States, racism, and black America longer or with more attention than Cuba's Nicolás Guillén, who was criticizing the United States even before the publication in 1930 of his *Motivos de son* (*Sound Motifs*), the black poems that first made him famous. His anti-imperialist mode was deep-rooted and long established, dating back to when his father was alive and duped by the United States:

> My father was a Liberal leader with a very active life, and a professional journalist of high standing. Having just returned from the War of Independence, in which he achieved the rank of second lieutenant, he founded, with a confederate of his named Pedro Mendoza—an orator who sometimes wrote poetry—a newspaper which they called "The Two Republics." It seems to me that both my father and his friend succumbed to a political mirage, the same one which deceived many Cubans when the Republic was established. There is little doubt in my mind that those "two republics" were Cuba and the United States, since as is well known the Yankees disguised their imperialist penetration in our country, directed towards the exploitation of our resources, under the cloak of a "protection" which never existed.[13]

Guillén published his memoirs, *Páginas vueltas*[14] (*Turned Pages*) in 1982. In this volume, which undoubtedly will generate continued interest in his prose, Guillén tried to set the record straight regarding his long-standing attitude toward the "Yankee presence." The book, one of Guillén's last publications, presented many new problems and challenges. The initial problem or challenge with the memoir was that it was written by a man who had already published a great deal about himself and the United States in prose and in poetry. His memoir would have to be seen in the context of other sources that cover the same ground, which include existing biographies of and published interviews with him, his speeches, his own three-volume *Prosa de prisa* (*Prose on the Run*), his poetry, and other autobiographical material previously published in newspapers. It would be rewarding to establish relationships among the material while documenting the problem of selectivity Guillén must have encountered in preparing this work.

Another challenge would have been to distinguish differences in style and narrative *persona* between this and his other work.

The lyric protagonist we came to know so well through Guillén's verse is here a narrative voice. The greatest challenge would have been to try to answer this question: Is this Guillén's novel? If so, what is the narrative line that gives the work unity? Is it sufficiently different from his journalism in perspective and narrative coherence to lend itself to "fiction"? Is he the "hero"? Does Guillén reshape history especially regarding the United States as he looks back on it from his fully formed position.

There are three overriding impressions one gets from the book: (1) throughout his early years Guillén was surrounded by blacks as well as whites, from his white uncle to his black *abuela*, (grandmother) and his racial consciousness was acute; (2) the "Yankee" presence was a factor early in his life and in his consciousness; and (3) his father was a strong formative force in his early years, and remained so throughout his life. Guillén conveys very well divisions and conflicts, not only among whites and blacks and mulattoes but also between liberals and conservatives and between Cuba and the United States. Especially interesting are those pages dealing with his father, with his family, with his neighborhood, and with societies based on color. There are good descriptions of these societies and of black characters out of his past. They are interesting because of how they were, how Guillén remembered them, and, most important, how he described his memories of them.

Regarding the United States, we are never allowed to lose sight of what was "the suffocating influence of the empire next door." There is much critical commentary in *Páginas vueltas* regarding his opposition to the U.S. presence in Cuba. We should notice, however, that while harsh at times, Guillén does show tact and discretion in his memoir with regard to the United States. He is careful, for example, to term his life-long opposition to the United States as *rebeldía* not *odio* ("rebellion" not "hate"), since he recognized that there are good people in the United States who react as he did against its negative aspects. His father— Guillén quite simply elevates to the status of martyr. There are many references throughout the book to his father's death, already immortalized in the dedication page of *Cantos para soldados* (*Songs for Soldiers*) in the words "To my father, killed by soldiers," words that are as well known as the poems in the collection themselves.

There are many serious and dramatic moments in the book, and there is, as well, an abundance of humor. Guillén's humor, especially when criticizing the United States, can be sharp. Stylistically, Guillén's language is elegant, almost floral, and full of charm. Structurally, the book is organized into four (untitled) parts, but the real divisions seem to focus on what I suspect Guillén himself considered his three most significant books: *Motivos de son* (1930), *West Indies Ltd.* (1934), and *Elegía a Jesús Menéndez (Elegy to Jesús Menéndez)* (1948–1951). In all of these key books the "Yankee presence" is decidedly strong. While a number of critics have confirmed that some of Guillén's poetry drew inspiration from his prose, we can also say that his memoirs grew out of, or were shaped by, his poetry. Guillén the poet had always been conscious of the *novedad* ("newness") of these works (and of *Sóngoro cosongo*, 1931), and of the new directions they heralded in his art and ideology. *Motivos de son* (and *Sóngoro cosongo* "which was a new kind of . . . book") marks "a deep dividing gap between my first attempts at poetry and the road I was to later follow." *West Indies Ltd.*, which he considered a "civic elegy," part of a *suite* of eight, represents his coming of age as a social poet. Guillén considered *Elegía a Jesús Menéndez*, quite simply, one of the "greatest poems in the Spanish language." Guillén recalls other literary "highlights" from his past ("Al margen de mis libros de estudio" and his poems on Che Guevara, for example), and he gives background material for some of his poems, not meaningful on a larger scale but significant to the poet personally, to clarify the circumstances of their composition. But the real milestones in his development must include *Motivos de son*, *West Indies Ltd.*, and *Elegía a Jesús Menéndez*.

Páginas vueltas, perhaps, could be the biggest milestone of all, especially if we consider Guillén's memoirs are a novel, but not a novel in the "mentira" sense or fiction as an invention but rather as a true, personal, social, and political history as Guillén, the narrative voice, remembers it. I have always thought of Guillén as the lyric protagonist of many of his poems, a heroic protagonist who in poetry reflects the courageous stands he has often taken in his journalism and speeches, his stand against the United States for one example. Guillén's memoirs are meant to entertain, but they have a decided ideological focus from the very first page, as he makes literature out of his life and his political beliefs. At times his memoirs read like an autobiographical novel or a political novel. His book is told in the first person, but there is re-created dialogue, good character description, and dramatic narration. Thus the book holds the reader's attention throughout because the author has lived the events narrated. This is not a "historical" novel of what might have been but a clear, chronological record of the circumstances that gave birth to his views.

Guillén's memoirs are not filled with ego or high self-regard. In fact, Guillén rarely presents himself or his views in isolation from the modern history of Cuba. In his memoirs, the man and the nation are inextricably linked because the conditions that influenced his development and especially his attitude toward the United States are the same ones that helped shape and influence his country. Guillén seems at all times to be aware that he is writing as much about his own birth and growth as about Cuba's, especially when he dwells on historical factors such as colonialism and slavery and on geographical factors such as the proximity of the United States. What gives the work coherence, unity, and a narrative line is Guillén's account of these factors and forces that shaped his personal and his political development from his early days in Camagüey, his *patria chica* ("hometown"), to revolutionary fulfillment in the "new Cuba," his *patria nueva*. These are his memoirs but they provide, like his poetry and his journalism, an overview of Cuba since his birth.

Guillén always presented himself in literature as witness, conscience, and participant in his historical time. But here he is not just a first-person reporter of journalism or a poetic *persona* of verse. In the narrative format of his memoirs, Guillén becomes the protagonist he has often been in his poetry. Here he is able to step outside poetry and journalism and to assume a linear, active, narrative *persona* who not only reports but also lives inside the subject of his reporting. Guillén manages to draw the reader inside his world and he makes the reader empathize with his long-standing opposition to the United States. Drawing readers intimately into his confidence was Guillén's way of convincing them that he and they are one. Guillén's obsession with the issue of racism spanned decades. While no other black Hispanic writer has been so obsessed over as long a time, there is general antagonism throughout the black Hispanic world toward the treatment of blacks in the United States. Racist policies associated with the United States affected blacks in Central America as well as those in the Caribbean. Most hurt were blacks of West Indian origin, especially those who worked for the United Fruit Company and the Canal Zone.

For many Hispanic blacks of West Indian descent, Marcus Garvey was a hero. Garvey was "the Jamaican Black of pure African blood, descended from Maroons, who founded the Universal Negro Improvement Association, an organization that preached black solidarity in the 1920s to an enthusiastic audience, including the Blacks of Limón and other parts of Spanish America."[15] There are many references in black Hispanic literature to Marcus Garvey, who worked for a time on a banana plantation in Limón, Costa Rica. Pedro Dull, the protagonist of *La paz del pueblo* (*The Peace of the People*) by the Afro-Costa Rican author Quince Duncan, is a follower of Garvey. Carlos Guillermo Wilson, the Panamanian black writer now living in the United States, uses some words from Garvey as an opening epigraph to his first novel *Chombo*: "A people without knowledge of their past history, origin, and culture is like a tree without roots."

Wilson, or "Cubena" as he prefers to be called, has also written a powerful little poem titled "Gatún,"[16] which begins:

	K	K	K
No queremos	o	o	r
	c	l	i
	a	a	n
			g
			a

	K	K	K
We don't want	o	o	r
	c	l	i
	a	a	n
			g
			a

Ian Smart, whose translation I am using here, was perhaps the first to comment extensively on this poem. Smart summarizes Wilson's attitude toward the United States presence in Panama as illustrated in this poem about Gatún. An important lake in the Panama Canal, Gatún is situated near the Caribbean end of the waterway, not far from the town of Colón:

> No reader can miss the basic sense of the material pun achieved by the clever configuration of the poem; the definitive rejection of the KKK, the Ku Klux Klan, the white terrorist group that many

people instinctively associate with the most hateful aspects of American racism. . . . "Koca" is simply a form of "Coca" that the poet has taken the liberty to spell with a "K," for obvious reasons. In like fashion, the word "gringo, a" (adjective or noun commonly used to refer primarily to white North Americans) is with poetic license transformed into "Kringa" through the simple step of unvoicing the initial velar stop. This physical and mental image translated into unpoetic Spanish is "No queremos Coca Cola gringa" (We don't want Yankee Coca Cola). In one clever swoop Cubena has riveted our attention onto the two most essential features of the American occupation of Panama and the consequent imposition of a new plantation system, namely, a vicious systematic racism, and a pernicious laissez-faire capitalism. . . .[17]

Just as Guillén in *West Indies Ltd.* characterizes the Caribbean as a big American enterprise, Cubena, as Smart has shown, attacks and resents the Panama-as-Plantation concept imposed on the country by the American presence. Wilson, called the most important black writer in Latin America today,[18] is certainly one of the most aggressive and uncompromising—in his attacks on racism both in the United States (his adopted country) and in his native Panama as well as in his determination to affirm the *chombo* contribution to America. By using *Chombo* as the title of his first novel, Wilson takes what normally would be a derogatory term for black Panamanians of West Indian ancestry and proudly moves it center stage.

Research on black journals from the 1930s and 1940s in Uruguay reveals a large number of references to black Americans in the United States. The Pilar Barrios poem "Voices" on Langston Hughes and Virginia Brindis de Salas's poem "Canto para un muchacho americano del Sur" ("Song for a Black American Boy from the South") are but two examples. These journals carried articles on George Washington Carver, Booker T. Washington, Claude McKay, Joe Louis, Jesse Owens, Marian Anderson, Ethel Waters, Paul Robeson, and Duke Ellington. There were even self-help organizations named after Booker T. Washington. One of the journals was called *Bahía Hulan Jack*, a name taken from the predominantly black state in Brazil and from a black New York politician. Black Americans in the United States clearly had a symbolic significance for blacks in Uruguay.

In Ecuador the novels of Nelson Estupiñán Bass often carry protests against United States imperialism and economic exploitation of Ecuador's natural resources. This is especially evident in *Senderos brillantes* (*Shining Paths*, 1974) and in *Bajo el cielo nublado* (*Under the Clouded Sky*, 1981) where the Afro-Ecuadorian writer creates the ultimate absurdity, namely, a Hispanic "gringoized" mulatto who did not just love everything "made in the U.S.A." but even changed his name from Roque Quintero to Rock King and went to the United States. The character learns how to "sell out" his country and he returns to Ecuador to exploit it. Estupiñán Bass has always shown solidarity with U.S. blacks. His message to them and to blacks everywhere is "Unámonos"[19] ("Let us Unite"), which seems to contrast sharply with that of his compatriot Adalberto Ortiz, who advised blacks in the United States not to put so much emphasis on racism. Not only does Ortiz not deal with racism in the United States, but also he advises U.S. blacks not to deal with it.[20]

Nelson Estupiñán Bass always manages to work black themes and characters into his novels. Ortiz, however, came to purposely avoid them, not only because he believed blacks in Ecuador and elsewhere should focus on class rather than race—a point he made consistently both in and since *Juyungo* (1943)—but also because he put his Esmeraldas roots behind him, having spent much of his time since his youth elsewhere in the world. Other black Hispanic writers in South America, however, have attacked racism in the United States as well as in their own countries, including the Peruvian black Nicomedes Santa Cruz. His best-known poem in this category is "De igual a igual," where the poet expresses a desire to take on George Wallace head to head in "savage" combat. "Muerte en el ring" ("Death in the Ring") also refers to the plight and suffering of blacks in the United States and to the racism and exploitation that victimize them. The Colombian black poet Helcías Martán Góngora has an entire group of poems in his *Mester de negrería* (*Black Verse*, 1966) that he places under the title "Made in U.S.A." They are "El buen pastor" ("The Good Pastor"), "Integración racial" ("Racial Integration"), "Negro espiritual," and "Made in U.S.A.," plus an epitaph "Epitafio negro" ("Black Epitaph") composed later, for Martin Luther King Jr.

Other Colombian blacks who were knowledgeable about racism and U.S. blacks include the novelist Arnoldo Palacios, whose black protagonist Irra, in *Las estrellas son negras* (*The Stars*

Are Black, 1949), read about KKK activity in the United States. Jorge Artel, Juan Zapata Olivella, and Manuel Zapata Olivella are perhaps best versed in the black experience in the United States, where all three have spent time. Marvin Lewis has said that the one salient characteristic of Artel's *Antología poética* (*Poetry Collection*, 1979) is that "it demonstrates how well versed Artel is in the black experience throughout the Americas instead of being limited to Colombia."[21] Artel has a Ph.D. in law and political science from the University of Cartagena, his home city, and has traveled widely. He has lectured at both Princeton and Columbia Universities and, in fact, lived in the United States for three years. Artel no doubt has some personal experience with the kinds of things he mentions in English in many of his poems that are in Spanish, terms such as *jazz bands, jazz sessions, waiting rooms, dancing, cowboy, gangster, ragtime, girls, furnished room, humming, clown,* and *Harlem,* the title of one of his poems. Artel focuses on aspects of the black experience in the United States from the "hot sex" and music of Harlem to lynchings: "Los recuerdo, silenciosos, / bajo la resignada indiferencia / en el 'waiting room,' / ... He visto perseguirlos como fieras / lincharlos / ...'[22] (I remember them, silent / with resigned indifference / in the *waiting room* / ... I've seem them hunted down like wild animals / lynched ...").

Artel understands the shared history of blacks in the Americas, and he communicates very well his identification with the "hombre oscuro del sur" ("black man of the South"). He becomes that person and feels with him "la mirada larga del hombre blanco / cayendo sobre mi carne / como un látigo"[23] ("the long blue-eyed stare of the white man / coming down across me / like a whip"). Considering his time spent in the United States partly in and around New York, it is not surprising to find a poem among his works on that city. In fact, "Palabras a la ciudad de Nueva York" is Artel's longest poem, one that refers to and captures the sights and geography of a city of "vice and virtue: Times Square, Brooklyn, Harlem, Lexington Avenue, the Bowery, the Village, the subway, Wall Street, Columbia University, Madison Square Garden, Manhattan, Chinatown, Radio City, the Empire State Building, the Hudson River and the East River, Coney Island, the East Side, and Broadway. All of these landmarks appear in the poem, together with references to statues, monuments, and museums, in what is clearly Artel's attempt to show that New York City is a place for everybody, one that generates every kind of emotional reaction. This poem, really a salute to a city known throughout the world, shows New York's role as a place of hopes and dreams, not always realized:

> Te hablo, Nueva York
> desde mi soledad
> compartida por diez millones de habitantes
> ....
> desde la risa o la lágrima
> que tiemblan en alguna guitarra latina,
> bajo las luces amarillas de Lexington Avenue;
> ....
> desde cualquier rincón de Harlem
> la orgullosa humanidad que espera y canta
> refugiada en sus blues de sarcástica tristeza.[24]

> (I speak to you, New York
> from my solitude
> shared by ten million people
> ....
> from the laughter and tears
> vibrating in some Latin guitar
> under the yellow lights of Lexington Avenue;
> ....
> from any street corner in Harlem
> where proud humanity hopes and sings
> taking refuge in the sarcastic sadness of the blues.)

"Palabras a la ciudad de Nueva York" is a poem on monuments, statues, and places, but it focuses on the human element as well, along with the effects of the city, "mezquina y generosa . . . leyenda y realidad"[25] ("stingy and generous . . . legend and reality"), on human lives. Although the poem is more picturesque than political, we can see in it the seed of the later poetry of Artel. When he writes "Wall Street, / pequeño grande imperio de impávidos mercaderes y eruditos profetas. / Son tuyos el 'trust,' el 'dollar,' . . ."[26] ("Wall Street, / a small great empire of intrepid merchants and erudite prophets. / The 'trusts' and the 'dollar' belong to you . . ."), we anticipate the poet who will later place anti-imperialistic sentiment at the core of what will become his political themes.

Evolution is characteristic of Artel's poetry, even from edition to edition of the same work. Laurence Prescott has noted that the second edition of *Tambores en la noche* (*Drums in the Night*, 1955) is "blacker" than the first edition published in 1940. Defending Artel's title of "the black poet of Colombia," Prescott says that the black poems of the second edition are certainly black poetry of the highest quality. Prescott has examined both editions and says that the 1955 edition has twenty-one new poems "bolder and more forceful" in tone and that they "bear witness to the poet's travels, experiences, and psychic developments both within and without Colombia."[27]

The "bolder and more forceful" second edition, it should be noted, was published following Artel's three-year stay in the United States. While the first edition corresponds to the period when poetic Negrism was rampant, the second contains poems that transcend cultural and literary movements—poems such as "Soneto más negro" ("The Blackest Sonnet"), "Al drummer negro de un jazz sessión" ("To the Black Drummer of a Jazz Session"), and "Poema sin odios ni temores" ("Poem With Neither Hate Nor Fear"), in which the poet builds on the title of "the black poet of Colombia," already conferred by earlier poems like "Negro soy" ("I Am Black") from the first edition. Now, Prescott correctly writes, Artel has broadened his view to include Africa, Harlem, and the Antilles, his point being that Artel now has moved beyond the picturesque part of black life and on to the tragedy and grief often associated with being black, especially in America.[28] In this second edition, Artel addresses the "great themes" of black poetry like affirmation of black identity and racial equality.

Prescott considers Artel's six-year period of travel outside Colombia between 1949 and 1955 to be an odyssey, which the poet translated into the twenty-one additional poems that prompted the second, revised edition of *Tambores en la noche*. Some of these poems, which were inspired by black people in the United States, enabled Artel to bridge the gulf between Ibero and Anglo America and to "unveil"[29] the fraternal bonds linking Americans of African descent. Prescott has also contrasted the "black poet" identity of Artel, who wanted to be known by that title, with Nicolás Guillén, who did not. Both Artel and Guillén started out in poetic Negrism and its rhythmic aspect, but both wanted to move on, to give another direction to black poetry, which they did, but they evolved differently. Guillén, "like a good Marxist," moves away from racial consciousness, Prescott says, and toward a national and political one, while Artel continued even more to embrace the title of "black poet." Prescott recognizes that Artel and Guillén are both "companions of the Marxist ideology," but he believes that in contrast to Guillén's work, politics is virtually nonexistent in Artel's black poetry. This might be true in poems like "Negro soy," but one cannot say, as Prescott does, that "Artel . . . was more concerned with spiritual emotion,"[30] especially judging from some of Artel's most recent poetry.

It seems, in fact, that Artel has surpassed even Guillén in his rage against the United States. In his poetry the African Colombian has gone from defense of blacks to defense of Castro, Cuba, and Lenin, which he combines with political and ideological attacks on the United States. Juvenal Herrera Torres[31] in his prologue to Artel's *Antología poética* (1979) gives an interpretation of Artel's poetry that contrasts sharply with Prescott's view.[32] Herrera presents Artel as a poet of blacks everywhere, mentioning New York where they are "spit on by mean, racist, fascist yankee idiots." Herrera presents Artel as an anti-imperialist and Third World poet who writes in praise of Lenin ("Credo" and "Canto a Lenin") and Castro and the Cuban Revolution ("Esquema para un canto a Fidel Castro" and "Fenecida emoción de Cuba") and who sings of peace ("Memorandum para un canto a la paz").

In "Credo" ("My Belief") Artel recalls Guillén at his most vitriolic: "Creo en / . . . la paz . . . / mas no es la paz de Mr. President / made in U.S.A. / a base de conquistas denigrantes / firmadas con la sangre de los pueblos más débiles, / después que haya hecho su good bussines / el mercader de armas / y en el violado territorio de Vietnam / la muerte, hablando inglés. . . . Creo en . . . la libertad de Puerto Rico . . . sin gringos / . . . en la desaparición definitiva de imperialistas . . ." ("I believe in / . . . peace . . . / but not the peace of Mr. President / made in the U.S.A. / through denigrating conquests, signed with the blood of weaker nations, / after the arms merchant / has done his *good bussines* / and in violated Vietnam / death, speaking English . . . / I believe in / . . . freedom in Puerto Rico . . . without gringos . . . in the disappearance of imperialists once and for all . . .").

In "Fenecida emoción de Cuba" ("Cuba's Dying Emotion") Artel, like Guillén before him, mocks those Cubans who fled to Miami abandoning the revolution: "Un morbo del Sur estadounidense / inoculo principios / de pretendidas castas superiores / a aquella seudoaristocracia / que se ufana de España entre sus venas . . ." ("A disease of the American South / contaminated principles / of a breed that thinks itself superior / that pseudo aristocracy / that boasts of having Spanish blood in its veins"). In "Memorandum para un canto a la paz" ("Memo for a Peace Song") he writes that "los dulces blues son sacrificados / por la noche sin rostro / y ensangrentada del Ku Klux Klan" ("the sweet blues are sacrificed / by a faceless night / bloodied by the Ku Klux Klan"), while "Black Power" is born in "Manhattan, Chicago, Kansas City" ("Volver") ("Returning").

Finally, Artel writes in "Este duro salitre que se extiende en mi pecho" ("This Hard Saltpeter That Is Filling My Chest"): "Debes preguntar / por Langston / . . . / para que con su voz de eternidad / te diga / que Allende está más vivo / que en todos sus inviernos / listo para morir cada primavera" (You must ask/ for Langston / . . . so that he can tell you / with his voice from eternity / that Allende is more alive / than in all his winters / ready to die each spring"). Earlier we saw English words in his poetry such as *waiting room, jazz band,* and *drummer.* Now he peppers his verse with pejorative and political allusions to Wall Street, Washington, the Pentagon, and the American dollar.

The African Colombian brothers Juan and Manuel Zapata Olivella are two of the black Hispanic writers with a good deal of experience in the United States, and their literature often reflects it. Juan Zapata Olivella's first novel, *Historia de un joven negro* (*A Young Black's Story,* 1983) is dedicated to the memory of Martin Luther King Jr.; his second novel, *Pisando el camino de ébano* (*Treading the Ebony Path,* 1984), carries an epigraph from Langston Hughes in the front and a picture of the author with the late Mayor Washington of Chicago on the back. His third novel, *Entre dos mundos* (*Between Two Worlds,* 1990), is set, in part, in the United States. His book of "liberated poetry" titled *Panacea: poesía liberada* (*Panacea: Liberated Poetry,* 1976) has a lead-off quote from Booker T. Washington. This volume also contains the poem "U.S.A. 200 años":

> Y llegaron los inmigrantes
> y vieron la nueva tierra
> ....
> y tras ellos
> otras gentes vinieron

de tierras lejanas y exóticas

....

y un buen día pensaron
en una patria propia y libre[33]

....

(And the immigrants came
and saw the new land

....

and after them
other people came
from exotic, far off places

....

and one good day they
thought about having a country of their own, free
............................)

This salute to America, reminiscent of Artel's salute to New York, is a history lesson but a curious one, conspicuous for what is not mentioned. How blacks came to this country is an example of the history that is missing. Nor are native Americans part of this commemorative exercise. One can see an irony here. Despite all the glorious terminology that defines the American experience during its 200 years since independence, the question remains: Are all the people really considered equal in this land whose charter says all people were born that way? Or do Americans trust in God and remain firm in their Christian principles in the same boastful way ex-President Botha and his South African brethren did?

Juan Zapata Olivella's interest in the United States, racism, and U.S. blacks is shared by his brother, Manuel. As I have already mentioned, Manuel met Langston Hughes in New York in the 1940s, a meeting he describes in *He visto la noche*, a little book that deals exclusively with his experiences in the United States. Manuel Zapata Olivella set a good deal of his other literature in the United States as well: A play titled *Hotel de vagabundos* (*Vagabond Hotel*), a couple of short stories titled "Un extraño bajo mi piel" ("A Stranger Under My Skin") and "¿Quién dio el fusil a Oswald?" ("Who Shot Oswald?"), and his big novel *Changó, el gran putas* (1983) are some examples. The novel he published in Cuba in 1962, *Chambacú, corral de negros*, was critical of the United States regarding the Peace Corps and the Alliance for Progress, which he saw as American pretexts to keep Latin

Americans from becoming Communist. The novel condemns the United States, its involvement in the Korean War, and its hypocrisy. *Chambacú* asks questions such as "How can they come and talk to us about schools when they deny a university education to James Meridith?"[34] As we saw earlier, *Chambacú* both in style and content is reminiscent of the "Turbulent Sixties" in the United States and of some of the militant, protest literature that the period produced.

Infused with "the souls of black folk" and with "soul-force"— the unbreakable courage and human spirit of the African that enabled him to survive in the New World—*Changó, el gran putas*[35] is also of interest to U.S. blacks. In this novel, Manuel Zapata Olivella traces the history of black survival from preslavery days in Africa to the black struggle in the United States today. The author, well versed in the subject, divides black history into five "sagas" or "novels" spanning different geographical areas and centuries. The five parts, or "distinct, separate novels,"[36] are (1) "Los orígenes," an overture in poetry that focuses on the mythological beginnings and the slave trade; (2) "El muntu americano," 100 years later in Cartagena, the first century of blacks in the New World; (3) "La rebelión de los vodú," the story of Haiti and the "soul-force" that led to independence; (4) "Las sangres encontradas," or the black influence in the liberation struggles in the nineteenth century led by Bolivar and others; and (5) "Los ancestros combatientes," set in the United States, where the black struggle, especially the Civil Rights Movement in the 1960s, is presented as the final battleground in the New World on the long journey from Africa to freedom in America. Part 5 of the novel is of interest to us because many of its characters are well-known U.S. black heroes—among them are Langston Hughes, Harriet Tubman, Nat Turner, Booker T. Washington, W. E. B. Du Bois, Marcus Garvey, Malcolm X, Frederick Douglass, and Martin Luther King Jr. In the same book they share the spotlight with Agne Brown, "a fictitious black North American militant from the 1960s who calls to mind Angela Davis."[37]

Part 5 can be read as the education of Agne Brown. She is a representative freedom fighter who is constantly being "taught" by various historical characters, who inspire her with accounts of black heroism. Agne Brown provides the glue that holds Part 5 together. What holds her together and maintains her steadfast in her purpose is the guidance or enlightenment she receives from all the "supporting" cast in the novel—heroes who have shaped American history and the black role in it. The novel—and Part 5—ends in a great show of "Muntu solidarity," characterized by the March on Washington, a time when *ekobios* (spiritual or "soul" brothers) of all races came together in a symbolic show of brotherhood.

It is inevitable that the search for freedom in the New World, which this novel traces, culminates in the United States, considering that the issue of racism has so dominated the black experience in that country. Part 5 of the novel is devoted to the history of the black struggle in the United States. The spirit of that struggle is as important as the history, and in this sense *Changó, el gran putas* recalls W. E. B. Du Bois, whose work *The Souls of Black Folk* is the custodian of that spirit. Zapata Olivella has said that he considers Du Bois to be the most important architectural pioneer of both the old and the new black renaissance movements, north and south, and that as a New World thinker he belongs with José Martí and Benito Juárez. He believes, in addition, that Octavio Paz was inspired by some of Du Bois's thought.[38]

What most impressed Zapata Olivella about Du Bois was Du Bois's support for a theory of art from the perspective of U.S. blacks. Du Bois realized early that blacks saw black life differently from whites, and that blacks should perpetuate their heritage by expressing the souls of black folk, which is what Zapata Olivella's novel does. "To be black is to be beautiful and strong and proud"[39]—a phrase Darwin Turner invents to apply to Du Bois—can be equally applied to all the black characters and protagonists in *Changó, el gran putas,* including Du Bois himself, who is a character in the book. Like Du Bois, the author interweaves poetry, history, philosophy, mythology, theology, and sociology into an aesthetic whole told from a black perspective: all of his major narrators are black. There is much in this novel that reminds us of Du Bois: the spiritual world in which blacks live and strive, the timeless soul of black folk, the need for blacks to be both black and American, the concept of slavery as "the sum of all villainies,"[40] the search for liberty and freedom, the one refrain that swells "in song and exhortation."[41] Zapata Olivella envelops his works with a mythic quality that suggests Du Bois's poetic and noble style and that gives a heroic dimension to the black experience. In the United States, Michael Harper[42] sees Du Bois as a cultural and artistic model. So does Manuel Zapata Olivella, in Latin America.

Changó, el gran putas covers a lot of ground, from Africa to the March on Washington, as the author links up "soul-force" from Africa with "the souls of black folk" in America. At times black American preachers preach the word of *Changó* as from their pulpits they light the fire of rebellion under their congregations. Consistent with the spirit of Du Bois, Zapata Olivella makes liberal use of the English word *soul* in his novel, as in, for example, "the soul of your mirror image," "the soul of your ancestors," "your soul," "your true soul," and "the happy soul." The word *ekobios*, which Zapata Olivella uses throughout, conveys the sense of "soul" or spiritual brother. He employs other English words as well to help capture the black experience in the United States: "the slums," "the slum," "the slum man," "my blues," "southern blues," and "they were singing the blues in the Cotton Club."

Zapata Olivella takes the reader into the major language cultures united by the African spirit in black America. Almost 300 pages of *Changó, el gran putas* are devoted to the struggle for liberty and equality in the United States. The author has researched his story well, and the U.S. black reader will find much of interest. Zapata Olivella began the novel more than twenty years ago during the heat of the struggle. It, like his *Chambacú*, was inspired not only by Du Bois's *Souls of Black Folk* but also by the impetus of the 1960s in the United States. Zapata Olivella sees the 1960s as the culmination of the struggle for freedom and black identity in the New World. It is appropriate, therefore, that he should end his novel with an account of that struggle.

THE HISPANIC BLACK WRITER IN THE UNITED STATES

I will close this chapter with some remarks on racism and black Hispanic writers in the United States. U.S. racism, according to Carlos Guillermo Wilson,[43] can more accurately be judged by the prejudice and discrimination directed at African Hispanics. *Los excluídos* is his term for this minority within minorities. Citing Roy Bryce Laporte, he reports that immigrants of African descent in the United States suffer double invisibility. This invisibility stems from being black and from being foreign. African

Hispanics—and this is Wilson's main point—are often forced to cope with a threefold rejection: The rejection of immigrants of African descent, of Spanish-speaking immigrants, and of Catholic immigrants. In his study, Wilson criticizes the racist attitude toward Haitian refugees, for example, and African Cubans. He also laments the lack of contact by Americans in this country with African Hispanics other than with "exotic" and "charming" personalities in African Cuban and African Brazilian music and sports.

Some African Hispanics like Wilson himself have written about their experiences living in the United States. Some were in the country for an extended time and some merely passed through. The work of this type by Juan and Manuel Zapata Olivella, Nicolás Guillén, and Jorge Artel has already been discussed. Other African Latin American writers who know this country firsthand include Quince Duncan, Nancy Morejón, Blas Jiménez, Norberto James, Adalberto Ortiz, and Abdias do Nascimento. Wilson, an African Panamanian, is the only "immigrant" in this group. He lives permanently in the United States, or "gringolandia," as he has called it. Wilson, or "Cubena," who writes in Spanish is in an excellent position to write about and reflect the feelings of *los excluídos*.

Ian Smart[44] has identified what he calls a new Hispanic literature, now being written by writers of West Indian descent in Central America. He sees Wilson as part of the West Indian aesthetic, but acknowledges that Wilson's perspective because he lives in the United States will be different. Wilson's novel *Chombo* (1981) is full of rage against racism both in the United States and in Panama. This same rage runs throughout his poetry as well. In his poems he recognizes the greatness of the United States, but sees the country undermined by small-minded people—people he holds responsible for the riots in Watts, for the war in Vietnam, and for the deaths of Martin Luther King Jr. and other freedom fighters. In his latest novel, *Los nietos de Felicidad Dolores*, Wilson is a little bit annoyed with U.S. blacks who, he believes, are not always sympathetic to blacks from other cultures.

Cubena's complaints bring to mind a report I read about the problems of Cuban blacks in Miami. According to Dr. Marvin Dunne, a black community leader in Miami, Cuban blacks are discriminated against by native U.S. blacks. Dunne, who is also an associate professor of psychology at Florida International

University, says that in Miami Cuban blacks feel like outsiders in that they live in a world isolated from the main black community and only peripheral to the Cuban community. Similar to Guillermo Wilson's discussion of double invisibility, Dunne describes the double burden this group's blackness carries: "They not only get it from whites who discriminate against them but also from the Cubans who don't want to be identified with them."[45] One of Dunne's Cuban black informants reported that he was never rejected on racial grounds until he came to Miami. "Here," he says, "there is a separation, because Cubans in Miami act more like white Americans than Latins."[46]

I also want to mention Guillermo Bowie, an African American poet who was born in Texas. Bowie writes in Spanish and in English, and he reclaims his Mexican heritage not only through extensive travel in Mexico but also by writing as an African Chicano. Bowie is not as well known as Cubena because the poetry he has written over the past few years, as far as I know, is still in the manuscript stage, although I did see his first published poem in an issue of the *Afro-Hispanic Review*,[47] along with a new poem by Cubena. Like Cubena, who holds an M.A. and a Ph.D., Bowie is a scholar. Bowie did graduate work at Columbia and at New York University, earning an M.A. from both institutions. He also has studied at the Du Bois Institute at Harvard and at the Union Theological Seminary. Among Bowie's poems is a long one in Spanish, "Harlem sueños del Congo a través de America" ("Thoughts of the Congo in America's Harlem"), which he addressed to a Latin American friend. This poem was published in the *Afro-Hispanic Review*. In another poem, "Los pasos perdidos," also addressed to a Latin American friend, he writes: "No te olvidaré / Cuando estoy en la estación de los subways / calle 125 / Harlem" ("I will not forget you / when I am in the subway station / 125th Street / Harlem").[48] His best poem, I believe, is one written in English and is called "River Harlem." It graphically captures the sights, sounds, and frustrations of life in Harlem. It is a powerful poem whose intensity builds right up to its prophetic conclusion: "Oh Harlem! / . . . / through you will sprout . . . / NEW AFRICA."

Carlos Guillermo Wilson and Guillermo Bowie—for the most part—write in Spanish. There are Hispanic black authors living in the United States who write in English and some who write in both languages. They include Carlos E. Russell, a West Indian

Panamanian whose book of poems *Miss Anna's Son Remembers* was published in New York (Bayano Publications) in 1976. There are the Puerto Rican poets who explore African Puerto Rican identity, among them Victor Hernandez Cruz, a well-known U.S. poet who was born in Aguas Buenas, Puerto Rico, as well as Felipe Luciano and Sandra María Esteves. All are well known in Nuyorican poetry circles. Hernández Cruz, who returned to Puerto Rico, has published several books of poetry since his first volume of poems, *Snaps*, was published in 1969. Some of his poems have been translated into Spanish. In one of them, "African Things," the poet asks: "What was Puerto Rico all about? / all about the / *indios* and you better believe it the African things / black and shiney / . . . latin boo-ga-loo . . . / conga drums in the islands / . . . black African things."[49]

Felipe Luciano was born in Manhattan and has written "You're Nothing but a Spanish Colored Kid," which I consider his signature poem. It is a perceptive statement that pointedly summarizes what it is like to be a Puerto Rican black in New York City.

> I see them
> Puerto Ricans/ Spanish niggers
> Bronzed farmers look silly being doormen
>
> ....
> C'mon spic
> . . . you're nothing but a Spanish colored kid
> unless you
> Get real nigger
> And stop making gestures.[50]

Sandra María Esteves's signature poem, I believe, is "My Name Is María Cristina." She writes: "I am the mother of a new age of warriors / I am the child of a race of slaves / . . . my soul reflects the strength of my culture."[51] Her poem and Luciano's are memorable, but Hernández Cruz is the best known of the Puerto Rican poets who are keeping alive the African heritage, background, and identity of the Puerto Ricans living in the United States. The work of this group relates to a growing body of literature that focuses thematically on the Puerto Rican black in New York.

Several works come to mind, among them Emilio Díaz Valcárcel's *Harlem todos los días* (*Harlem Everyday*, 1978), Manuel

Manrique's *Una isla en Harlem* (*Island in Harlem*, 1965) and Stan Steiner's *The Islands* (1974). Some of this literature shows conflict, disunity, and alienation among native and immigrant blacks, and some of it tries to correct this alienation. Passages such as the following are typical:

> In the Bronx High School of Science, where young Guzmán had once been an honours student, he too had sought to "be accepted": he was a handsome, darkskinned boy too darkskinned to "be accepted" by either the Whites or the few middle-class Ricans in his class. The Blacks knew from his name and accent that he was not one of them.[52]

Luciano's poem "You're Nothing but a Spanish Colored Kid" touches on the dilemma and alienation faced by the "dark-skinned boy" in the passage above. Manuel Manrique tries to correct that kind of alienation. In his novel, unity is forged through a freedom march and a subsequent battle in the streets. In the English translation of his novel we read:

> And the battle began. . . . Antonio felt that he was truly one of them and that they belonged to him. . . . He rushed out into St. Nicholas Avenue to fight the police like the others. He was in the middle of the street, in the middle of a crowd of American Negroes, fighting like them. And for the first time in his life he— a Puerto Rican—felt glad that he was a Negro and an American. . . . And it was a real fight. Blows rained down from every side, and those who received the worst ones were the nameless, sweating Negroes—his people and himself.[53]

Manrique's novel reflects the Turbulent Sixties complete with freedom marches, the singing of "We Shall Overcome" and violent confrontations such as the one described above. In Manrique's novel, the black immigrant "felt proud" because he knew he was not alone and that he had friends. His people and himself—U.S. blacks and Puerto Rican blacks—were one and the same, certainly in the eyes of the police raining the blows down on their heads. Black Power and the Civil Rights Movement of the 1960s inspired Puerto Ricans who are black and, in Felipe Luciano's view, should inspire those who might as well be to "Get real nigger / And stop making gestures."

Clara Rodríguez calls attention to some of the early literature on the Puerto Rican racial experience in the United States,
literature that focuses on the "two paths" offered the Puerto
Rican in the United States—"one to the White world and one
to the not-White world."[54] Rodriguez discusses the literature
of Jesús Colón. His book of stories set in the 1950s, *A Puerto
Rican in New York and Other Sketches* (1982), deals with Puerto
Ricans who are considered "colored" and with others who are
not. Also set in the 1950s and early 1960s, Piri Thomas's book
Down These Mean Streets (1967) is discussed as well. His book is
considered to be the major, most widely read work of the second generation of Puerto Ricans in the United States.
Rodríguez also mentions Edward Rivera's *Family Installments:
Memoirs of Growing Up Hispanic* (1983). What all of these works
have in common is that they reveal "the imposition of the
bifurcated race order."[55] They show that Puerto Ricans are
being identified in the United States by "the divisive racial
perception of Americans,"[56] which means being identified
racially by color and not by culture. These literary works show
the resulting confusion in the minds of the books' characters.
Wilson's "double invisibility," Dunne's "double burden," and
Rodriguez's "two paths" (or the "bifurcated race order") are
all variations on the same obstacles facing Hispanic blacks in
the United States.

Determining the debt that Puerto Rican poets in the United
States owe to the black community could well become one of
the critical challenges in American contemporary poetry. A
nonstandard English has increasingly replaced Spanish as the
dominant mode of communication in some of the poetry. The
proximity of the Puerto Rican and the black communities provides an explanation. According to Martin Espada, "El Barrio
[in New York] is called Spanish Harlem for a reason. It shares a
lot of space with the black community."[57] Sandra María Esteves
also has written that "the Puerto Rican community has merged
with the black community in terms of how we are treated by
the dominant society. . . . The black community here has been
dealing with language issues for a long time. That provides a
focus for us to deal with the English language."[58] Esteves and
Espada seem to agree that black words, black music, and black
rhythms are the strongest influences from the black community
on Puerto Rican poetry.[59]

Notes

1. Laurence E. Prescott, "A Conversation with Nicolás Guillén," *Nicolás Guillén: A Special Issue*, ed. Vera Kutzinski, *Callaloo* 10, no. 2 (1987): 354.
2. Renée Larrier, "Racism in the United States: An Issue in Caribbean Poetry," *Journal of Caribbean Studies* 2, no. 1 (1981): 51–71.
3. Nicolás Guillén, *Páginas vueltas. Memorias* (Havana: Ediciones Unión, 1982): 277.
4. Ibid.
5. Nicolás Guillén, "Camino de Harlem," *Prosa de prisa 1929–1972*, vol. I (Havana: Editorial de Arte y Literatura, 1975): 3–6.
6. See, for example, Nicolás Guillén, "Del problema negro en los Estados Unidos," *Prosa de prisa, 1929–1972*, vol. II (Havana: Editorial de Arte y Literatura, 1975): 66–68.
7. Miriam deCosta Willis, "Nicolás Guillén and His Poetry for Black Americans," *Black World* 22 (1973): 12–16.
8. Amiri Baraka, *Daggers and Javelins: Essays, 1974–1979* (New York: William Morrow, 1984): 186.
9. Joseph Pereira, "Raza el la obra de Nicolás Guillén después de 1959." *Sin nombre* 13, no. 3 (1983): 41.
10. Ibid.
11. Nicolás Guillén, *Obra poética 1958–1972*, vol. II (Havana: Editorial de Arte y Literatura, 1974): 1972.
12. Harvey Johnson, "Nicolás Guillén, Poet of Protest," *Folio* 16 (December 1984): 156.
13. Dennis Sardinha, *The Poetry of Nicolás Guillén* (London: New Beacon Books, 1976), 59.
14. Nicolás Guillén, *Páginas vueltas: Memorias* (Havana: Ediciones Unión, 1982). All further quotations are from this edition.
15. Lisa Davis, "The World of the West Indian Black in Central America: The Recent Works of Quince Duncan," in *Voices From Under: Black Narrative in Latin America and the Caribbean*, ed. William Luis (Westport, Conn.: Greenwood Press, 1984); 158.
16. Carlos Guillermo Wilson ("Cubena"), *Pensamientos del negro Cubena* (Los Angeles: published by author, 1977), 19.
17. Ian Smart, *Central American Writers of West Indian Origin: A New Hispanic Literature* (Washington, D.C.: Three Continents Press, 1984), 101.
18. Julio Finn, *Voices of Negritude* (London: Quartet Books, 1988), 169.
19. Michael Walker, "The Black Social Identity in Selected Novels of Nelson Estupiñán Bass and Adalberto Ortiz," (Ph.D. diss., University of California, Riverside, 1977), 197.
20. Ibid., 194.
21. Marvin Lewis, *Afro-Hispanic Poetry, 1940–1980: From Slavery to "Negritude" in South American Verse* (Columbia: University of Missouri Press, 1983), 146.
22. Jorge Artel, *Tambores en la noche* (Guanajuato: Ediciones de la Universidad de Guanajuato, 1955): 105–6.
23. Ibid., 118.
24. Ibid., 121.

25. Ibid., 123.
26. Ibid., 124.
27. Laurence Prescott, "*El tambor*: Symbol and Substance in the Poetry of Jorge Artel," *Afro-Hispanic Review* 3, no. 2 (1984a): 12.
28. Laurence Prescott, "Jorge Artel y sus tambores en la noche," *El Caribe*, 15 October 1975, 4.
29. Laurence Prescott, "Spirit Voices: Jorge Artel's Poetic Odyssey of the Afro-Amerian Soul," *Perspectives on Contemporary Literature* 8 (1982): 75.
30. Laurence Prescott, "Jorge Artel frente a Nicolás Guillén: dos poetas mulatos ante la poesía negra hispanoamericana," *Ensayistas de literatura colombia*, ed. Raymond Williams (Bogotá: Plaza y Janés, 1984b): 136.
31. Juvenal Herrera Torres, "Prólogo," Jorge Artel, *Antología poética* (Bogotá: Ecoe Ediciones, 1979), v–xiv.
32. Ibid., viii.
33. Juan Zapata Olivella, *Panacea: Poesía liberada* (Cartagena: Ediciones Capricornio, 1976), 11.
34. Manuel Zapata Olivella, *Corral de negros* (Havana: Casa de las Américas, 1962), 199.
35. Manuel Zapata Olivella, *Changó, el gran putas* (Bogotá: Editorial la Oveja Negra, 1983).
36. Gilberto Gómez and Raymond Williams, "Interview with Manuel Zapata Olivella," *Hispania* 67, no. 4 (1984): 657.
37. Ian Smart, review of "*Changó, el gran putas* by Manuel Zapata Olivella," *Afro-Hispanic Review* 3, no. 2 (1984): 31.
38. Yvonne Captain-Hidalgo, "Conversación con el doctor Manuel Zapata Olivella, Bogotá, 1980; 1983," *Afro-Hispanic Review* 4, no. 1 (1985): 28.
39. Darwin Turner, "W. E. B. Du Bois and the Theory of a Black Aesthetic," *Studies in the Literary Imagination* 7, no. 2 (1974): 21.
40. Ibid., 18.
41. Ibid., 7.
42. Michael Harper, "Magic: Power: Activation," *Acts of Mind: Conversations with Contemporary Poets*, ed. Richard Jackson (University, Ala.: University of Alabama Press, 1983): 1983–90.
43. Carlos Guillermo Wilson, "Afro-Hispanics: A Challenge for Multicultural Education," *Schools in Crisis. A Socio-Psychological View*, ed. Alfred Lightfoot (Lexington: Mass.: Ginn Custom Pub., 1985), 78–97.
44. Smart, *Central American Writers*, 101.
45. Jon Nordheimer, "Black Cubans: Apart in Two Worlds," *New York Times*, 2 December 1987, D26.
46. Ibid. Also see Roberto Rodríguez, "FIU Professors Seek Answers to Complex Black/Cuban Relations," *Black Issues in Higher Education*, 25 February 1993, 16–17. Rodríguez reiterates recent research that shows Afro-Cubans feel discriminated against by light-skinned Cubans and not accepted by African Americans.
47. Guillermo Bowie, "Harlem sueños del Congo a través de América (poema)," *Afro-Hispanic Review* 8, no. 1 & 2 (1989): 20.
48. All quotes are from manuscript.
49. Translated by Carmen Valle and Julio Marzán, in *Inventing a Word: An*

Anthology of Twentieth Century Puerto Rican Poetry, ed. Julio Marzán (New York: Columbia University Press, 1980), 170. Several of his poems are bilingual, written in Puerto Rican slang and black English. He recently published *Red Beans* (Coffee House Press) in 1991. Also see Elizabeth Alexander, "Living in Americas," *Voice Literary Supplement* (November 1991): 36. Alexander reports on a telephone conversation with Hernandez Cruz, who defines the language used in *Snaps* as a combination of Puerto Rican slang and black English.

50. Arnold Adoff, ed., *The Poetry of Black America* (New York: Harper and Row, 1973), 501–2.

51. Sandra María Esteves, "My Name Is María Cristina," in *Herejes y mitificadores: Muestra de poesía puertorriqueña en los Estados Unidos*, ed. Efraín Barradas and Rafael Rodríguez (San Juan: Ediciones Huracán, 1980), 112. Also see Asunción Horno-Delgado et al., eds., *Breaking Boundaries. Latina Writing, and Critical Readings* (Boston: University of Massachusetts Press, 1989); and Yamila Azize, "Poetas puertorriqueñas en Nueva York," *Revista de la Universidad Metropolitana* 4, no. 1 (1987): 17–24.

52. Stan Steiner, *The Islands: The Worlds of the Puerto Ricans* (New York: Harper and Row, 1974), 445. Diaz Valcárcel's latest novel, translated by Tanya T. Fayen, is called *Hot Soles in Harlem* and was published by the Latin American Literary Review Press in 1993.

53. Manuel Manrique, *Island in Harlem* (New York: John Day Co., 1966), 195–96. Also see Juan Flores, " 'Que assimilated, brother, yo soy assimilao': La estruturación de la identidad puertorriqueña en los Estados Unidos," *Casa de las Americas* 26, no. 152 (1985). Yet, despite such idealistic identification with blacks, there are racial tensions grounded, in part, in economic competition today between blacks and Hispanics, or Latinos. See Jack Miles, "Blacks vs. Browns: The Struggle for the Bottom Rung," *The Atlantic Monthly* (October 1992): 41–68.

54. Clara Rodríguez, *Puerto Ricans Born in the United States* (Boston: Unwin Hayman, 1989): 56.

55. Ibid., 59.

56. Ibid. Martin Espada addresses the Puerto Rican attempt to escape this divisiveness on the race question in a poem where the speaker, grabbing at the plastic identification bracelet marked "Negro," shouts: "I'm not / Take it off! / I'm Other!" (In Earl Shorris, "In Search of the Latino Writer," *New York Times Book Review*, 15 July 1990, 27.) The divisive racial perceptions of Americans affect not only Puerto Ricans but also others. The Dominican writer Sherezade (Chiqui) Vicioso acknowledges that in the United States there is no space for fine distinctions of race. During her travels in this country, she discovered herself "as a Caribbean *mulata* and adopted the black identity as a gesture of solidarity." (In Rosemary Geisdorfer Feal, "Bordering Feminism in Afro-Hispanic Studies: Crossroads in the Field," *Latin American Literary Review* 20, p. 40 (1992): 41–45.

57. Martin Espada, "Documentaries and Declamadores: Puerto Rican Poetry in the United States," in *A Gift of Tongues: Critical Challenges in Contemporary American Poetry*, ed. Marie Harris and Katheleen Aguero (Athens:

University of Georgia Press, 1987), 257–66. Also see Martin Espada and Juan Flores, eds., *Puerto Rican Literature: A Special Focus*. Special issue of *Callaloo* 15, no. 4 (1992), for the following: Edna Acosta-Belén, "Beyond Island Boundaries: Ethnicity, Gender, and Cultural Revitalization in Nuyorican Literature," 979–98; Juan Flores, "'It's a Street Thing!' An Interview with Charlie Chase," 999–1021; and William Luis, "From New York to the World: An Interview with Tato Laviera," 1022–33. Acosta-Belén writes that the bilingualism in Nuyorican literature "nurtures itself from the interaction with jive, Black English, and, most recently, the rap phenomenon." To some blacks rap is "a black thing," but Juan Flores makes the point that there are Hispanics who do it as well. Tato Laviera talked about the rap quality of black America rooted lyrics in Nuyorican writing, telling Luis that in his oral recitals he reads "an hour in Spanish and an hour in Black."

58. Sandra María Esteves in Espada, "Documentaries and Declamadores," 259. Also see Asela Rodríguez Laguna, ed., *Images and Identities: The Puerto Rican in Two World Contexts* (New Brunswick: Transaction Books, 1987), especially Miguel Algarín's views on Nuyorican aesthetics and Sandra María Esteves' assertion that Neo Rican or New Rican language is street rooted, evolving from natural mixing plus the anger.

59. For other good discussions of black poetry, music, and Hispanic culture in the United States, see Ed Morales, "(M)other Tongues: Writing the Future of Puerto Rican Poetry," *Village Voice*, 24 May 1992, 74–75; and Peter Watrous, "Bilingual Music Is Breaking Down Cultural Barriers," *New York Times*, 2 September 1990, A19. Morales reviews Faythe Turner, ed., *Puerto Rican Writers in the U.S.A.* (Seattle: Open Hand Publishing 1991) and Pedro López-Adorno, ed., *Papiros de Babel: antología de la poesía puertorriqueña en Nueva York* (San Juan: Editorial de la Universidad de Puerto Rico 1991). Morales addresses the question raised by these recent publications, namely, is Puerto Rican poetry in the United States a new, bilingual hybrid that draws largely on the oral tradition of African people? Morales sees this poetry as a challenge to the Eurocentric canon. Watrous discusses several Chicano or Hispanic rap groups that draw on black American music. He also discusses the merging of Afro-American and Chicano cultures in rap music.

FIVE

Black Writers in Latin America Today

> All over America a new kind of
> black is coming forward with
> a new outlook and a new
> determination.
> —Nelson Estupiñán Bass[1]

FROM OLD GUARD TO NEW

It has been said that among the younger generation in Latin America, Cuban writers are the most interested in the black presence.[2] This assertion is not altogether true, although the assumption is understandable because black themes continue to be explored by Cuban writers.[3] The fact is, however, that today most black writers throughout Latin America proclaim their black identity and their national identity. Fully aware of the courage and example U.S. blacks displayed in the 1960s, today's young Latin American writers, as well as some of the not-so-young, are showing similar heroism. Many of them are relentless in their recognition and condemnation of racism and injustice—in their homelands and in the United States. Black writers in Latin America today are just as insistent in their determination to be heard as the old guard was in its quest for social justice and visibility.

Some of the older black writers who started publishing in the 1940s, such as Jorge Artel, Adalberto Ortiz, and Manuel Zapata,[4] continued to produce, as did Nelson Estupiñán Bass, who started in the 1950s. Even Nicolás Guillén, whose adolescent verse dates back to 1917, was still publishing well into the 1980s. Antonio Preciado, Carlos Guillermo Wilson, Nancy Morejón, Blas Jiménez, and Quince Duncan are some of the contemporary writers whose works are becoming more familiar in the United States and around the world. Antonio Preciado, for example, is getting attention in France,[5] as are other established African Hispanic writers. Aside from being a fertile decade for black writers in Latin America, many of the writers we are seeing today were born in the 1940s: Quince Duncan (Costa Rica, 1940); Carlos Guillermo Wilson

(Panama, 1941); Gregorio Martínez (Peru, 1942); Pedro Pérez Sarduy (Cuba, 1943); Nancy Morejón (Cuba, 1944); Tito Junco (Cuba, 1944); Carlos Rigby (Nicaragua, 1944); Gerardo Maloney (Panama, 1945); and Norberto James (Dominican Republic, 1945). Of all these black writers, Nancy Morejón, "the best Cuban poet"[6] writing today, is the most widely known.

NANCY MOREJÓN, THE "NEW WOMAN" IN CUBA, AND THE FIRST GENERATION OF BLACK WRITERS OF THE REVOLUTION

Langston Hughes, the "traveling star" of black America, was the "best-loved star"[7] of the Harlem Renaissance. Nancy Morejón, the traveling star of Castro's Cuba, is becoming the "best-loved star" among black writers in Latin America today. Born in 1944, this African Cuban poet was fifteen at the time of the triumph of the Cuban Revolution, and much of her young adult life has been spent supporting it. Morejón, who belongs to what has been called the first generation of the Cuban Revolution,[8] is an exciting poet whose diversity and multiple talents command respect. Morejón is definitely the best known of black writers in Cuba today who have an awareness of the world at large, including the United States. Like Guillén, these writers reach inward and write of the Cuban Revolution. They also write to set the world right, for example, by decrying racism in the United States.

Morejón is a specialist on Guillén, whose work she continues in her own. Like Cuba's national poet, Morejón is a poetic spokesperson claimed by blacks, an apologist for Castro's Cuba, and a crusader for the Third World. In addition, as a Cuban black woman writer, Morejón is lionized by feminists interested in women writers in general. For all of these reasons, Roberto Márquez speaks of her not only as "the New Man" but also as "the New Woman"[9] in Cuba. She affirms both Cuba's black cultural heritage and her own. Morejón writes in Spanish, has a doctorate in French from the University of Havana, and is fast becoming known in English, since her works are appearing in translation in the United States. A small collection of her poems has been published by the Center for Cuban Studies in New York.[10]

Morejón has published several volumes of poetry[11] since 1962, and the bilingual anthology titled *Where the Island Sleeps Like a Wing* (1985)[12] highlights much of it. Despite several printing errors, this volume is valuable not only because it covers her first twenty-five years through a representative cross-section of her poetry, but also because it arranges the selections in four organizational groupings that clearly define her thematic range: (1) un patio de la Habana (family, home, and community); (2) donde duerme la Isla como un ala (country); (3) el sueño de la razón produce monstruos (love relationships); and (4) mujer negra (race and gender). These categories show the reader clearly why Morejón is acclaimed by Cubans, the Third World, blacks, and feminists alike.

Morejón is a classic model for the black "womanist" perspective in that she, like June Jordan, has responded admirably to the demands made on black women by race, gender, and politics. Morejón may be best known for "Mujer negra" ("Black Woman"), which includes the lines:

> Me dejaron aquí y aquí he vivido.
> Y porque trabajé como una bestia,
> aquí volví a nacer.
> A cuanta epopeya mandinga intenté recurrir.
> Me rebelé.[13]

> (They left me here and here I've lived.
> And, because I worked like an animal,
> here I came to be born.
> How many Mandinga epics did I look to for strength.
> I rebelled.)

In a conversation with Rafael Rodríguez, she has talked at length about this poem:

> I remembered someone asking me whether I had written it more as a woman than as a black. Believe me, that was a very eloquent question but at the same time very unsettling. I told them that . . . I hadn't been able to divide myself up like that since both things are one and the same. . . . The title "Black Woman" is symbolic, universal, and unlimited. An artist cannot be bound by "I did this for the liberation of women" or "I did such and such to combat racial prejudice." Those kinds of things are implicit.[14]

It is easy to understand why Morejón does not write from the viewpoint of a feminist only or of a black only. It is equally understandable why black and female readers identify with her poetry. In her work, black and female characters are fully realized human beings, though they are shown to be exploited because of color and gender. Morejón's poetic voices are always those of the abused, the underdog, and the mistreated. "Mujer negra" is a significant and symbolic title, not only for the poem but also for an entire section of poems. Naturally she writes about blacks and females because in doing so she is able to express an important part of her identity. She does this consistently in poems on family, race, country, and women.

This essence or sense of identity is reflected in her praise poems on the black woman in history, on the black man reviled, on black rebels in the United States and the Caribbean, on the black ghetto in the United States, on black couples, and on black dancers. It is especially evident in her praise poem written from a daughter to her black mother. In "Madre" ("Mother") she writes: "Mi madre no tuvo jardín / sino islas acantiladas / flotando, bajo el sol, / en sus corales delicados. / . . . Ella no tuvo el aposento de márfil, / ni la sala de mimbre / . . ."[15] ("My mother had no patio garden / but rocky islands / floating in delicate corals / under the sun. / . . . She had no ivory-inlaid bedroom, / no drawing-room with wicker chairs / . . .") The poem is especially reminiscent of Langston Hughes's "Mother to Son," which begins "Well, son, I'll tell you: / Life for me ain't been no crystal stair. . . ."[16]

The "black" essence of her work, together with her "Cubanness," attracted Guillén to "Nancy," as he once called her. In his short descriptive prose piece about her, Guillén focuses on these twin poles that, he believes, lie at the heart of her being: "I think that the essence of her poetry is black like her skin. It is also Cuban for that same reason, so firmly rooted with roots planted so deep that they come out on the other side of the planet. I love her smile, her dark skin, her African hair."[17] Guillén then levels criticism at the custom among blacks of pressing (frying hair): "I say unstraightened hair in reference to those hair straighteners and hair straightened middle class blacks who straighten their hair every week and live slaves to a hairdresser they want to work miracles."[18]

The "negritude" aspect of Morejon's work is one of its most obvious traits, and many observers—Nicolás Guillén among them—consider her "blackness" and her "Cubanness" to be one and the same. Any reading, for example, of "Richard trajo su flauta"[19] (1967), one of her earliest poems, will reveal how closely

eric
ne
in
t

linked the two are to each other and indeed to the Third World in general. "Richard trajo su flauta" is really a poem about a black family imitating white American middle-class society in which Mozart and jazz take precedence over African Cuban popular music. "Richard" shows how things used to be in the black family in Cuba before the revolution, when black values were tied to foreign models from the United States and Europe. Morejón uses music to illustrate the options for Cubans: European (Mozart), United States (jazz), and Cuban (popular African Cuban). Cuban is the most natural of the three, though Cuban blacks at the time were reluctant to admit it.

"Richard trajo su flauta," like Guillén's prose portrait of "Nancy," contains some criticism of the United States. Some of Morejón's poems are reminiscent of Guillén's in the choice of subject though not in the form of expression—Guillén uses more humor and sarcasm than Morejón. Also in contrast to Guillén, Morejón does not concentrate on attacking the United States. She does defend Grenada,[20] however, and she has written such "political" poems as "Abril," a reference "to both the Bay of Pigs (Playa Girón) invasion attempted by the United States in April 1961 and to the so-called Free Flotilla (Mariel) exodus of the Cuban citizens to the United States in April 1980."[21]

There are angry poems like "Freedom Now,"[22] which Morejón dedicated to SNCC and to the black struggle in the United States—a poem that Renée Larrier[23] links to other Caribbean poems on the U.S. Civil Rights Movement. Though Morejón is never consistently on the same high level of *rabia* ("rage") as Guillén, J. Kubayanda was right when he said that Morejón is inspired by some of the best poems of Guillén.[24] Poems such as "Freedom Now" also link Morejón to other African Hispanic authors who have addressed the issue of racism and the U.S. black. Her treatment of this topic in her work is impressive. What most impresses the reader, however, is how aware she is of what makes her country meaningful to her: its people—natural, beautiful—its ideology, its history, and especially its promise, which is based on the sacrifices and faith of those who went before. Morejón's poetry sings of hope and expresses appreciation of individuals and of groups that have helped bring the country its good fortune. Her "Mujer negra" and other poems (like "Parque central, alguna gente") are updated versions of Guillén's "Tengo." When she writes of the masses or when she writes of individual heroes or of the generic "black woman" or "black man," we know that to her each one represents many more who are similar. Heroes are symbolic in her poetry, but Morejón humanizes symbols and reminds us that heroes and martyrs are people too who lived and died, people like Antonio Maceo and Camilo Cienfuegos and others unnamed.

Morejón's love and appreciation of history embrace race, family acquaintances, and even city, as in "Amor, ciudad atribuida" ("Love, Attributed City"): "aquí vuelvo a decir: el corazón de la ciudad no ha muerto todavía . . . / ahora mi corazón se hospeda en la ciudad y su aventura . . ."[25] ("here I say again: the heart of the city has not yet died . . . / my heart is lodged in the city and its adventure . . ."). Her poetry remains personal and always full of love and memory, although her subjects are sometimes political. She is clearly inspired by the history of her race and its experiences in both Africa and America, including the United States. She has dedicated her poems not only to SNCC and to the black struggle in the United States but also to Angela Davis: "Un manzano de Oakland" ("An Oakland Apple Tree").

Such poems as Morejón's "Amo a mi amo" ("I Love My Master") and her "Mujer negra," which view history through the eyes of one individual, also describe experiences that were common to many. More important, in telling these stories of adversity, her poems trace the development of the human heart, which suffers affront, questions, and proudly endures. They also serve to link history to the immediate present. Morejón is able to show history as the human drama it must have been for the slave concubine, for the *cimarrón*, and for all who were victims of their time and condition. In a style similar to that of Manuel Zapata Olivella and Carlos Guillermo Wilson, Morejón takes the reader "below deck" on the slave ship and inside the mind of the slave, a mind the slave master cannot even begin to understand. Morejón gives voice to the slave woman who curses "esta lengua abigarradamente hostil que no mastico"[26] ("this language so stubbornly hostile I can't spit it out").

Morejón's poem "Negro" ("Black Man") is a natural complement to "Mujer Negra" ("Black Woman"). In this praise poem she writes: "Nosotros amaremos por siempre / tus huellas y tu ánimo de bronce / porque has traído esa luz viva del pasado / fluyente . . ."[27] ("Forever we will love your footprints / and your bronze spirit, / for you have brought that living light / of the fluid past . . ."). "Negro" shows Morejón's appreciation of the black man in history and of the pain, anguish, and hell he had to endure for being black and African, while recognizing always his arrogance, his rebelliousness, and his ability to love and show affection despite his suffering.

Morejón's poetry expresses appreciation and gratitude because she feels truly blessed for having inherited strength from her family, pride from her race, and political satisfaction from her country. And Morejón is always aware that the suffering of her predecessors is partly responsible for her good fortune. For this reason, memory is a recurring motif in her poetry. Her poems are filled with phrases relating to memory: "limpio recuerdo"[28] ("I clearly remember"), "En tu recuerdo"[29] ("In your memory"), "pero no olvido"[30] ("but I will not forget"), "no he olvidado"[31] ("I haven't forgotten"). She is conscious of her role as poet and accepts the responsibility to portray feelings—hers and those of others like her—whose world she shares. She writes of "mi acto de poesía"[32] ("my poetry writing") and of "esta página blanca vibra"[33] ("this blank sheet of paper comes alive"). In "Amor, ciudad atribuida" she writes that "la poesía viene sola como un pájaro"[34] ("poetry comes freely like a bird"). To Morejón, the ability to write is a precious gift, and she shows as much gratitude for that ability as for the values she has inherited from the past. Africa in America is a history of horror and hell, but it is also one of struggle and resistance. This history is the source of her strength, independence, and freedom.

Other black writers in Cuba, some of them acquiring exposure in the United States, include the poet Pedro Pérez Sarduy. His poetry, like Morejón's has appeared in the pages of The Black Scholar.[35] In this journal he is presented as a young African Cuban writer whose work in Cumbite (1976) retraces his ancestral Yoruba ties, through "the rich use of African mythology achieving a syncretism of Cuba's African and Spanish roots."[36] The selection from Sarduy's work titled "Riddled with Insult" and published in English is, however, a political poem he wrote in 1983. This poem about Grenada is filled with condemnation for the "traders of sorrow"—the "invaders" from the United States—and praise for "the great Black Bishop, the head brother . . . no longer there."[37]

"New theater" is also of great interest to Cuban black writers. Tito Junco, actor turned author, is a voice of this theater. As he has told Nancy Morejón,[38] his prize-winning play titled *Asalto a las guardias* (*Attacking*) is dedicated to Nicolás Guillén, to Guillén's work and to their friendship. Junco is a true product of the Cuban Revolution, whose goals he feels he must express in his work. He credits the revolution for his opportunity to write plays today.

Eugenio Hernández Espinosa's play titled *María Antonia* (1967) was revived in the 1980s. It was produced for the Third Festival of Latin American Theater in Havana in January 1984. Yvonne Yarbro-Bejaramo, who attended and reported on the festival, found Espinosa's work—because of its blending of European scene design, Brechtian alienation techniques, and African Cuban elements—to be the most satisfying of all the plays she saw.[39] Yarbro-Bejaramo considers *María Antonia* to be a high point in the history of Cuban theater because it portrays blacks with human dignity.

Despite the positive examples we have seen, not all observers feel that Cuba has been free of racism and sexism since the revolution. Film director Tomás Gutiérrez Alea, reporting in April 1986, had this view:

> "Officially in Cuba," he says, "there is no racism (the country is 40 percent black); in reality, on the contrary, there is always racism; historically and culturally it is so strong. In the first years of the revolution there was a very important speech from Fidel on television about this issue. After that, nobody talked racist—it was all settled. But it was not, of course. People continued acting the same way, though they did not talk about it. Now, it is being talked about again, and we feel there is a need to discriminate *in favor* of blacks and women, because if you don't, it is too easy for there to be no change."[40]

BLACK WRITERS IN CENTRAL AMERICA, THE DOMINICAN REPUBLIC, AND SOUTH AMERICA

Revolution came later to Nicaragua. In July 1979, twenty years after Castro's triumph in Cuba, the revolution in Nicaragua ousted Somoza, bringing to power the Sandinista government. So in contrast to the first generation of black writers in revolutionary Cuba, the Nicaraguan black writers David McField— born in 1936—and Carlos Rigby—born in 1944—had already published before the triumph of their country's revolution. According to Ian Smart,[41] who has written a pioneering book on black Central American writers of West Indian origin, their work is reconciled with the larger society. Yet, though Smart has difficulty identifying any West Indian elements in their writing, we should recognize the tremendous pride in black accomplishment David McField displays in the poem "Cuando el equipo de Leon" ("When León Was the Team"):

> Cuando el equipo de León
> fue campeón nacional
> de la liga del béisbol profesional,
> Duncan Campbell,
> la revelación del año,
> conectó batazos sin cuento.
>
> ....
> Duncan Cambell era nombre pronunciado con respecto
> . . . y todos los costeños somos . . . /
> primos y hermanos de Duncan Campbell . . .[42]
>
> (When Leon was the championship team
> of the professional baseball league
> Duncan Campbell,
> the find of the year
> had so many base hits you couldn't count them.
>
> ....
> Duncan Campbell was a name you said with respect
> . . . and all us coast people say we are
> kin to Duncan Campbell . . .)

Also, reading about the hard times of the Atlantic coast people under the Sandinistas,[43] one is reminded of Carlos Rigby's "Palabras del campesino en la inauguracion del palo de mayo" ("Words from a farmer on the occasion of the inauguration of the Maypole"), which effectively catalogues the complaints of a farmer who after so many seasons of hunger decides to protest:

> fíjense hermanos
> que ahora
> en vez de pedirle a Dios
> por mi pan de todos los días
> es el presidente a quien mando a molestar[44]
>
> (take note brothers
> now
> instead of asking God

> for my daily bread
> it's the president I want bothered for it).

The poem captures the urgency of one who wants changes made and promises kept. Fed up with dictatorship, he does not want another year of "la misma vaina," the same hypocrisy of before. Both Rigby and McField are from the Atlantic coast, and "Coast people are used to good times,"[45] one of the local residents recently said. Rigby's poem captures this sentiment exactly.

Central American black writers as a group represent for Smart the most important black writers in contemporary Spanish America because they, he says, "are the most intelligent in terms of the black experience."[46] This assessment, though some might dispute it, underscores the active presence of a new generation of black writers in Central America. Most of these writers present a black perspective, including David McField whose poem "Black Is Black" contains the bilingual message "black is black / full time; / por dentro y por fuera."[47] While acknowledging their West Indian background and the African past, such writers as Carlos Guillermo Wilson strongly identify with their countries of citizenship. Cubena's Panamanian compatriot Alberto Smith-Fernández expresses it best in "Panamá, la patria nuestra" ("Panama, Our Native Land"): "Nací de Panama. . . . Soy negro panameño. . . . Somos todos de aquí ¡Todos!"[48] ("I was born in Panama. . . . I am a Panamanian Black. . . . We are all from here, all of us!").

The Panamanian black poet Gerardo Maloney published *Juega vivo* (1984), his first book of poems that, according to Smart, Maloney translates as *Get Hip*, "thereby linking his work with the North American black poetry of the '60s and subsequent periods."[49] Smart's study of this work focuses on some of the formal aspects of Maloney's poetry, but compares, in one instance, the didactic humor of "Cogiéndolo suave" ("Playing It Cool") to Gwendolyn Brooks's poem "We Real Cool." Thematically Maloney's poem "Amo a mi raza" ("I Love My Race") is one of the most eloquent statements on behalf of black people ever written in Spanish:

> Amo a mi raza
> porque ha sido odiada
> de siglos en siglos
> ....

Amo a mi raza
negra, fuerte y vigorosa[50]
(I love my race
because it has been hated
for centuries

....

I love my race
black, strong, and vigorous)

Maloney's poems are consistently positive; he reminds blacks, as in "Cambios" ("Changes"), of how far they have come and the changes they have undergone since slavery: "Ya somos diferentes / . . . bien diferentes / bien hablados / cultos, / imaginativos, / doctos y preparados, / . . . Estamos repensando esta Patria / repensando a nosotros mismos / . . ."[51] ("We are different now / . . . very different / Now we are educated, ready, creative. . . . / We are rethinking this country / and our place in it"). Smart, with good reason, believes Maloney with his "fresh and much hoped-for voice"[52] will become one of Central America's most interesting literary figures.

Some of Maloney's work falls very much in the tradition of Pilar Barrios, who in the 1940s regularly addressed his black poetry to the black youth of his native Uruguay. Maloney's poetry today recalls Barrios's concern for black self-improvement. It is designed to motivate black people to take control of their future and their history. I especially like his poem "Invasion"[53] where he exhorts blacks to take over not just their little plots of land but history as well, and to establish their presence in it. Maloney's poetry covers a good deal of black history from the first slave ship to today, and it clearly establishes his ties with Africa, with the West Indies, and with his race. But mainly, Maloney is a poet of change and renewal. Poems like "Líder," "Cambios," and "Cogiéndolo suave" are among his most significant. These poems show his outstanding contribution to the new black consciousness. His message is an inspiring one designed to encourage all black people to join hands and forces for the common goal of developing black potential to the fullest.

Maloney is very conscious of where blacks came from and where they should be heading, and for this reason he wants each black to examine his or her own life. Perhaps more intensely than any other black writer in Latin America today, Maloney has his eye on the future; his poetry constantly points to tomorrow. His is a poetry of example, which is why there are so many poems about individual people in his work, real people whose example he poeticizes. There are references to "Miss Aines," "Mista Lambert," "Aunt May," "Willy," "Leroy," and "Brayan" because they are the embodiment of the people. In his desire to bring blacks to the realization that times have changed, Maloney is indeed a spokesperson for today's generation of Latin American black writers.

Another Central American black writer, Eulalia Bernard, has published her first book *Ritmohéroe* (*Rhythm King*, 1982). She dedicated her book to family members who helped build Costa Rica, "our country." Bernard's poetry is infused with love: of her province Limón, of her country, and of the people in it. Celebration of the "West Indian essence" ("esencia antillana"), however, is a recurring motif: "¡No! antillano / necio eres si enterrar / tu etnia prefieres" ("No! West Indian / you are a fool if you prefer / to hide your ethnic background"). Bernard was born in Limón to Jamaican parents and her ties to "Jamaica / tierra negra" ("Jamaica / black land") in "Himno a Jamaica" ("Hymn to Jamaica") were further strengthened during her period as Costa Rica's cultural attaché to Jamaica. Her work stands as "a source of sustenance for West Indian culture"[54] in the heavily black Caribbean province of Limón. Bernard's new voice is a strong one even when she overlays her poetry with a tenderness, sometimes maternal, that recognizes the fragile nature of the black experience in Costa Rica.

Although the "race question" is a thematic concern of Costa Rican black writers, Quince Duncan stepped outside the West Indian experience in writing *Final de calle* (*Dead End Street*, 1980), deliberately suppressing, for the most part, all overt references to blackness. Duncan is proud of the acclaim this novel received since his purpose was to write "a significant novel without capitalizing on the black theme."[55] Duncan submitted his novel anonymously and won both the Editorial Costa Rica in-house prize in 1978 and the Aquileo Echeverría National Prize for Literature the following year. The publisher, Editorial Costa Rica, Duncan tells us, made five thousand rather than the normal three thousand copies per edition for his novel that, he adds, has already gone through two editions.[56] Born in 1940, Duncan is the oldest of the 1940s-born black writers in Latin America. *Final de calle*, his ninth book in a body of work that includes short stories and novels among other publications, looks back on the civil war in 1948 and its effects on his generation. Duncan published several new items in the 1980s, among them *Los cuentos do Jack Mantorra* (1989), and in 1990 he published his recent novel titled *Kimbo*.

In the Dominican Republic, Norberto James published his collected works in the volume *Hago constar (poemas 1969–1982) (I State My Case [Poems 1969–1982]*, 1983). In his poem "Los inmigrantes" ("The Immigrants"), immediately recognizable as a tribute to his West Indian ancestry, James states a claim for his "pedazo de Patria" ("piece of the country"). Speaking for his generation, James has written: "Hoy nos sobran las palabras / y nos piden que bajemos la voz. / Que callen. / Es hora de iniciar el canto. . . ." ("Today we have so much to say / and they ask us to keep quiet. / Let them keep quiet / It's time to begin the song. . . ." James realizes that his is a "nueva voz" ("new voice"), and he uses it to give his people hope. James dedicated one of his poems to Juan ("Juancho") Sánchez Lamouth, the older-generation Dominican black poet who published several volumes of poetry in the 1950s. Lamouth died in 1968 at the age of thirty-nine. In one of the few studies on both these poets, James Davis writes that James's poetry, like that of his predecessor, shows a genuine concern for poor people and blacks and includes the themes of human suffering, oppression, injustice, inequality, and alienation.[57] James understands the sense of alienation some non–Spanish-speaking immigrants feel, and he demands recognition of their rights in Dominican society.

James, who has some experience in the United States, has acknowledged that seeing the racial problem in that country close up has helped him understand the problem of race in his native Dominican Republic.[58] One of the most interesting revelations of Dominicans, James Davis has written, is "that they do not consciously concern themselves with the issue of race until they come into contact with Afro-Americans."[59] Davis goes on to cite Frank Moya Pons, a renowned Dominican historian, who asserted that a major impact of the relationship between the United States and the Dominican Republic was the discovery of the concept of negritude by Dominican blacks living in the United States. "Something new" is going on in the Dominican Republic, Moya Pons has written. "More and more Dominicans now dare to say that they are not white, certainly those from among the younger generation who have been raised in the cities of the East and have grown up with colored Puerto Ricans, West Indians, and Black Americans."[60]

Blas Jiménez, James's compatriot, is becoming increasingly more visible and vocal. His work, perhaps more than that of any other new Hispanic black writing today, recalls the very strong black consciousness literature of the 1940s, represented best by Jorge Artel's *Tambores en la noche* (*Drums in the Night* [1940], 1955). This memorable book of verse by Artel—later enlarged—contains oft-quoted poems such as "Negro soy" ("I Am Black"). Writing forty years later, Jiménez peppers the poetry from his first book, *Aquí . . . otro español* (*Another . . . Spaniard Here*, 1980), with such phrases as "soy un negro," "soy negro," "yo quiero ser negro," "Que me deje ser / negro y nada más," "tengo que sentirme negro," and "el negro que soy." ("I am a black person," "I am black," "I want to be black," "Let me be black / black and nothing more," "I have to feel black," and "the black person that I am"). From the beginning Jiménez makes it clear that his work is made up of "negros cantos / cantos negros / de los negros / para negros."[61] Jimenez asks searching questions about black and national identity in the Dominican Republic. There is no hesitancy in proclaiming his own black identity, and the poet takes as his mission the task of forcing others to do the same. His primary objective is to upgrade not only black identity but also the image of the black as Dominican.

Jiménez feels a strong obligation to write, to reclaim a voice, and to express his black vision of the future and his hope for a better tomorrow. There is some pessimism clouding his belief in a brighter future in his later work, but this does not prevent him from making a claim on behalf of all those black voices lost in the Middle Passage and beyond whom he represents and for whom he writes. Jiménez writes because he does not wish for black voices to ever again be forfeited or to be made over in someone else's image. Jiménez's poetry inspires black pride in self and in black history, but his poetry also has a social and nationalistic goal, which is to give hope to those without it and an identity to those who are still unsure. Jiménez's poem "Tengo," recalls Nicolás Guillén's composition of the same name, but unlike the Cuban black poet's better-known poem, Jiménez's version is much more black-based than ideologically appreciative. "Tengo que sentirme negro" ("I have to feel black"), he writes, because that is his first obligation. One must feel black to truly fight an inferiority complex of blackness and an image of servility.

Jiménez has published three volumes of poetry in this decade. His other two are *Caribe africano en despertar* (*African Caribbean Awakening*, 1984) and *Exigencias de un cimarrón (en sueños)* (*A Rebel's Demands [Imagined]*, 1987). In these more recent volumes Jiménez writes of change, pride, black history, rebellion, freedom, personal growth, and the beauty of blackness. As a new generation black writer, Blas Jiménez is most concerned with projecting an image of black people come of age, especially those in his country—a country, he argues, whose culture is as much black as anything else. In *Caribe, africano en despertar*, Jiménez expresses his concern for young people, for the child "sin mañana y sin historia"[62] ("without a tomorrow and without a yesterday"), and for a people who have yet to define themselves realistically and who are reluctant to work at that definition. The culminating statement the poet makes in *Exigencias de un cimarrón (en sueños)*, his third volume of poetry, can be found in the poem "Indio claro"[63] ("Light-Skinned Indian"). Although exposing (and condemning) the wish to be white characterized his earlier work, this most recent volume highlights the light-skinned person who identifies with blacks and who willingly accepts and chooses to be black in an act of consciousness that could have trend-setting repercussions in the Dominican Republic.

Recently published black writers in Latin America outside Cuba, then Dominican Republic, and Central America include the Colombian black Yvonne América Truque, whose work is published in a bilingual edition titled *Proyección de los silencios* (*Projection of Silence*, 1986). Truque, who is the daughter of the Colombian black writer Carlos Arturo Truque, writes about love, tenderness, freedom, grief, bitterness, hope, and other abstract concepts that are difficult to express because words do not always capture adequately what one feels inside one's soul. Yet she tries as she moves about in the world in search of "nueva vida" ("new life"). She looks "en lo profundo de mi alma" ("in the deepest recesses of her soul") for inspiration and guidance. Happiness in a new life is her hope, and she is determined to have it. Yvonne América Truque is, indeed, a "mujer futuro" ("woman of the future"), a "mujer mañana" ("a woman of tomorrow").

For a long time the late Nicomedes Santa Cruz, who wrote not just about blacks but as a black, was the best-known publishing black author in Peru. Now with Gregorio Martínez's fiction, there is a new black image emerging in Peruvian literature. *Canto de sirena* (*Siren's Song*, 1977) is his first novel, but Martínez's first work on black life in coastal Peru is the book of short stories, *Tierra de caléndula* (*Caléndula Land*, 1975). His experiments with language and word formation in this book had already attracted critical attention and acclaim. Martínez was born in Coyungo, a small village in the Nazca region on the Pacific coast of Peru. He gives this same background to Candelario Navarro, the old black protagonist in *Canto de sirena*. Martínez considers his protagonist to be a representative collective voice of the region, and the character shares to some degree the author's own world vision. For that reason, Martínez describes his main character as somewhat autobiographical. His own way of life, certainly in sexual matters, is not too different from that of his protagonist, whose characterization was based on an actual person.[64]

The excessive sexual nature of this novel has generated the question, as posed by Marvin Lewis: "If, as Martínez maintains, Candelario represents the collective consciousness of the region, are we to assume that coastal Blacks were/are concerned only with satisfying physical needs?"[65] Martínez has said that his protagonist ideologically is backward like most of the people he represents. It is this absence of ideological content that Lewis criticizes. We can say that in a way Martínez's character is a new variation on Adalberto Ortiz's 1943 African Ecuadorian novel titled *Juyungo*. This character's ideological base was minimal, as indeed was the case for some of Nicolás Guillén's early black characters. Latent or covert discontent is a quality all these fictional characters have in common. Martínez's intent was to make Candelario authentic and, like Ascensión, primarily motivated by feelings rather than by theory or ideological platform.

In Venezuela, Antonio Acosta Márquez's book of poetry, *Yo pienso aqui donde . . . estoy* (*I Think Here Where . . . I Am*, 1981), is "the most recent literary assessment of Afro-Venezuelan culture from a black perspective."[66] His Venezuelan black poetry is affirmative and is, perhaps, a bit more exuberant than most of his Hispanic black counterparts. Acosta Márquez has an eye on the future, taking his inspiration from the people who are the main subjects of his poetry. He specifically ties black liberation to the inspiration he feels as a poet. He is inspired by the efforts of the people, and his poetry sings as much of their efforts to overcome hardship as it does about black culture. The exuberance in Acosta Márquez's poetry derives from its essentially oral nature. Much of it seems

designed to be sung, and many of his poems immediately sound
like black rhythms of Venezuela, recalling Nicomedes Santa Cruz's
black rhythms of Peru. Both of these writers are black-poet singers
whose appeal lies partly in their preference for the popular forms
of verse that invoke black music and black dance. Acosta
Márquez's poetry is a poetry of *coplas, romances, contrapunteos, joro-
pos, décimas,* and *refranes*; of dance, of *tambor, ritmo, calor, and sol.*
Like Nicomedes Santa Cruz, Márquez does not shy away from the
political statement. And like Marcelino Arozarena in Cuba,
Márquez knows how to "cantar opinando" ("sing passing judgment"), which he occasionally does.

Antonio Acosta Márquez is concerned with the oral and
rhythmic cadence of poetry, but most of all he seems to pride
himself on his total identification with his people, his region ("mi
Barlovento"), and his country ("mi bella Venezuela"). To the
poet, song and verse are one. They are the medium he uses to
capture the words, music, and thought of his people, which he in
turn transmits back to them, his source. The Venezuelan poet, in
fact, does not really consider himself a poet but rather "un
obrero, que no sabe nada de letras" ("a worker, who does not
know anything about literature"). Aníbal Nazoa,[67] in an overly
apologetic prologue, underscores the popular nature of the
poetry of Antonio Acosta Márquez, who much to the consterna-
tion of some *precetistas* ("academicians"), does not concern himself too much with form. Like Blas Jiménez and others, "El Negro
Acosta," as he is called, is clearly more concerned with complexion than with complexity.

While some think the Caribbean black and the Central
American black authors are the most active or promising among
the 1940s-born group, Heriberto Dixon believes that black literature in Ecuador is the most courageous, best documented, and
most committed in all of Latin America.[68] The Ecuadorian black
contingent is a strong one with Adalberto Ortiz, Nelson Estupiñán
Bass, and Antonio Preciado leading the way. One of the remarkable aspects of the Ecuadorian black group is the ability of several
writers to produce authentic black literature while at the same
time making efforts to put negritude behind them. Adalberto
Ortiz, for example, felt he had broken new ground with *Juyungo* in
1943, but once he left the province of Esmeraldas, he thought it his
obligation to grow into other things and other themes. Antonio
Preciado, a new voice in Ecuador, brings the rhythm of black

music to some of his poems, but Preciado himself believes he has evolved from an Africanist tradition to one designed to bring people together, not separate them. He thinks it possible to leave one's own world behind without losing one's identity.[69]

In Brazil, black intellectuals brought up during the late 1960s are responsible for a cycle of black Brazilian consciousness. Started in the second half of the 1970s, this cycle, as yet, has not lost its impetus. David Brookshaw, who reports on this process, points to the establishment of centers and institutes in Rio and Sao Paulo for research into black art and culture as evidence of this development. The most significant initiative of this period, he writes, has been the yearly publication since 1978 of *Cadernos negros* ("Black Notebooks"), reminiscent in some ways of the Broadside Press in the United States during the 1960s, which provided a mouthpiece for black writers and activists.[70] Black poets in Brazil call for a common acceptance of their country's pluri-cultural identity.[71]

A witness to many of the changes in Brazil, Anani Dzidzienyo is one of the fewer than fifteen experts around the world in Afro-Brazilian history.[72] He has been to Brazil many times since 1970, and he is the author of academic studies in African Brazilian race relations. What is more important, he can give an eye-witness account of the many changes in Brazil that reflect the African Brazilians' growing awareness of their position in society: "I think from about '74 to '78 you could see some changes. . . . As I traveled through Brazil and talked to people both black and white, I came to form the impression that we had entered a new era. . . . From about '74, little things began to appear here and there; publications, etc. I think it all comes to a head in August of 1978. . . ."[73] Black writers who produce *Cadernos negros* are also partly responsible for *Jornegro*, a black newspaper. Since March 1978, *Jornegro* has been publishing the poetry of Brazilian blacks from several regions of Brazil as an integral part of its program to increase the awareness of African Brazilian culture among its readers.

Abelardo Rodrigues was considered by Phyllis Reisman, who interviewed him in Sao Paulo in July 1979, to be the most promising poet to appear during those years.[74] Jane McDivitt agrees that Rodrigues, who began publishing in the late 1970s, was the most important poet of that generation. She adds that he, like other black Brazilian poets today, has received the encouragement of Oswaldo de Camargo, who has been the dean of African

Brazilian letters since the death of Solano Trindade in 1974. McDivitt also believed that the most talented African Brazilian writer today is Angela Lopes Galvao, the first female poet of genuine promise to emerge in modern African Brazilian verse.[75] McDivitt and Reisman are generating interest in these writers just as Ann Venture Young did with black poetry written in Spanish. Even though her bilingual anthology, *The Image of Women in 20th Century South American Poetry*,[76] does not contain the work of any of the 1940s-born black authors who write in Spanish, it is a valuable addition to the field of Hispanic literature.

TRADITION AND RENEWAL

Black writers are continuing the black literary tradition in Latin America but are bringing to it at the same time their own contemporary perspectives. Such writers as Nancy Morejón, Quince Duncan, Gerardo Maloney, Blas Jiménez, Antonio Acosta Márquez, and Gregorio Martínez are noteworthy not only for their unique contributions but also for how their work recalls earlier masters such as Nicolás Guillén, Jorge Artel, Pilar Barrios, Nicomedes Santa Cruz, Adalberto Ortiz, Nelson Estupiñán Bass, and Manuel Zapata Olivella. The thematic range of these writers is broad, but what are some of the overriding black images taking shape in their literature? What are some of the dominant impressions they leave us? Gregorio Martínez's Candelario in *Canto de sirena* (1977) could strike us as a new macho black who, reminiscent of Adalberto Ortiz's *Juyungo* (1943), has little or no revolutionary orientation or ideology. Morejón's black characters can be found at the other end of the political spectrum. Quince Duncan's Charles McForbes in *Los cuarto espejos* (1973) is a classic example of a black man trying to come to terms with his identity. This character type is repeated in the work of other Latin American black authors, most visibly in Nelson Estupiñán Bass's *El último río* (1966).

Throughout Hispanic black literature, memorable black characters are portrayed, ranging from the brute to the intellectual, to revolutionary leaders and individuals. One of the most notable qualities I find in this literature is black anger, combined with indignation and bitterness. There is some gentleness and sensitivity in Morejón, Bernard, and Truque, but there is also black aggressiveness in this literature. Litó, Wilson's angry young protagonist in *Chombo*, is a black hero for our time. Noticeable anger is in the poetry of Blas Jimenez, one of the strongest new black voices around, and few poets have expressed anger the way Nancy Morejón has in "Freedom Now," her poem to black student leaders in the United States. Black writers today are trying to overcome frustration and are urging black readers to become serious. Gerardo Maloney urges his black character to stop "cogiéndolo suave" ("playing it cool"). Eulalia Bernard wants her black heroes to be something more than a "ritmoheroe," more than a carnival king, which is really what Nicolás Guillén had been saying all along. In the 1940s-born generation of Hispanic black writing, we are seeing the continuation of a tradition plus a renewal.

Hispanic black writers are indeed coming into their own.[77] Major black writers who, like Nicolás Guillén, had been working for a while are now gaining some recognition. It is increasingly evident, however, that since the 1960s and 1970s, Latin American black writers have been expressing a new black consciousness. Edward Mullen[78] surveyed the proliferation in the 1970s and 1980s of black-based anthologies. The difference between these anthologies and earlier ones published in the 1930s and 1940s is that now more black authors are represented. This explicit desire "to radicalize the traditional canon,"[79] however, is not limited to anthologies, nor is it one-dimensional. Clearly, one of the most striking characteristics in Hispanic black literature today is the height to which black consciousness is being raised. Black consciousness in Hispanic literature dates back to the past century, and Hispanic black authors writing in the first half of this century kept the tradition alive. Hispanic black writers today continue that tradition.

All over Latin America, as Nelson Estupiñán Bass[80] wrote, a new black is emerging with a new outlook and a new consciousness, aware of his civil rights and claiming a rightful place in society. Antonio Acosta Márquez raises this very point in his poem titled "Yo pienso aquí en donde estoy" in which he asks "es que no tengo derechos . . . de vivir en esta tierra?" ("do I not have the right . . . to live here?") Clearly black writers today have done a lot of thinking on this topic, and their determination to claim a place as black citizens is reflected in their work. Individually, black writers seem to sense that their work is being heard and read, not as a passing diversion but as a voice of hope.

A focus on the future is another trait that bonds all of these 1940s-born black writers together. We are the builders of tomorrow, Norberto James has said, of a new order. Nancy Morejón underscores in her poetry her belief that she is the "New Woman" in the "new day" of Cuba. Yvonne América Truque considers herself to be a woman of the future. Blas Jiménez writes of a new day coming. In his work *Juega vivo*, Gerardo Maloney calls Part 3 "Toward Tomorrow." In this generation's literature, black consciousness at times runs triple deep. Central America, where black writers feel ties to Central America, to the West Indies, and to Africa, is an example. This literature, some of it reminiscent of the Turbulent Sixties, shows no signs of abating. A new toughness is exhibited by the aggressive and angry tone the writing sometimes takes. These black poets are especially concerned with speaking in a clear voice that reflects the will of the people for whom they write. They do not stifle creativity with complexity, nor do they pretend that complexion does not matter. There is genuine racial feeling in much of their work, and they strongly feel that there is as much room for black literature as there is for black people in their countries of birth. Since the 1960s, black writers in Latin America have conveyed the message that blacks are willing to participate as blacks, "without feeling that to do so makes them any less Latin American, nationalist, revolutionary, human, or refined."[81]

Yet, although the overwhelming trend among Latin American black writers is the cultivation of a literature that gives expression to a black perspective, black writers such as Quince Duncan in Costa Rica have at times intentionally tried to transcend black themes by writing works on completely separate subjects (even under anonymous authorship). This decision to write on any topic of their choosing is itself a measure of a new consciousness, especially among black female writers of the 1940s-born generation. Examples are Yvonne América Truque of Colombia, Nancy Morejón of Cuba, and Eulalia Bernard of Costa Rica. As Marvin Lewis[82] demonstrated, some black writers may supplement literary blackness with national concerns, especially in Colombia. Violence and ideology, he has discovered, are the two rhetorical symbols that structure the literature of Colombian black writers of fiction, who embrace both literary blackness and literary Americanism.

Hispanic black literature emerged as an area for literary research in the late 1960s. Critics were propelled to research and to develop criticism to keep pace with the literature being produced. In the aftermath of the 1960s, Hispanic black literature became a new frontier for critics, some of whom brought what has been called a North American perspective to bear on issues of race and color in Latin America. Others brought deeper reflection and closer reading to the Hispanic black text. What all of them found were Hispanic black writers eagerly researching their past, while aggressively looking to the future.

Notes

1. Nelson Estupiñán Bass, "La lira negra," *Revista Colegio Nacional 5 de Agosto* 7 (1981): 11.
2. Roberto Márquez, "Zombi to Synthesis: Notes on the Negro in Spanish American Literature," *Jamaica Journal* 11, no. 1 (1977): 30.
3. Constance S. de García-Barrios, "The Black in Post-Revolutionary Cuban Literature," *Revista/Review Interamericana* 8 (1978): 263–70.
4. See Richard L. Jackson, *Black Literature and Humanism in Latin America* (Athens: University of Georgia Press, 1988).
5. See *Notre Librairie* 80 (1985). This entire issue is devoted to Hispanic black writers.
6. Roberto González Echeverría, ed. *Hispanic Caribbean Literature*, special issue of *Latin American Literary Review* 7, no. 16 (1980): 241.
7. Gwendolyn Brooks, "The Darker Brother," *New York Times*, Book Review section, 12 October 1986, 7.
8. Roberto Márquez, ed., *Latin American Revolutionary Poetry. A Bilingual Anthology* (New York: Monthly Review Press, 1974), 200.
9. Márquez, "Zombi," 30.
10. *Nancy Morejón* (New York: Center for Cuban Studies, 1983).
11. Her works include *Mutismos* ("Silences") 1962; *Amor, ciudad atribuída* ("Love, Attributed City") 1964; *Richard trajo su flauta* ("Richard Brought His Flute") 1967; *Parajes de una época* ("Parameters of an Epoch") 1979; *Octubre imprescindible* ("Essential October") 1982; *Cuaderno de Grenada* ("Grenada Notebook") 1984; and *Piedra Pulida* ("Polished Stone") 1986.
12. *Where the Island Sleeps Like a Wing: Selected Poetry by Nancy Morejón*, trans. Kathleen Weaver (San Francisco: Black Scholar Press, 1985).
13. *Where the Island*, 86.
14. Rafael Rodríguez, "Nancy Morejón en su Habana," *Areito* 8, no. 32 (1983): 25.
15. *Where the Island*, 2.
16. Langston Hughes, "Mother to Son" ("No Crystal Stair"), in *Selected Poems of Langston Hughes* (New York: A. A. Knopf, 1959). Reprinted in *Ebony* (May 1982), 54.
17. Nicolás Guillén, *Obra poética, 1958–1972*, vol. II (Havana: Editorial Arte y Literatura, 1974): 334.
18. Guillén, 334.

19. Nancy Morejón, *Richard trajo su flauta y otros argumentos* (Havana: Instituto del Libro, 1967): 27–35.

20. See Nancy Morejón, "Warrior's Brief Song," *The Black Scholar* (May/June 1984): 19, and her *Cuaderno de Grenada* (1984).

21. *Where the Island* 90.

22. Ibid., 84.

23. Renée Larrier, "Racism in the United States: An Issue in Caribbean Poetry," *Journal of Caribbean Studies* 2, no. 1 (1981): 61.

24. Josephat B. Kubayanda, *The Poet's Africa: Africanness in the Poetry of Nicolás Guillén and Aimé Césaire* (Westport, Conn.: Greenwood Press, 1990), 118.

25. *Where the Island*, 20.

26. Ibid., 76.

27. Ibid., 72.

28. Ibid., 136.

29. Ibid., 58.

30. Ibid., 86.

31. Ibid., 80.

32. Ibid., 60.

33. Ibid., 58.

34. Ibid., 20.

35. *The Black Scholar* (May/June 1984): 18–19.

36. Ibid., 56. *Cumbite* has been published in English. See Pedro Pérez Sarduy, *Cumbite and Other Poems* (New York: Center for Cuban Studies, 1990). Here he is described as a "child of the Revolution."

37. *The Black Scholar* (May/June 1984): 18.

38. Nancy Morejón, "Asalto a Tito Junco," *La gaceta de Cuba* 157 (December 1976): 8.

39. Yvonne Yarbro-Bejarano, "Cuban Theater Today: Report on Third Festival of Latin American Theater Today," *Metamorphosis: Northwest Chicano Magazine of Art and Literature* 5, no. 2; 6, no. 1 (1984–1985): 44–51.

40. Jay Scott, "Cuba's Foremost Filmmaker Travels Independent Route," *Globe and Mail* (Toronto), 7 April 1986, A26.

41. Ian Smart, *Central American Writers of West Indian Origin: A New Hispanic Literature* (Washington, D.C.: Three Continents Press, 1984), 115.

42. David McField, *Poemas para el año del elefante* (Managua: Artes Gráficas, 1970), 12.

43. Stephen Kinzer, "In Nicaragua, Reggae, and Resentment," *New York Times*, 15 October 1986, 10.

44. Carlos Rigby, "Palabras del campesino en la inauguración del Palo de Mayo," *Poesía nicaragüense*, ed. Ernesto Cardenal (Havana: Casa de las Americas, 1973), 549.

45. Kinzer., 10.

46. Ian Smart, "The Literary World of Quince Duncan: An Interview," *College Language Association Journal* 28, no. 3 (1985): 283.

47. Francisco de Asis Fernández, ed., *Poesía política nicaragüense* (Managua: Ministerio de Cultura, 1986), 169.

48. Alberto Smith-Fernández, "Panama, la patria nuestra," *Afro-Hispanic Review* 3, no. 1 (1984): 10.

49. Ian Smart, "Popular Black Intellectualism in Yerardo Maloney's *Juega Vivo*," *Afro-Hispanic Review* 5, nos. 1, 2, & 3, (1986): 43.
50. *Afro-Hispanic Review* 3, no. 1 (1984): 29.
51. *Afro-Hispanic Review* 1, no. 3 (1982): 9.
52. Ian Smart, "A New Panamanian Poet's Promising Quest for Identity," *Plantation Society in the Americas* 1 (1981): 386.
53. Gerardo Maloney, *Juega vivo* (Panama: Ediciones Formato, 1984), 85. All quotations are from this edition.
54. Ian Smart, "Religious Elements in the Narrative of Quince Duncan," *Afro-Hispanic Review* 1, no. 2 (1982), 31.
55. Ibid.
56. Ian Smart, "The Literary World of Quince Duncan: An Interview," *College Language Association Journal* 28, no. 3 (1985): 283.
57. James Davis, "On Black Poetry in the Dominican Republic," *Afro-Hispanic Review* 1, no. 3 (1982): 29.
58. See James J. Davis, "Entrevista con el dominicano Norberto James Rawlings," *Afro-Hispanic Review* 6, no. 2 (1987): 18.
59. James J. Davis, Review of *Poems of Exile and Other Concerns: A Bilingual Selection of the Poetry Written by Dominicans in the United States* by Daisy Cocco de Filippis and Emma Jane Robinett (New York: Ediciones Alcance, 1988) in *College Language Association Journal* 33, no. 3 (1989): 383.
60. Quoted in E. Valerie Smith, "A Merging of Two Cultures: The Afro-Hispanic Immigrants of Samana, Dominican Republic," *Afro-Hispanic Review* 8, nos. 1 & 2 (1989): 9.
61. Blas Jimenez, *Aquí . . . otro español* (Santo Domingo: Editorial Incoco, 1980), 3. All quotations are from this edition.
62. Blas Jiménez, *Caribe, africano en despertar* (Santo Domingo: Nuevas Rutas, 1984), 11. All quotations are from this edition.
63. Blas Jiménez, *Exigencias de un cimarrón (en sueños)* (Santo Domingo: Editora Taller, 1987), 100. All quotations are from this edition.
64. Luis Freire, "La sirena popular de Gregorio," *Runa* 6 (1977): 33–35.
65. Marvin Lewis, "From Chincha to Chimbote: Blacks in the Contemporary Peruvian-Novel," *Afro-Hispanic Review* 3, no. 2 (1984): 9.
66. Marvin Lewis, "Afro-Venezuelan Literature: A Cultural Perspective," in *Abstracts/Resúmenes* (Amsterdam: 46th International Congress of Americanists, 1988), 797. Also see his *Ethnicity and Identity in Contemporary Afro-Venezuelan Literature. A Culturalist Approach* (Columbia: University of Missouri Press, 1992).
67. Aníbal Nazoa, "Un poeta del pueblo," in *Yo pienso aquí donde estoy* by Antonio Acosta Márquez (Medellín: Ediciones Cascabel, 1977): 1–3. All quotations are from this edition. A second edition was published in 1981 by Editorial Trazos in Caracas, Venezuela.
68. Heriberto Dixon, "Folklore afro-ecuatoriano reflejado a través de la literatura," *Círculo: Revista de cultura*, Verona, N.J.: 13 (1987): 71–77.
69. Ester de Crespo, "Les racines africaines d'Antonio Preciado, poète equatorien," *Notre librairie* 80 (1985): 96–98.
70. David Brookshaw, *Race and Color in Brazilian Literature* (Metuchen, N.J.: Scarecrow Press, 1986): 286. Fifteen of these "Black Notebooks" have been

published thus far. See Carolyn Richardson Durham, "Hunger, Racism, and Abandoned Children: Topics of Poetry Readings by Afro-Brazilian Literary Groups," *Hispania* 75 (December 1992): 1225. She discusses *Quilombhoje Literatura*, an organization of Afro-Brazilian writers whose members give poetry readings. This group has also taken over responsibility for the publication of *Cadernos negros*.

71. Brookshaw, *Race and Color*, 306.
72. John D. Huddles, "Afro-Brazilian Race Relations: An Interview with Insider Anani Dzidzienyo," *Issues Monthly* (Brown University) (March 1984): 15.
73. Ibid., 16–17.
74. See Jane M. McDivitt, "Contemporary Afro-Brazilian Protest Poetry," *Caribe* (April 1980): 9.
75. Jane M. McDivitt, "Modern Afro-Brazilian Poetry," *Callaloo* 3, nos. 1–3 (1980): 59. For a recent study of the upsurge in Afro-Brazilian literary production in the late 1970s and early 1980s, see James H. Kennedy, "Political Liberalization, Black Consciousness, and Recent Afro-Brazilian Literature," *Phylon* 48, no. 3 (1986): 199–209. Also see his comprehensive bibliography of contemporary Afro-Brazilian literature: "Recent Afro-Brazilian Literature: A Tentative Bibliography," *A Current Bibliography on African Affaires* 17, no. 4 (1985): 327–45.
76. Ann Ventura Young, *The Image of Black Women in 20th Century South American Poetry: A Bilingual Anthology* (Washington, D.C.: Three Continents Press, 1987).
77. William Siemens, review of *Afro-Hispanic Poetry 1940–1980: From Slavery to "Negritud" in South American Verse* by Marvin Lewis in *Revista de estudios hispánicos* 22 (1988): 146.
78. Edward Mullen, "The Emergence of Afro-Hispanic Poetry: Some Notes on Canon Formation," *Hispanic Review* 56, no. 4 (1988): 435–53.
79. Ibid., 449.
80. Nelson Estupiñán Bass, "Aristas negras," *Cultura*, 4, no. 10 (1981): 63.
81. Cited in Pierre-Michel Fontaine, "Research in the Political Economy of Afro-Latin America," *Latin American Research Review* 15, no. 2 (1980): 134.
82. Marvin Lewis, *Treading the Ebony Path: Ideology and Violence in Contemporary Afro-Colombian Prose Fiction* (Columbia: University of Missouri Press, 1987).

CONCLUSION

Hispanic Black Criticism and the North American Perspective

Several years ago, criticism on Hispanic black literature fell roughly into four main categories: (1) black criticism, (2) negristic or socio-negristic criticism, (3) socialist or Marxist or nationalist criticism, and (4) universal criticism. These categories had, I thought, racial overtones, sociological or ethnological connotations, and political implications (the latter with a decidedly nonracial emphasis).[1] Black criticism looks at black authors subjectively or from a black ethnic point of view, reevaluating in the process the black person's image in literature and in criticism. Black criticism recognizes the role ethnicity plays in evaluation. Negristic or socio-negristic criticism is interested mainly in the folkloric and atavistic aspects of black literature or in defending blacks. Marxist, socialist, and nationalist criticism, by emphasizing revolutionary solidarity or *mestizaje*, are aimed, like universal criticism, at "whitening" black authors by playing down their black ethnic identity.

Things have not changed greatly over the years, although there are some new developments. Avant garde criticism is on the rise.[2] This new criticism, which admires the complexity of the text, is aimed, like the last two types, at whitening the black author even though, unlike the others, it is not concerned with ideology and politics. Another new development, this one a type of black criticism, falls at the other end of the spectrum. I refer to the prominence of the African critic of Hispanic black literature. Examples are the late J. Bekunuru Kubayanda of Ghana and Ohio State University, Sierra Leone's Lemuel Johnson of the University of Michigan, and Ghana's Anani Dzidzienyo of Brown University. Their unique worldview and comparative knowledge of African writers and linguistics have enriched our discipline.

Kubayanda specialized in clarifying the African sources of Latin American black literature. The body of writing he left us shows that principles of African versification are more appropriate than traditional European meter in analyzing poems such as

Guillén's "Negro bembón." He also challenged the acceptance of white (European) or "universal" models that have characterized Latin America since Columbus. Kubayanda's work stands as a constant repudiation of colonialism or neo-colonialism or any of the other theories that support the view that Western whites have a monopoly on beauty, virtue, and intelligence. The African reading that Kubayanda gave to Latin American black literature went beyond "literary blackness" to seek the African source of this blackness manifest in African principles such as ancestrality, drum communication, ideophonic expression, plant symbolism, and heroic codes.[3]

The debates on black criticism and on literary blackness in Latin America are ongoing affairs. Contributions made by Kubayanda, by Ian Smart,[4] and certainly by Hispanic black writers themselves take these debates to higher ground. In fact, my primary focus in this concluding chapter will be on the increasing availability of critical commentary about Hispanic black literature from Hispanic black writers themselves. Of all such critical writings, perhaps the best-known essay belongs to Adalberto Ortiz, whose treatise on negritude in Latin America has been translated into English and published in an easily available and prestigious collection of critical essays.[5] Nelson Estupiñán Bass has also produced criticism. On at least four separate occasions, he has expanded his ideas on black literature and black writers, concentrating on Ecuador and more specifically on his home province of Esmeraldas.[6] Manuel Zapata Olivella[7] has published several critical statements and many of his interventions in conferences have been published, as have some by Nicomedes Santa Cruz.[8] In addition, numerous published interviews, conversations, and other items (some of them mentioned below) have provided the reader with insights into the authors' thoughts on their own literature and on that of others.

Much of this commentary writing addresses negritude, slavery, and the black image in literature. Much of it questions whether white writers can create credible and authentic images of nonwhite people. This "contentious" issue was raised vociferously at the recent PEN meeting in Toronto. Jeanette Armstrong, an Okanagan Indian writer from British Columbia, attacked white Canadian writers who use Indian terms, themes, legends, myths, motifs, and point of view in their fiction. "You have no right to steal what is important to us and reinterpret it for your own use,"[9] she has said. Armstrong strongly believes that nonnatives "should keep their hands off these myths and legends,"[10] claiming they distort such myths and prevent native writers with the genuine article from being heard. This discussion on the question of whether white writers should even write about black or native characters led another congress participant to admit: "I would feel terribly uneasy writing about the experience of a black woman because I'm not black."[11] This issue most relates to the distinction we must make between *negrismo* and negritude, one that Hispanic black writers themselves certainly make. The Hispanic black writer as critic views the issues of credibility and authenticity, particularly in *negrista* texts, as crucial.

The critic of Hispanic black literature must also determine whether the Hispanic black writer is more concerned with class than with race or vice versa. We must make this determination because it is of uppermost concern to black writers themselves. What we find, certainly in reading Manuel Zapata Olivella, is that some Hispanic black writers rarely make a distinction between the two and that others are concerned with both. Nicolás Guillén, Adalberto Ortiz, and Nelson Estupiñán Bass often see issues more in terms of class than of race, but these three are at the same time best known for their race literature and for being strong proponents of the positive black image. This aggressiveness on race carries over into their criticism.

Another major question that arises as we read Hispanic black literature is whether we approach it simply as writing (a position that would render the race and the color of the author irrelevant) or whether we continue to consider the ethnicity factor to be as important as technique. This question dovetails into the modern, or avant-garde, concern with complexity (more than with complexion) and with its assertion. Hispanic black writers, especially Nicolás Guillén and Adalberto Ortiz, are themselves very concerned with this matter. In contrast, black writers such as Blas Jiménez in the Dominican Republic and Antonio Acosta Márquez in Venezuela clearly are more concerned with complexion than with complexity, and they clearly tell us so right in their poetry. Both emphasize that they write poetry as a means to an end. This aim is to address human needs; their objective is to do it clearly, not with a complexity that confounds the issues. Both emphasize, as we saw, that there should be more to poetry than erudite terms and pretty phrases.

Some critics today continue to view Hispanic black literature through a *mestizo* prism. They believe that in Latin America, black literature cannot be seen in black and white as it is in the United States. At best, it is in black, brown, and white or in black, white, and Hispanic. To discuss literary blackness, they would argue, is to bring a North American perspective to the issues of race and color in Latin America, where such a perspective has no place. In Latin America, the widespread perception is that racial mixing has blurred the lines between black and white. Can black criticism be used to assess Latin American black literature? This is, perhaps, the leading question. How, then, should we answer it? First, we should look at how Hispanic black writers themselves handle the question. We will find that they have resolved the *mestizo*/black dichotomy, and we in North America should keep in mind the critical perspective these Hispanic black writers bring to bear on the black literature of their own countries.

Much of their commentary writing tells us that acceptance of one's origins—and accommodating that acceptance to a new-world reality that often denies it validity—is an overriding principle guiding not only their aesthetics as Hispanic black writers but also their critical literature. Much of their criticism, which is often an extension of the ideas that shape their creative work, confirms that the black critical perspective in Latin America is not too different from that found in the racially polarized North. Hispanic black writers resolve their own black perspective in a *mestizo* reality, finding their own solutions to what has been called "an insoluble identity question."[12] Miscegenation, of course, is a key factor here. As Marvin Lewis has written, black writers such as Nicomedes Santa Cruz, Adalberto Ortiz, and Nelson Estupiñán Bass have "passionately grappled"[13] with the identity problem it presents. The determination to maintain black consciousness is often stronger in Latin American society precisely because blacks there have to contend with constant pressures to minimize or to distort their presence. This struggle, which was recently labeled a struggle "against invisibility,"[14] is best illustrated in the following quotation: "As a child, I looked through Peruvian history books. All the famous blacks came out as whites."[15] These are the words of Andrés Mandros Gallardo, cultural secretary of the Francisco Congo Black Movement in Peru. Based in Lima, this group is part of several attempts by blacks to reassert African identity in Latin America.

The *mestizo* factor clearly is the source of some racial ambivalence, but Hispanic black writers have found ways to work through it. Stanley Cyrus discussed the cultural and racial ambivalence of some Hispanic black writers (especially Adalberto Ortiz) whose mixed ancestry or "allegiance" to the concept of *mestizaje* forces them to confront psychological dualism in their works.[16] Nicolás Guillén, Adalberto Ortiz, and Manuel Zapata Olivella— the three leading proponents of *mestizaje* (*mulatez*)—are at the same time the leading Hispanic black writers in Latin America. Clearly, they have recognized, confronted, and resolved the problem of identity. What I find remarkable is that while acknowledging the fact of racial mixture, they are at the same time able to give their work a black perspective. They accomplish this partly by honoring the black ancestors and partly by raising contemporary black consciousness. And they bring a vindicationist perspective toward black history to their way of fighting the legacy of the slave past—in their creative work and in their historical, sociological, and critical writings as well.

Black writers who are clearly black have no trouble proclaiming their black identity or their West Indian heritage. What is surprising is how firmly *mestizo* black writers have fought off the "anything but black"[17] syndrome to give equal if not superior time to the black part of the racial equation. Writers do this by taking a critical approach to black history and literature, an approach that includes attacking "white" writings and myths about blacks while recognizing the authenticity and credibility of their own black literature. From Guillén's early *son* poems in the 1930s to Ortiz's *Juyungo* in the 1940s to Manuel Zapata Olivella's *Changó, el gran putas* in the 1980s, black *mestizo* writers in Latin America have strengthened the black image in literature and have underscored and protected that image in their critical writings.

Throughout his life, Guillén produced poetry and prose that touched on these black, brown, and white issues. Ortiz, after grappling with the subject and creating in the process some enduring creative and critical works on blacks, moved away from the "black" province of Esmeraldas and away from black literature. Manuel Zapata Olivella, conversely, continues to address these issues in *Nuestra voz* (*Our Voice*, 1987) in his essay, "Negritud, indianidad y mestizaje en Latinoamerica" (1987), as well as in *Lève toi, mulâtre* (1987), his autobiography. In these more recent works, as in *Changó, el gran putas* (1983), Manuel

Zapata Olivella acknowledges and elevates all three of his ancestors to equal status. Triethnicity is Manuel Zapata Olivella's latest campaign. As a Colombian black he has gone beyond the
dualism of *mestizaje* to pose a *trietnicidad americana*, not only in
his personal history but also for Latin America. To support his
contention that writers can be black (in a North American sense)
and *mestizo* (in a triethnic sense), Manuel Zapata Olivella points
to Langston Hughes and to Jorge Artel as examples of writers
who clearly want to be remembered as black writers, but who
have testified to a triethnic, biological past.[18]

   Hispanic black writers believe their personal experience and
their identification with blacks enable them to give the most
accurate portrayal of the black experience. They take this position in assessing *negrismo*, or poetic Negrism. One of the primary
tasks of the black writer as a critic of Latin American literature
has been to attack the false black images of poetic Negrism.
Interested in a true black self-identity, Hispanic black writers feel
it is their duty to protect the black image from distortion. To this
end, Hispanic black criticism—like Hispanic black creative literature—often reacts against what nonblack writers have written
about blacks, questioning matters of both style and content.
Hispanic black writers question, for example, the auditive and
rhythmic devices and the imagery used by white *negrista* poets,
believing that white writers do not portray blacks with the same
authenticity, sensitivity, and accuracy as they themselves do.

   Many Latin American black writers have responded to the portrayal of the black experience by a nonblack writer. Martin Morúa
Delgado questioned Villaverde's antislavery novel in the late
nineteenth century and set about writing a better one of his own.
Juan Pablo Sojo in the early twentieth century attacked Rómulo
Gallego's depiction of blacks in Barlovento, eventually writing his
own novel on the same subject. Quince Duncan lambasted whites
who write about black life from a distance. And Nicolás Guillén
roundly rejected the superficiality of poetic *negrismo* and the dam-
aging image of blacks that white *negrista* poets from the 1920s,
1930s, and beyond have left. Guillén singled out the "black"
poetry of Luis Palés Matos for criticism, despite Anibal González
Pérez's recent attempt to bring these two poets closer together.[19]

   When asked whether he thought the *negrista* poems of José
Zacarías Tallet, Ramón Guirao, and Palés Matos gave a false
image of blacks, Guillén responded that the false image appeared

because the poems were badly focused. He added that Palés Matos presents "a superficial black, a black man without any human problems at all,"[20] one satisfied "with the rhythmic thing, which by the way is very beautiful . . . but he did not go any deeper than that."[21] Guillén's main objection to Palés Matos, a Puerto Rican poet, was that Palés Matos failed to give his black verse a human content, "and when there is no human content, horrible things come out."[22] Guillén believed that white writers using folkloric elements and the language of blacks must go deeper, must go beyond the superficial and the picturesque.

Guillén is not the only Hispanic black writer to criticize white poetic Negrism. Even while acknowledging that the *negrista* movement in the Antilles awakened the consciousness of many blacks and people of color, Manuel Zapata Olivella is adamant that the black poetry the movement produced was more problematic and exotic than an authentic expression of true black identity.[23] Adalberto Ortiz even criticized his own early black poetry written in the 1940s because, as he later realized, that kind of rhythmic poetry should have had more soul, more depth, and more profundity than he and others had given it.[24] Nelson Estupiñán Bass has argued that there is more to authentic black verse than the rhythmic onomatopeia found in *negrismo*. He recognizes that Hispanic black writers such as Guillén, Helcias Martán Góngora, and Adalberto Ortiz are also fond of onomatopeia, formal decoration, and *jitanjáforas*, for example, but he believes that they go beyond the sound, the ornamental, the picturesque, and the festive to express profundity and rage.[25]

Nelson Estupiñén Bass rejected Borges, writing that we should not pay any attention to a man who has made disparaging remarks about blacks.[26] In an equally protective or critical mood, Nicomedes Santa Cruz took Mariátegui to task for negative comments the Peruvian Marxist wrote about black people.[27] Hispanic black writers launch critical attacks wherever and whenever warranted, but the *negrista* poets seem to receive the lion's share of their rebuttals. When the subject of authenticity in Tallet's "Rumba" surfaced in a conference session, Nicomedes Santa Cruz replied: "I don't see it. No black is going to look at things from within with such a white description as 'y hay olor a grajo' ('there is a bad smell') and 'las nalgas bambolean' ('rumps swaying')."[28] His point is that this is not negritude because black writers do not describe their reality in such terms.

Nicomedes Santa Cruz intensified his campaign for clarity on the black image in a strongly outspoken essay on the historical contribution of blacks, especially Peruvian blacks. In addition to taking on the *negrista* poets, Mariátegui, and the literary establishment in Peru (which he believed dismissed him pejoratively as simply a "popular" poet),[29] he took on history as well. He researched in depth the slave history ("our history") of the African in America, paying particular attention to Peru. Labeled the "new Nicomedes," following his move from *décimas* into social protest poetry, he was just as effective in discussing the human tragedy of slavery as he was in writing poems about it. His essay, "El negro en Ibero-america"[30] ('Blacks in Iberian America'), published on the centenary of the abolition of slavery in Brazil, is an emotional and vindicationist reading of historical texts on slavery. Nicomedes Santa Cruz was proud of his new image as he stated in the introduction to an edition of his work that contains his poems on the "black problem."[31] He knew that he was accomplishing a worthy task, because it was the first time such vital questions about Africa and black America had been taken up in Peru by a black writer.

In addition to protecting the black image from abuse, black writers are also assessing their own work. Adalberto Ortiz, Quince Duncan, Antonio Preciado, and Nancy Morejón, among others, have offered self-assessments at one time or another. Nancy Morejón, for example, has made as many substantive comments about her famous poem "Mujer negra" as anyone else.[32] The same can be said of Guillén about his *son*. Norberto James guides the reader to his social and political poetry[33] and Preciado[34] to the negritude elements in his own work. Finally, Manuel Zapata Olivella in several interviews[35] has talked extensively about his novel *Changó, el gran putas*.

Hispanic black writers also have had a good deal to say about each other. Nancy Morejón[36] is as well known for her critical work on Guillén as for her own poetry. And Guillén had some laudatory things to say about the pioneering work of Candelario Obeso, though he was not too kind to Obeso's compatriot Jorge Artel, considering him too cynical, disenchanted, and defeatist.[37] Carlos Arturo Truque outlined what he believed authentic Colombian national literature should be.[38] Nelson Estupiñán Bass has made a careful assessment of his contemporaries Guillén and Ortiz, concluding that their black poetry has the proper rhythmic effect as well as profundity. In his critical essays, Estupiñán Bass has also tried to give some direction to black writers in Ecuador, urging them to honor their black heritage. Both Estupiñán Bass and Ortiz are clearly impressed with the potential of the younger black writers in Ecuador and have tried to give their work more exposure. Carlos Guillermo Wilson has tried to do the same for some of his fellow black compatriots in Panama,[39] and in Costa Rica Quince Duncan has prologued the work of Eulalia Bernard.[40]

The point being made is that blackness is as viable a concept in Latin America as it is in North America, both in literature and in criticism. And instead of assuming that North American black and Latin American black perspectives are different, we should concentrate more on what Hispanic black writers themselves are saying about their own Hispanic black literature. Their critical views clearly give us clues to help in our understanding of their creative literature.

Notes

1. Richard L. Jackson, *The Afro-Spanish American Author: An Annotated Bibliography of Criticism* (New York: Garland Publishing Co., 1980), xiii.
2. Richard L. Jackson, "Afro-Hispanic Literature: The New Frontier of Avant-Garde Criticism," *Callaloo* 12, no. 1 (1989a): 255–60.
3. See, for example, Kubayanda's article "Notes on the Impact of African Oral-Traditional Rhetoric on Latin-American and Caribbean Writing," *Afro-Hispanic Review* 3, no. 3 (1984): 5–10.
4. Ian Smart, *Central American Writers of West Indian Origin: A New Hispanic Literature* (Washington, D.C.: Three Continents Press, 1984).
5. Adalberto Ortiz, "Negritude in Latin American Culture," in *Blacks in Hispanic Literature: Critical Essays*, ed. Miriam DeCosta (Port Washington, N.Y.: Kennikat Press, 1977), 74–82.
6. These works were published as "Apuntes sobre el negro de Esmeraldas en la literatura ecuatoriana," *Norte* 7, no. 5 (1967): 101–9; "Aristas negras," *Cultura: Revista del Banco Central del Ecuador* 4, no. 10 (1981): 51–80; "La lira negra," *Revista Colegio Nacional 5 de Agosto de Esmeraldas* 7 (5 August 1981): 6–14; and "Esmeraldas: su politica y su literatura," in *Las 2 caras de la palabra* (Quito: Ediciones Contragolpe, 1982): 11–22.
7. See, for example, Manuel Zapata Olivella's book titled *Nuestra voz. Apuntes del habla popular latinoamericana al idioma español* (Bogotá: Ecoe Ediciones, 1987), which includes a section on the black in Spanish American literature. See the article "Negritud, indianidad y mestizaje en Latino America," *Présence africaine*, 145 (1988): 57–66, which discusses negritude and black oral expression.

8. See, for example, their interventions in discussions at the Dakar conference in 1974 published in *Négritude et Amérique Latine* (Dakar: Les Nouvelles Editions Africaines, 1978), 172–76.

9. Mark Abley, "Little-Known Canadian Law Has PEN Delegates Up in Arms," *Gazette* (Montreal), 27 September 1989, B5.

10. Philip Marchand, "Long Debates Fizzle Out Exactly as Planned," *Toronto Star*, 27 September 1989, C3.

11. Ibid.

12. Marvin Lewis, *Afro-Hispanic Poetry, 1940–1980: From Slavery to "Negritud" in Spanish American Verse* (Columbia: University of Missouri Press, 1983), 176.

13. Ibid., 156.

14. James Brooke, "Blacks of South America Fight 'a Terrible Silence,' " *New York Times International*, 28 September 1989, A4.

15. Ibid.

16. Stanley Cyrus, "Ethnic Ambivalence and Afro-Hispanic Novelists," *Afro-Hispanic Review* 1, no.1 (1982): 29–32.

17. Louise Byrne, "Black Spot on Brazil's Record," *Globe and Mail (Toronto)*, 10 May 1988, A7.

18. Zapata Olivella's autobiography titled *Lève toi, mulâtre* (Paris: Payot, 1987) was published in Spanish as *¡Levántate, mulato!* (Bogotá: Rei Andes, 1990).

19. For Guillén's comments, see Laurence Prescott, "A Conversation with Nicolás Guillén," in *Nicolás Guillén: A Special Issue*, ed. Vera M. Kutzinski, *Callaloo* 10, no. 3 (1987): 352–54. See also in that issue Anibal González Pérez, "Ballad of the Two Poets: Nicolás Guillén and Luis Palés Matos," pp. 285–301.

20. Prescott, "Conversation with Guillén," 353.

21. Ibid.

22. Ibid.

23. Yvonne Captain-Hidalgo, "Conversación con el doctor Manuel Zapata Olivella," Bogota, 1980; 1983, *Afro-Hispanic Review* 4, no. 1 (1985): 32.

24. See Adalberto Ortiz, "La negritud en la cultura latinoamericana," *Expresiones culturales del Ecuador* 1 (June 1972): 17. Also see the bibliography for the English translation of this article.

25. Estupiñán Bass, "La lira negra," (1981): 9.

26. Ibid., 11.

27. See Wolfgang A. Luchting, "Mariátegui a Racist," *Hispania* 51, no. 3 (1968): 562–63.

28. *Négritude et Amerique Latine*, 175.

29. Elena Poniatowska, "Habla el peruano Nicomedes Santa Cruz," *Siempre!* 103 (14 August 1974): 39–41, 70.

30. Nicomedes Santa Cruz, "El negro en Iberoamerica," *Los negros en America*, special issue of *Cuadernos hispanoamericanos* 451–52 (1988): 7–46.

31. Nicomedes Santa Cruz, *Antología: Décimas y poemas* (Lima: Campodónico Ediciones, S.A., 1971): 15–16.

32. See, for example, Rafael Rodríguez, "Nancy Morejón en su Habana," *Areito* 8, no. 32 (1983): 25.

33. See interview with James Davis, "Entrevista con el dominicano Norberto James Rawlings," *Afro-Hispanic Review* 6, no. 2 (1981): 16–18.

34. See Ester de Crespo, "Les racines africaines d'Antonio Preciado, poète equatorien," *Notre librairie* 80 (1985): 96–98.

35. See Yvonne Captain-Hidalgo, "Conversaciones con el doctor Manuel Zapata Olivella, Bogotá 1980; 1983," *Afro-Hispanic Review* 4 (1985): 26–32; Rosalía Cortés, "L'Epopée du noir dans le nouveau monde selon Manuel Zapata Olivella," *Notre librairie* 80 (1985): 99–101; and Gilberto Gómez and Raymond Williams, "Interview with Manuel Zapata Olivella," *Hispania* 67, no. 4 (1984): 657–58.

36. Nancy Morejón, *Nación y mestizaje en Nicolás Guillén* (Havana: Ediciones Unión, 1982).

37. Prescott, "A Conversation with Guillén."

38. Carlos Arturo Truque, "Mi testimonio," *Afro-Hispanic Review* 1, no. 1 (1982): 17–22.

39. Carlos Guillermo Wilson, "Sinopsis de la poesia afro-panameña," *Afro-Hispanic Review* 7, no. 2 (1982): 14–16.

40. Quince Duncan, "Prólogo," in Eulalia Bernard, *Ritmohéroe* (San José: Editorial Costa Rica, 1982): 7–18.

Selected Bibliography

Abley, Mark. "Little-Known Canadian Law Has PEN Delegates Up in Arms." *Gazette* (Montreal), 27 September 1989, B5.

Acosta-Belén, Edna. "Beyond Island Boundaries: Ethnicity, Gender, and Cultural Revitalization in Nuyorican Literature." In *Puerto Rican Literature: A Special Focus.* Special issue. Edited by Martín Espada and Juan Flores. *Callaloo.* 15, no. 4 (1992): 979–98.

Acosta Márquez, Antonio. *Yo pienso aquí donde estoy.* Caracas: Editorial Trazos, 1981.

Adoff, Arnold, ed. *The Poetry of Black America.* New York: Harper and Row, 1973.

L'Afrique et les Ameriques. Special issue. *Nôtre Librairie* 80 (July–September 1989).

Aguirre, Mirta. *Un poeta y un continente.* Havana: Editorial Letras Cubanas, 1982.

Ai, *Sin.* Boston: Houghton Mifflin, 1986.

Ako, Edward. "Langston Hughes and the Negritude Movement: A Study in Literary Influences." *College Language Association Journal* 28, no. 1 (1984): 46–56.

Alegría, Carmen. *The Black Scholar* 16, no. 4 (1985): 54–60.

Ambrose, Margaret Styles. "*Roots*: A Southern Symposium." *Callaloo* 2 (1978): 124–26.

Arozarena, Marcelino. *Canción negra sin color.* Havana: Ediciones Unión, 1966.

Artel, Jorge. *Antología poética.* Bogotá: Ediciones Ecoe, 1979.

———. *Tambores en la noche.* [1940]. 2d ed., rev. and enlarged Guanajuato: Ediciones de la Universidad de Guanajuato, 1955.

———. *No es la muerte, es el morir.* Bogotá: Ediciones Ecoe, 1979.

Azize, Yamila. "Poetas puertorriqueñas en Nueva York." *Revista de la Universidad Metropolitana* 4, no. 1 (1987): 17–24.

Baker, Houston A. Jr. *Modernism and the Harlem Renaissance.* Chicago: University of Chicago Press, 1987.

Bakish, David. *Richard Wright.* New York: Frederick Ungar Publishing Co., 1973.

Ballagas, Emilio, ed. *Antología de la poesía negra americana.* Madrid: Aguilar, 1935.

———, ed. *Mapa de la poesía americana.* Buenos Aires: Editorial Pleamar, 1946.

Balseiro, José A. *The Americas Look at Each Other: Essays on the Culture and Life of the Americas.* Coral Gables, Fla.: University of Miami Press, 1969.

Bambara, Toni Cade. *The Sea Birds Are Still Alive.* New York: Random House, 1977.

———. *The Salt Eaters.* New York: Random House, 1980.

Baraka, Amiri. *Home: Social Essays.* New York: William Morrow and Co., 1966.

———. *The Autobiography of LeRoi Jones.* New York: Freundlich Books, 1984a.

———. *Daggers and Javelins: Essays, 1974–1979.* New York: William Morrow and Co., 1984b.

Baraka, Amiri, and Amina Baraka, eds. *Confirmation: An Anthology of African American Women.* New York: Quill, 1983.

Barnet, Miguel. "The Poetry of Nancy Morejón." In *Where the Island Sleeps Like a Wing: Selected Poetry by Nancy Morejón,* translated by Kathleen Weaver, ix–xi. San Francisco: Black Scholar Press, 1985.

Barradas, Efraín. "La negritude hoy: Nota sobre la poesía de Nancy Morejón." *Areito* 6, no. 24 (1980): 33–38.

Barradas, Efraín, and Rafael Rodríquez, eds. *Herejes y mitificadores: Muestra de peosía Puerto Riqueño en los Estados Unidos.* San Juan: Ediones Huracán, 1980.

Barrax, Gerald. "The Early Poetry of Jay Wright." *Callaloo* 6, no. 3 (1983): 85–102.

Barrett, Yvonne Gullon. "Nicolás Guillén y el movimiento de arte negro." *Iris* 3 (1982): 47–55.

Barrios, Pilar. *Piel negra*. Montevideo: Nuestra Raza, 1947.

Bernard, Eulalia. *Ritmohéroe*. San José: Editorial Costa Rica, 1982.

Berry, Faith, ed. *Langston Hughes—Good Morning Revolution: Uncollected Writings of Social Protest*. Westport, Conn.: Lawrence Hill and Co., 1973.

———. *Langston Hughes Before and Beyond Harlem*. Westport, Conn.: Lawrence Hill and Co., 1983.

Bienvenu, German J. "The People of Delany's *Blake*." *College Language Association Journal* 36, no. 4 (1993): 406–29.

Birmingham-Pokorny, Elba, ed. *Denouncement and Reaffirmation of the Afro-Hispanic Identity in Carlos Guillermo Wilson's Works*. Miami: Ediciones Universal, 1993.

Bowie, Guillermo. "Harlem sueños del Congo a través de America (poema)." *Afro-Hispanic Review* 8, no. 1 & 2 (1989): 20.

Brooke, James. "Blacks of South America Fight 'a Terrible Silence.' " *New York Times, International* section, 28 September, 1989, A4.

———. "The New Beat of Black Brazil Sets the Pace for Self-Affirmation." *New York Times*, 11 April 1993, E7.

Brooks, Gwendolyn. "The Darker Brother." *New York Times, Book Review* section, 12 October 1986, 7.

Brookshaw, David. *Race and Color in Brazilian Literature*. Metuchen, N.J.: Scarecrow Press, 1986.

Brookshaw, Michael. "Protest, Militancy, and Revolution: The Evolution of the Afro-Hispanic Novel of the Diaspora." Ph. D. Diss., University of Illinois, 1983.

Brown, Beth. "Book Review," Review of *A Daughter's Geography* by Ntozake Shange, *Black Woman Writers at Work* by Claudia Tate, and of *Our Nig. Sketches from the Life of a Free Black*. *College Language Association Journal* (1984): 378–86.

———. "Four from Lotus Press." Review of *The Watermelon Dress* by Paulette Childress White, *Breaking Camp* by Jill Witherspoon Boyer, *Elegies for Patrice* by T. H. Kiarri , and *Now Is the Thing to Praise* by Delores Kendrick. *College Language Association Journal* 29 (1985): 250–56.

Byrne, Louise. "Black Spot on Brazil's Record." *Globe and Mail* (Toronto). 10 May 1988, A7.

Canley, Anne. "A Definition of Freedom in the Fiction of Richard Wright." *College Language Association Journal* 19, no. 3 (1976): 327–46.

Captain-Hidalgo, Yvonne. "Conversación con el doctor Manuel Zapata Olivella, Bogotá, 1980, 1983." *Afro-Hispanic Review* 4, no. 1 (1985): 26–32.

———. *The Culture of Fiction in the Works of Manuel Zapata Olivella*. Columbia: University of Missouri Press, 1993.

Cassells, Cyrus. "To the Cypress Again and Again." *Callaloo* 9, no. 1 (1986): 20–23.

Castañeda, Digna, and Lisa Brock. *The Unbroken Cord: African-Americans and Cubans in the Nineteenth and Twentieth Centuries*. Forthcoming.

Chapman, Abraham, ed. *New Black Voices: An Anthology of Contemporary Afro-American Literature*. New York: New American Library, 1972.

Chrisman, Robert. "Impressions of Cuba: Revolutionaries and Poets." *The Black Scholar* 11, no. 3 (1980): 12–25.

———, ed. "Langston Hughes: Six Letters to Nicolás Guillén." Translated by Carmen Alegría. *The Black Scholar* 16, no. 4 (1985): 54–60.

Clark, John Henrik. "Langston Hughes and Jesse B. Semple." *Freedomways* 8, no. 2 (1968): 167–69.

Clytus, John. *Black Man in Red Cuba*. Miami: University of Miami Press, 1970.

Cobb, Martha. *Harlem, Haiti, and Havana: A Comparative Critical Survey of Langston Hughes, Jacques Roumain, and Nicolás Guillén*. Washington, D.C.: Three Continents Press, 1979.

Collier, Eugenia. "The Closing of the Circle: Movement from Division to Wholeness in Paule Marshall's Fiction." *Black Women Writers (1950–1980)*, edited by Mari Evans, 303–34. Garden City, N.Y.: Anchor Books, 1984.

Colón, Jesús. *A Puerto Rican in New York and Other Sketches*. New York: International, 1982.

Cook, Mercer. "Some Literary Contacts: African, West Indian, Afro-American." In *The Black Writer in Africa and the Americas*, edited by Lloyd W. Brown, 119–40. Los Angeles: Hennessey and Ingalls, 1973.

Cortés, Rosalía. "L'Epopée du noir dans le nouveau monde selon Manuel Zapata Olivella." *Nôtre librairie* 80 (1985): 99–101.

Cortez, Jayne. *Coagulations and Selected Poems*. New York: Thunder Mouth Press, 1984.

———. "When I Look at Wilfredo Lam's Paintings." *Callaloo* 9, no. 1 (1986): 26.

Crespo, Ester de. "Les racines africaines d'Antonio Preciado, poète équatorien." *Nôtre librairie* 80 (1985): 96–98.

Cunard, Nancy. "Three Negro Poets." *Left Review* 2 (October 1937): 529–36.

Cyrus, Stanley. "Ethnic Ambivalence and Afro-Hispanic Novelists." *Afro-Hispanic Review* 1, no. 1 (1982): 29–32.

Dathorne, O. R. *Dark Ancestor: The Literature of the Black Man in the Caribbean*. Baton Rouge: Louisiana State University Press, 1981.

Davis, Arthur P. *From the Dark Tower: Afro-American Writers, 1900 to 1960*. Washington D.C.: Howard University Press, 1974.

———. "Novels of the New Black Renaissance, 1960–1970: A Thematic Survey." *College Language Association Journal* 21, no. 4 (1978): 457–90.

Davis, James. "Entrevista con el dominicano Norberto James Rawlings." *Afro-Hispanic Review* 6, no. 2 (1981): 16–18.

———. "On Black Poetry in the Dominican Republic." *Afro-Hispanic Review* 1, no. 3 (1982): 27–30.

———. "Review of *Poems of Exile and Other Concerns: A Bilingual Selection of the Poetry Written by Dominicans in the United States*" by Daisy Cocco de Filippis and Emma Jane Robinett. *College Language Association Journal* 33, no. 3 (1989): 383.

Davis, Lisa. "The World of the West Indian Black in Central America: The Recent Works of Quince Duncan." In *Voices from Under: Black Narrative in Latin America and the Caribbean*, edited by William Luis, 147–62. Westport, Conn.: Greenwood Press, 1984.

DeCosta Willis, Miriam. "Nicolás Guillén and His Poetry for Black Americans." *Black World* 22 (September 1973): 12–16.

Delany, Martin Robison. *Blake, or the Huts of America: A Tale of the Mississippi Valley, the Southern United States. and Cuba*. [1859]. Reprint. Boston: Beacon Press, 1970.

Diaz Valcárcel, Emilio. *Hot Soles in Harlem*. Pittsburgh: Latin American Literary Review Press, 1993.

Dickerson, Donald. *A Bio-Bibliography of Langston Hughes, 1902–1967*. Hamden, Conn.: Shoe String Press, 1967.

Dissanayake, Wimal. "Richard Wright: A View from the Third World." *Callaloo* 9, no. 3 (1986): 481–89.

Dixon, Heriberto. "Folklore afro-ecuatoriano reflejado a través de la literatura." *Círculo: Revista de cultura* (Verona, N.J.) 13 (1987): 71–77.

Dixon, Melvin. "Rivers Remembering Their Sources: Comparative Studies in Black Literary History—Langston Hughes, Jacques Roumain, and Negritude." In *Afro-American Literature: The Reconstruction of Instruction*, edited by Dexter Fisher and Robert B. Stepto, 25–43. New York: Modern Language Association, 1979.

Dos Passos, John. *47th Parallel in U.S.A*. Boston: Houghton Mifflin, 1930.

Douglass, Frederick. *Life and Times of Frederick Douglass*. [1892]. Reprint. London: Collier Books, 1962.

———. *Narrative of the Life of Frederick Douglass, An American Slave: Written by Himself*. [1845]. Edited by Houston Baker Jr. New York: Penguin, 1982.

Drainie, Bronwyn. "Minorities Go Toe to Toe with Majority." *Globe and Mail*, 30 September 1989, C1.

Drake, St. Clair. "Introduction." In *Claude McKay: A Long Way from Home*. New York: Harcourt Brace and World, Inc., 1970, ix.

Du Bois, W. E. B. *The Souls of Black Folk.* [1903]. Reprint. Greenwood, Conn.: Fawcett Publishing Co., 1967.

Dumas, Henry. "Mexico Through a Clear Window." *Play Ebony, Play Ivory: Poetry by Henry Dumas.* Edited by Eugene Redmond, 37. New York: Random House, 1974.

Duncan, Quince. *Los cuatro espejos.* San José: Editorial Costa Rica, 1973.

———. *Final de calle.* San José: Editorial Costa Rica, 1980.

———. Prólogo to Ritmohéroe by Eulalia Bernard. San José: Editorial Costa Rica, 1982, 7–18.

———. *Los cuentos de Jack Mantorra.* San José: Editorial Nueva Década, 1989.

———. *Kimbo.* San José: Editorial Costa Rica, 1990.

Durham, Carolyn Richardson. "Hunger, Racism, and Abandoned Children: Topics of Poetry Readings by Afro-Brazilian Literary Group." *Hispania* 75 (December 1992): 1225.

Ellis, Keith. *Cuba's Nicolás Guillén: Poetry and Ideology.* Toronto: University of Toronto Press, 1983.

———. *Nicolás Guillén. New Love Poetry. Nuevo Poesía de Amor.* Toronto: University of Toronto Press, 1994.

Ellison, Katherine. "Rap Finds a Proud Niche: Musical Form Has Become Brazilian Blacks Art of Protest." *Gazette* (Montreal), 14 July 1994, B5.

Emanuel, James. *Langston Hughes.* New York: Twayne Publishers, Inc., 1967.

Espada, Martín. "Documentaries and Declamadores: Puerto Rican Poetry in the United States."In *A Gift of Tongues Critical Challenges in Contemporary American Poetry,* edited by Marie Harris and Kathleen Aguero, 257–66. Athens: University of Georgia Press, 1987.

Espada, Martín, and Juan Flores, eds. *Puerto Rican Literature: A Special Focus.* Special issue. *Callaloo* 15, no. 4 (1992).

Esteves, Sandra María. "My Name Is María Cristina." In *Herejes y mitificadores: Muestra de poesía puertorriqueña en los Estados Unidos,* edited by Efraín Barradas and Rafael Rodríguez. San Juan: Ediciones Huracán, 1980.

Estupiñán Bass, Nelson. *El último río.* Quito: Editorial Casa de la Cultura Ecuatoriana, 1966.

———. "Apuntes sobre el negro de Esmeraldas en la literatura ecuatoriana." *Norte* 7 (1967): 101–9.

———. *Senderos brillantes.* Quito: Casa de la Cultura Ecuatoriana, 1974.

———. *El desempate.* Portoviejo, Ecuador: Editorial Gregorio, 1980.

———. "Aristas negras." *Cultura: Revista del Banco Central del Ecuador* 4 (1981): 51–80.

———. "La lira negra." *Revista Colegio Nacional 5 de Agosto de Esmeraldas* 7 (1981): 6–14.

———. *Bajo el cielo nublado.* Quito: Editorial Casa de la Cultura Ecuatoriana, 1981.

———. "Esmeraldas: su política y su literatura."In *Las 2 caras de la palabra,* 11–22. Quito: Ediciones Contragolpe, 1982.

———. "Invitación cordial." *Afro-Hispanic Review* 1, no. 2 (1985): 25.

———. "Otras malas palabras." *Afro-Hispanic Review* 1, no. 2 (1985): 25.

———. *Curfew.* Translated by Henry J. Richards. Washington, D.C.: Afro-Hispanic Institute, 1992.

———. *Pastrana's Last River.* Translated by Ian Smart. Washington, D.C.: Afro-Hispanic Institute, 1993.

Ettrick, Patrick A., and Roman Foster. "The Making of 'Diggers.'" *Panama Chronicle,* New York, (Winter 1984): 9–10.

Fabre, Michel. "Entretien avec Frank Yerby." *Nôtre librairie* 77 (November–December 1984): 101–3.

———. "Richard Wright et l'Afrique." *Nôtre librairie* 77 (November–December 1984): 41–46.

Fernández, Francisco de Asis, ed. *Poesía política nicaragüense.* Managua: Ministerio de Cultura, 1986.

Fetrow, Fred M. *Robert Hayden.* Boston: Twayne, 1984.

Finn, Julio. *Voices of Negritude.* London: Quartet Books, 1988.

Flores, Juan. " 'It's a Street Thing!' An Interview with Charlie Chase." In *Puerto Rican Literature: A Special Focus*. Special issue. Edited by Martín Espada and Juan Flores. *Callaloo* 15, no. 4 (1992): 999–1021.

———. "'Que assimilated, brother, yo soy assimilao': La estructuración de la identidad puertorriqueña en los Estados Unidos." *Casa de las Americas* 26, no. 152 (1985): 54–63.

Fontaine, Pierre-Michel. "Research in the Political Economy of Afro-Latin America." *Latin American Research Review* 15, no. 2 (1980): 111–34.

Fowler, Carolyn. "The Shared Vision of Langston Hughes and Jacques Roumain." *Black American Literature Forum* 15, no. 3 (1981): 84–88.

Freire, Luis. "La sirena popular de Gregorio." *Runa* 6 (1977): 33–35.

García-Barrios, Constance S. de. "The Black in Post-Revolutionary Cuban Literature." *Revista/Review Interamericana* 8 (1978): 263–70.

Gayle, Addison Jr. *Claude McKay: The Black Poet at War*. Detroit: Broadside Press, 1972.

Geisdorfer Feal, Rosemary. "Bordering Feminism in Afro-Hispanic Studies: Crossroads in the Field." *Latin American Literary Review* 20, no. 40 (1992): 41–45.

Giovanni, Nikki. *Gemini*. New York: Penguin Books, 1971.

Goldman, Francisco. "Poetry and Power in Nicaragua." *New York Times Magazine*, 9 March 1987, 44–50.

Gómez, Gilberto, and Raymond Williams. "Interview with Manuel Zapata Olivella." *Hispania* 67, no. 4 (1984): 657–58.

González Echeverría, Roberto, ed. *Hispanic Caribbean Literature*. Special issue. *Latin American Literary Review* 7, no. 16 (1980).

González Pérez, Anibal. "Ballad of the Two Poets: Nicolás Guillén and Luis Palés Matos." *Nicolás Guillén: A Special Issue*. Special issue. Edited by Vera Kutzinski. *Callaloo* 10, no. 2 (1987): 285–301.

Greenlee, Sam. *The Spook Who Sat by the Door*. New York: R. W. Baron, 1969.

Guillén, Nicolás. *Obra poética, 1920–1972*, vols. I & II. Edited by Angel Augier. Havana: Editorial de Arte y Literatura, 1974.

———. *Prosa de prisa, 1929–1972*, vols. I, II, & III. Havana: Editorial de Arte y Literatura, 1975.

———. *Páqinas vueltas: Memorias*: Havana: Ediciones Unión, 1982.

Gunn, Drewey Wayne. *American and British Writers in Mexico, 1559–1973*. Austin: University of Texas Press, 1974.

Hale, Thomas. "From Afro-America to Afro-France: The Literary Triangle Trade." *The French Review* 49 (1976): 1089–96.

Haley, Alex. *Roots*. Garden City, N.Y.: Doubleday, 1976.

Hammon, Briton. *A Narrative of the Uncommon Sufferings and Surprising Deliverances of Briton Hammon*. Boston, 1760.

Hansell, William H. "The Spiritual Unity of Robert Hayden's *Angle of Ascent*." *Black American Literature Forum* 13 (1978): 24–27.

Harper, Michael S. *Dear John, Dear Coltrane*. Pittsburgh: University of Pittsburgh Press, 1970.

———. "Review of Robert Hayden, *Angle of Ascent*." *Obsidian* 2, no. 3 (1976): 90–92.

———. "Magic: Power: Activation." In *Acts of Mind: Conversations with Contemporary Poets*, edited by Richard Jackson, 183–90. University, Ala.: University of Alabama Press, 1983.

Harper, Michael S., and Robert Stepto, eds. *Chant of Saints*. Urbana: University of Illinois Press, 1979.

Hatcher, John. *From the Auroral Darkness: The Life and Poetry of Robert Hayden*. Oxford: George Ronald, 1984.

Hayden, Robert. *Selected Poems*. New York: October House, 1966.

———. "Robert Hayden–The Poet and His Art: A Conversation with Paul McClusky." In *How I Write/1*. New York: Harcourt Brace and Jovanovich, 1972.

———. *Angle of Ascent. New and Selected Poems*. New York: Liveright, 1975.

Hellwig, David, ed. *African-American Reflections on Brazil's Racial Paradise*. Philadelphia: Temple University Press, 1992.

Hernandez Cruz, Victor. *Snaps*. New York: Vintage Books, 1969.

———. *Red Beans*. Minneapolis: Coffee House Press, 1991.

Hernández Espinosa, Eugenio. *María Antonia*. Havana: Editorial Letras Cubanas, 1979.

Herrera Torres, Juvenal. "Prólogo to *Antología poética*" by Jorge Artel. Bogotá: Ecoe Ediciones, 1979: v–xiv.

Herron, Carolivía. "That Play." *Callaloo* 10, no. 3 (1987): 391–413.

Himes, Chester. *The Quality of Hurt: The Autobiography of Chester Himes*, vol. I. New York: Doubleday and Co., 1972.

———. *My Life of Absurdity: The Autobiography of Chester Himes*, vol. II. New York: Doubleday and Co., 1976.

Horno-Delgado, Asunción; Eliana Ortega; Nina M. Scott,; and Nancy Saporta Sterubach,. eds. *Breaking Boundaries: Latina Writing and Critical Readings*. Boston: University of Massachusetts Press, 1989.

Huddles, John D. "Afro-Brazilian Race Relations: An Interview with Insider Anani Dzidzienyo." *Issues Monthly*, (Brown University) (March 1984): 15–17.

Hughes, Carl Milton. *The Negro Novelist*. New York: Citadel Press, 1953.

Hughes, Langston. *The Big Sea*. New York: A. A. Knopf, 1942.

———. *I Wonder as I Wander*. New York: Rinehart, 1956.

———. *Selected Poems of Langston Hughes*. New York: A. A. Knopf, 1959.

———. *An African Treasury*, ed. New York: Crown, 1960.

———, ed. *Poems from Black Africa*. Bloomington: Indiana University Press, 1963.

———. *The Panther and the Lash*. New York: A.A. Knopf, 1967.

———. *Good Morning Revolution: Uncollected Social Protest Writing by Langston Hughes*. Edited by Faith Berry. New York: Lawrence Hill and Co., 1973.

Huidobro, Vicente. *Obras completas de Vicente Huidobro*, vol. I. Santiago: Ziz-Zag, 1963.

Jackson, Richard. *Acts of Mind: Conversations with Contemporary Poets*. University, Ala.: University of Alabama Press, 1983.

Jackson, Richard L. "La presencia negra en la obra de Rubén Darío." *Revista iberoamericana* 33, no. 64 (1967): 395–417.

———. *The Black Image in Latin American Literature*. Albuquerque: University of New Mexico Press, 1976.

———. *Black Writers in Latin America*. Albuquerque: University of New Mexico Press, 1979.

———. *The Afro-Spanish American Author: An Annotated Bibliography of Criticism*. New York: Garland Publishing Co., 1980.

———. "The Shared Vision of Langston Hughes and Black Hispanic Writers." *Black American Literary Forum* 15, no. 1 (1981): 89–92.

———. "Myth, History, and Narrative Structure in Manuel Zapata Olivella's *Changó, el gran putas*." *Revista/Review Interamericana* 3, no. 1–4 (1983): 108–19.

———. "The *Afrocriollo* Movement Revisited." *Afro-Hispanic Review* 3 (1984): 5–9.

———. "Langston Hughes and the African Diaspora in South America." *The Langston Hughes Review* 5, no. 1 (1986): 23–33.

———. *Black Literature and Humanism in Latin America*. Athens: University of Georgia Press, 1988.

———. "Afro-Hispanic Literature: The New Frontier of Avant-Garde Criticism." *Callaloo* 12, no. 1 (1989a): 255–60.

———. *The Afro-Spanish American Author II: The 1980s*. West Cornwall, Conn.: Locust Hill Press, 1989b.

Jahn, Janheinz. *A History of Neo-African Literature*. Translated by Oliver Coburn and Ursula Lehrburger. London: Faber and Faber, 1968.

James, Norberto. *Hago constar (poemas 1969–1982)*. Santo Domingo: Editora Taller, 1983.

Jiménez, Blas. *Aquí . . . otro español*. Santo Domingo: Editorial Incoco, 1980.

———. *Caribe, africano en despertar*. Santo Domingo: Nuevas Rutas, 1984.

———. *Exigencias de un cimarrón (en sueños)*. Santo Domingo: Editora Taller, 1987.

Johnson, Harvey. "Nicolás Guillén Poet of Protest." *Folio* 16 (December 1984): 127–59.

Jones, Gayle. "*Corregidora*. New York: Random House, 1975.

———. "Work in Progress." *Obsidian* 2, no. 3 (1976): 38–46.

———. "Almeyda." In *Chant of Saints*, edited by Michael Harper and Robert Stepto. Urbana: University of Illinois Press, 1979.

———. *Song for Annino*. Detroit: Lotus Press, 1981.

———. "Ensinança." In *Confirmations: An Anthology of African American Women*. New York: Quill, 1983: 174–76.

———. "From the Machete Woman: A Novel." *Callaloo* 17, no. 2 (1994): 399–404.

Jordan, June. *Civil Wars*. Boston: Beacon Press, 1981.

———. *Living Room*. New York: Thunder Mouth Press, 1985.

Kakutani, Michiko. "La Baker, the Twentieth Century's Empress Josephine." *New York Times, Word and Image* section, 13 October 1989.

Kendrick, Delores. *Now Is the Thing to Praise*. Detroit: Lotus Press, 1984.

Kennedy, James H. "Political Liberalization, Black Consciousness, and Recent Afro-Brazilian Literature." *Phylon* 48, no. 3 (1986): 199–209.

———. "Recent Afro-Brazilian Literature: A Tentative Bibliography." *A Current Bibliography on African Affaires* 17, no. 4 (1985): 327–45.

Kinzer, Stephen. "In Nicaragua, Reggae and Resentment." *New York Times*, 15 October, 1986, 10.

Klinkowitz, Jerome. "Clarence Major: An Interview with a Post-Contemporary Author." *Black American Literature Forum* 12 (1978): 32–37.

Komanyakaa, Yusef. "Mexico Memorabilia." *Obsidian* 1, no. 2 (1982): 79.

———. *Neon Vernacular: New and Selected Poems*. Middletown, Conn. Wesleyan/University Press of New England, 1993.

Kubayanda, J. Bekunuru. "The Drum Poetics of Nicolás Guillén and Aimé Césaire." *Prismal/Cabral* 7–8 (1982a): 37–55.

———. "The Linguistic Core of Afro-Hispanic Poetry: An African Reading." *Afro-Hispanic Review* 1, no. 3 (1982b): 21–26.

———. "Notes on the Impact of African Oral-Traditional Rhetoric on Latin-American and Caribbean Writing." *Afro-Hispanic Review* 3, no. 3 (1984): 5–10.

———. "Polyrhythmics and African Print Poetics: Nicolás Guillén, Aimé Césaire, and Atukwei Okai." In *Interdisciplinary Dimensions of African Literature*. Washington, D.C.: Three Continents Press, 1985.

———. *The Poet's Africa: Africanness in the Poetry of Nicolás Guillén and Aimé Césaire*. Westport, Conn.: Greenwood Press, 1990.

Kurlansky, Mark. "The Dominican Republic: In the Land of the Blind Caudillo." *New York Times Magazine*, 6 August 1989, 43.

Kutzinski, Vera. "The Logic of Wings: Gabriel García Márquez and Afro-American Literature." *Latin American Literary Review* 13 (1985): 133–46.

———. *Against the American Grain: Myth and History in William Carlos Williams, Jay Wright, and Nicolás Guillén*. Baltimore: Johns Hopkins University Press, 1987.

———. *Sugar's Secrets: Race and the Erotics of Cuban Nationalism*. Charlottesville: University Press of Virginia, 1993.

Larrier, Renée. "Racism in the United States: An Issue in Caribbean Poetry." *Journal of Caribbean Studies* 2, no. 1 (1981): 51–71.

Laryea, Doris. "A Black Poet's Vision: An Interview with Lance Jeffers." *College Language Association Journal* 26, no. 4 (1983): 422–33.

Leavitt, Sturgiss. "Latin American Literature in the United States." *Revue de littérature comparée* 11 (1931): 126–48.

———. *Hispano-American Literature in the United States*. Cambridge: Harvard University Press, 1932.

Lewis, Marvin. *Afro-Hispanic Poetry, 1940–1980: From Slavery to "Negritude" in South American Verse*. Columbia: University of Missouri Press, 1983.

————. "From Chincha to Chimbote: Blacks in the Contemporary Peruvian Novel." *Afro-Hispanic Review* 3, no. 2 (1984): 5–10.

————. *Treading the Ebony Path: Ideology and Violence in Contemporary Afro-Colombian Prose Fiction.* Columbia: University of Missouri Press, 1987.

————. "Afro-Venezuelan Literature: A Cultural Perspective." *Abstracts/ Resúmenes.* Amsterdam: 46th International Congress of Americanists, 1988, 797.

————. *Ethnicity and Identity in Contemporary Afro-Venezuelan Literature.* Columbia: University of Missouri Press, 1992.

————. *Afro-Argentine Discourse: Another Dimension of the Black Diaspora.* Columbia: University of Missouri Press, 1995.

Lewis, Richard O. "A Literary Psychoanalytic Interpretation of Robert Hayden's 'Market.'" *Negro American Literature Forum* 9, no. 1 (1975): 21–24.

Litto, Frederick M. "Some Notes on Brazil's Black Theater." In *The Black Writer in Africa and the Americas,* edited by Lloyd W. Brown, 199–222. Los Angeles: Hennessey and Ingalls, 1973.

Lively, Adam. "Singing Stereotypes." *Times Literary Supplement,* 13–19 January 1984, 30.

López-Adorno, Pedro, ed. *Papiros de Babel: Antología de la poesía puertorriqueña en Nueva York.* San Juan: Editorial de la Universidad de Puerto Rico, 1991.

Lorde, Audre. *The Cancer Journals.* Duluth, Minn.: Spinsters Ink, 1980.

————. *Zami: A New Spelling of My Name.* Trumansburg, N.Y.: Crossing Press, 1982.

Luchting, Wolfgang A. "Mariateguí a Racist." *Hispania* 51, no. 3 (1968): 562–63.

Luis, William, ed. *Voices from Under: Black Narrative in Latin America and the Caribbean.* Westport, Conn.: Greenwood Press, 1984.

————. *Literary Bondage: Slavery in Cuban Narrative.* Austin: University of Texas Press, 1990.

————. "From New York to the World: An Interview with Tato Laviero." In *Puerto Rican Literature: A Special Focus.* Special issue. Edited by Martin Espada and Juan Flores. *Callaloo* 15, no. 4 (1992): 1022–33.

Major, Clarence. *All Night Visitors.* New York: Olympia, 1969.

————. *No.* New York: Emerson Hall, 1973.

Maloney, Gerardo. *Juega vivo.* Panama: Ediciones Formato, 1984.

Malveaux, Julianne. "Widening the Lens of Black History." *Black Issues in Higher Education* (25 Feburary 1993): 30.

Manrique, Manuel. *Island in Harlem.* New York: John Day Co., 1966.

Manzano, Juan Francisco. *Autobiografía de un esclavo.* Edited by Ivan Schulman. Madrid: Ediciones Guadarrama, 1975.

Marchand, Philip. "Long Debates Fizzle Out Exactly as Planned." *Toronto Star,* 27 September 1989, C3.

Margolies, Edward. *The Art of Richard Wright.* Carbondale: Southern Illinois University Press, 1969.

Márquez, Roberto, ed. *Latin American Revolutionary Poetry: A Bilingual Anthology.* New York: Monthly Review Press, 1974.

————. "Zombi to Synthesis: Notes on the Negro in Spanish American Literature." *Jamaican Journal* 11, no. 1 (1977): 22–31.

Marshall, Paule. "Brazil." In *Dark Symphony,* edited by James A. Emanuel and Theodore L. Gross, 398–426. New York: Collier-MacMillan, 1968.

Martán Góngora, Hélcias. *Suma poética.* Bogotá: Rdiciones de la Revista Ximenez de Quesada, 1969.

Martin Ogunsola, Dellita. "In Our Own Black Images: Afro-American Literature in the 1980s." *Melus* 8, no. 2 (1981): 65–71.

————. "Langston Hughes and the Musico-Poetry of the African Diaspora." *The Langston Hughes Review* 5, no. 1 (1986): 1–17.

Martínez, Gregorio. *Canto de sirena.* Lima: Editorial Mosca Azul, 1977.

————. *Tierra de caléndula.* Lima: Milla Batres, 1975.

Marzán, Julio, ed. *Inventing a Word: An Anthology of Twentieth Century Puerto Rican Poetry.* New York: Columbia University Press, 1980.

Mc Divitt, Jane M. "Contemporary Afro-Brazilian Protest Poetry." *Caribe* (April 1980): 6–10.

———. "Modern Afro-Brazilian Poetry." *Callaloo* 3, nos. 1–3 (1980): 43–61.

McField, David. *Poemas para el año del elefante.* Managua: Artes Gráficas, 1970.

McKay, Claude. *A Long Way from Home.* New York: Harcourt Brace and World, 1970.

———. *The Passion of Claude McKay. Selected Poetry and Prose, 1912–1948.* Edited by Wayne F. Cooper. New York: Schocken Books, 1973.

Miles, Jack. "Blacks vs. Browns: The Struggle for the Bottom Rung." *Atlantic Monthly* October 1992, 41–68.

Miller, R. Baxter. "'For a Moment I Wondered': Theory and Symbolic Form in the Autobiographies of Langston Hughes." *The Langston Hughes Review* 3, no. 4 (1984): 1–6.

———. "Double Mirror: George E. Kent and the Scholarly Imagination." *Studies in Black American Literature* 2 (1986): 239–53.

Moore, Zelbert. "Solano Trindade Remembered, 1908–1974." *Luso-Brazilian Review* 16, no. 2 (1979): 234–35.

Morales, Ed. "(M)other Tongues: Writing the Future of Puerto Rican Poetry." *Village Voice,* 24 May 1992, 74–75.

Morejón, Nancy. *Mutismos.* Havana: Ediciones El Puente, 1962.

———. *Amor, ciudad atribuída.* Havana: Ediciones El Puente, 1964.

———. "Asalto a Tito Junco." *La gaceta de Cuba* 157 (December 1976): 8.

———. *Richard trajo su flauta y otros argumentos.* Havana: Instituto del Libro, 1967.

———. *Parajes de una época.* Havana: Editorial Letras, 1979.

———. "Cuerda veloz." In *Hispanic Caribbean Literature.* Edited by Roberto González Echeverría, 269. Special issue. *Latin American Literary Review* 7, no. 16 (1980): 269.

———. *Nación y mestizaje en Nicolás Guillén.* Havana: Ediciones Unión, 1982.

———. *Elogio de la danza.* Mexico City: Universidad Nacional Autónoma de México, 1982.

———. *Poemas.* Mexico City: Universidad Nacional Autónoma de México, 1982.

———. *Octubre imprescindible.* Havana: Ediciones Unión, 1982.

———. *Nancy Morejón.* New York: Center for Cuban Studies, 1983.

———. *Grenada Notebook (Cuadernos de Grenada).* Translated by Lisa Davis. New York: Círculo de Cultura Cubana, 1984.

———. "Warrior's Brief Song." *The Black Scholar* 15, no. 3. (May/June 1984): 19.

———. *Where the Island Sleeps Like a Wing.* Translated by Kathleen Weaver. San Francisco: Black Scholar Press, 1985.

———. *Piedra pulida.* Havana: Editorial Letras Cubanas, 1986.

Morganthau, Tom. "Decade Shock." *Newsweek,* 5 September 1988, 15.

Morrison, Toni. *Song of Solomon.* New York: A. A. Knopf, 1977.

Mullen, Edward. *Langston Hughes in the Hispanic World and Haiti.* Hamden, Conn.: Archon Books, 1977.

———, ed. *The Life and Times of a Cuban Slave: Juan Francisco Manzano, 1797–1854.* Hamden, Conn: Archon Books, 1981.

———. "The Emergence of Afro-Hispanic Poetry: Some Notes on Canon Formation." *Hispanic Review* 56, no. 4 (1988): 435–53.

Nascimento, Abdias do, ed. *Dramas para negros e prologo para brancas.* Rio de Janeiro: Teatro Experimental de Negro, 1964.

Nascimento, Elisa Larkin. *Pan-Africanism and South America: Emergence of a Black Rebellion.* Buffalo: Afrodiaspora, 1980.

Nazoa, Anibal. "Un poeta del pueblo." In *Yo pienso aqui donde estoy,* edited by Antonio Acosta Márquez. Medellín: Ediciones Cascabel, 1977: 1–3.

Négritude et Amérique Latine. Dakar: Les Nouvelles Editions Africaines, 1978, 172–76.

Nicholas, Charles A., ed. *Arna Bontemps-Langston Hughes Letters, 1925–1967.* New York: Dodd Mead and Co., 1980.

Nordheimer, Jon. "Black Cubans: Apart in Two Worlds." *New York Times*, 2 December 1987, D26.

"Notes and Reports." *The Langston Hughes Review* 5, no. 1 (1886): 47.

O'Brien, John. *Interviews with Black Writers*. New York: Liveright, 1973.

Oden, G. C. "A Private Letter to Brazil." In *Kaleidoscope: Poems by American Negro Poets*, edited by Robert Hayden. New York: Harcourt Brace and World, 1967, 185.

Onís, José de. *The United States as Seen by the Spanish American Writers, 1776–1890*. New York: Gordon Press, 1975.

Orjuela, Hector H. *Imagen de los Estados Unidos en la poesía de Hispanoamérica*. Mexico City: Universidad Nacional Autónoma de México, 1980a.

———. "Imagen de los Estados Unidos en la poesía de Hispanoamérica." In *Literatura hispanoamérica: Ensayos de interpretación y de crítica*, 121–46. Bogotá: Publicaciones del Instituto Caro y Cuervo, 1980.

Ortiz, Adalberto. "Negritude in Latin American Culture." In *Blacks in Hispanic Literature: Critical Essays*, edited by Miriam DeCosta, 74–82. Port Washington, N.Y.: Kennikat Press, 1977. Originally published in Spanish as "La Negritud en la cultura latin americana." *Expresiones culturales del Ecuador* 1 (June 1972): 10–22.

———. *Juyungo*. Translated by Susan Hill and Jonathan Tittler. Washington, D.C.: Three Continents Press, 1982.

———. *La envoltura del sueño*. Núcleo del Guayas: Casa de la Cultura, 1982.

Othow, Helen Chavis. "Roots and the Heroic Search for Identity." *College Language Association Journal* 26, no. 2 (1983): 311–24.

Ovington, Mary White. *Portraits in Color*. New York: Viking, 1927.

Palacios, Arnoldo. *Las estrellas son negras*. Bogotá: Editorial Iqueima, 1949.

Pardo García, Germán. "Honrando la memoria de Langston Hughes." *Nivel* 65 (15 February 1963): 1.

Patterson, Lindsay. "Langston Hughes—An Inspirer of Young Writers." *Freedomways* 8, no. 2 (1968): 179–81.

Payne, James Robert. "Afro-American Literature of the Spanish-American War." *Melus* 10, no. 3 (1983): 19–32.

Pedroso, Regino. *Poemas*. Havana: Ediciones Unión, 1966.

Pereda Valdés, Ildefonso. *Antología de la poesíía negra americana*. Santiago: Ediciones Ercilla, 1936. Reprint. Montevideo: Biblioteca Uruguaya de Autores, 1953.

———. *Línea de color*. Santiago: Ediciones Ercilla, 1938.

Pereira, Joseph. "Raza en la obra de Nicolás Guillén después de 1959." *Sin nombre* 13, no. 3 (1983): 30–38.

Pérez Sarduy, Pedro. "Riddled with Insult." *The Black Scholar* (May/June 1984): 18.

———. *Cumbite and Other Poems*. New York: Center for Cuban Studies, 1990.

Planells, Antonio. "Adalberto Ortiz: El hombre y la creación literaria." *Afro-Hispanic Review* 4, no. 2 (1985): 29–33.

Podesta, Guido A. "An Ethnographic Reproach to the Theory of the Avant-Garde: Modernity and Modernism in Latin America and the Harlem Renaissance." *Modern Language Notes* 106, no. 2 (March 1991): 395–422.

Poniatowska, Elena. "Habla el peruano Nicomedes Santa Cruz." *Siempre!* 103 (14 August 1974): 39–41, 70.

Prescott, Laurence. "Jorge Artel y sus tambores en la noche." *El Caribe* (5 October 1975): 1, 4.

———. "Spirit Voices: Jorge Artel's Poetic Odyssey of the Afro-American Soul." *Perspectives on Contemporary Literature* 8 (1982): 67–75.

———. "*El tambor*: Symbol and Substance in the Poetry of Jorge Artel." *Afro-Hispanic Review* 3, no. 2 (1984a): 11–14.

———. "Jorge Artel frente a Nicolás Guillén: Dos poetas mulatos ante la poesía negra hispanoamericana." In *Ensayistas de literatura colombiana*, edited by Raymond Williams, 129–36. Bogotá: Plaza y Janées, 1984b.

————. "A Conversación with Nicolás Guillén." *Nicolás Guillén*. Special issue. Edited by Vera Kutzinski. *Callaloo* 10, no. 2 (1987): 352–54.

Pyros, John. "Richard Wright: A Black Novelist's Experience in Film." *Negro American Literature Forum* 9, no. 2 (1975): 53–54.

Race Relations in the International Arena, 1940–1955. Ann Arbor: University Publications of America, 1993.

"Racial Gap Grows Wider in Brazil." *Globe and Mail* (Toronto), 24 May 1986, A9.

Rampersad, Arnold. "The Universal and the Particular in Afro-American Poetry." *College Language Association Journal* 25, no. 1 (1981): 1–17.

————. *The Life of Langston Hughes, Vol. 1: 1902–1941: I, Too, Sing America*. New York: Oxford University Press, 1988.

Randall, Dudley. "The Black Aesthetic of the Thirties, Forties, and Fifties." In *The Black Aesthetic*, edited by Addison Gayle Jr., 224–34. Garden City, N.Y.: Doubleday and Co., 1971.

Redmond, Eugene. *Drum Voices: The Mission of Afro-American Poetry*. Garden City, N.Y.: Doubleday and Co., 1976.

Reedy, Daniel. "Visión del caribe en las novelas de Frank Yerby." In *Homenaje a Lydia Cabrera*, edited by Reinaldo Sánchez, José Antonio Madrigal, Ricardo Viera, and José Sánchez-Boudy. Miami: Ediciones Universal, 1978.

Reeves, Sandra. "Following the Poet: Glimpses of Michael S. Harper." *Brown Alumni Monthly* 76 (1975): 8–15.

Reid, John T. *Spanish American Images of the United States*. Gainesville: University Presses of Florida, 1977.

Reilly, John M. "Richard Wright's Discovery of the Third World." *Minority Voices* (1978): 47–53.

————, ed. *Richard Wright: The Critical Reception*. New York: Burt Franklin, 1978.

————. "History Making Literature." In *Studies in Black American Literature II: Belief Versus Theory in Black American Literary Criticism*, edited by Joe Weixlmann and Chester J. Fontenot, 85–120. Greenwood, Fla.: Penkevill Publishing Co., 1986.

————. "Richard Wright and the Art of Non-Fiction: Stepping Out on the Stage of the World." *Callaloo* 9, no. 3 (1986): 507–20.

Richards, Henry J. "Entrevista con Nelson Estupiñán Bass." *Afro-Hispanic Review* 4, no. 2 & 3 (1985): 34–35.

Rigby, Carlos. "Palabras del campesino en la inauguración del Palo de Mayo." In *Poesía nicaragüense*, edited by Ernesto Cardenal. Havana: Casa de las Américas, 1973, 549.

Rivera, Edward. *Family Installments: Memoirs of Growing Up Hispanic*. New York: Penguin, 1983.

Rivera-Rodas, Oscar. "La imagen de los Estados Unidos en la poesía de Nicolás Guillén." *Casa de las Américas* 120 (1980): 154–60.

Ro, Sigmond. "'Desecrators' and 'Necromancers': Black American Writers and Critics in the Nineteen-Sixties and the Third World Perspective." *Callaloo* 8, no. 3 (1985): 563–76.

Robinson, Cecil. *Mexico and the Hispanic Southwest in American Literature*. Tucson: University of Arizona Press, 1977.

Robinson, Lori S. "The Two Faces of Brazil." *Emerge* (October 1994): 38.

Rodriguez, Abelardo. *Memorias de noite*. Sao Jose dos Campos: Author's Edition, 1978.

Rodríguez, Clara E. *Puerto Ricans Born in the U.S.A.* Boston: Unwin Hyman, 1989.

Rodríguez, Rafael. "Nancy Morejón en su Habana." *Areito* 8, no. 32 (1983): 25.

Rodríguez, Roberto. "FIU Professors Seek Answers to Complex Black/Cuban Relations." *Black Issues in Higher Education*, 25 February 1993, 16–17.

Rodriguez Laguna, Asela, ed. *Images and Identities: The Puerto Rican in Two World Contexts*. New Brunswick: Transaction Books, 1987.

Rose, Phyllis. *Jazz Cleopatra: Josephine Baker in Her Time*. New York: Doubleday and Co., 1989.

Rowell, Charles H. "The Unraveling of the Egg: An Interview with Jay Wright." *Callaloo* 6, no. 3 (1983): 3–15.

Roy, Joaquin, ed. *La Imagen de los Estados Unidos en Hispano America*. Special issue. *Ensayistas* 12–13 (1982).

Ruiz, William. "100 Years After Slavery Abolished, Racism Continues in Brazil." *Gazette* (Montreal), 3 August, 1989, A2.

Ruiz del Vizo, Hortensia, ed. *Black Poetry of the Americas (A Bilingual Anthology)*. Miami: Ediciones Universal, 1972.

Russell, Carlos E. *Miss Anna's Son Remembers*. New York: Bayano Publications, 1976.

Santa Cruz, Nicomedes. *Antología: Décimas y poemas*. Lima: Campodónico Ediciones, S.A., 1971: 15–16.

———. "El negro en Iberoamerica." *Los negros en America*. Special issue. *Cuadernos hispanoamericanos* 451–52 (1988): 7–46.

Sardhina, Dennis. *The Poetry of Nicolás Guillén*. London: New Beacon Books, 1976.

Scott, Jay. "Cuba's Foremost Filmmaker Travels Independent Route." *Globe and Mail* (Toronto) 7 April 1986, A26.

Shange, Ntozake. *A Daughter's Geography*. New York: St. Martin's Press, 1983.

Shorris, Earl. "In Search of the Latino Writer." *New York Times, Book Review* section, 15 July 1990, 27.

Siemens, William. "Review of *Afro-Hispanic Poetry, 1940–1980: From Slavery to 'Negritud'* in South American Verse by Marvin Lewis." *Revista de estudios hispánicos* 22 (1988): 146.

Smart, Ian. "A New Panamanian Poet's Promising Quest for Identity." *Plantation Society in the Americas* 1 (1981): 376–86.

———. "Religious Elements in the Narrative of Quince Duncan." *Afro-Hispanic Review* 1, no. 2 (1982): 27–31.

———. "Review of *Changó, el gran putas* by Manuel Zapata Olivella." *Afro-Hispanic Review* 3, no. 2 (1984): 31–32.

———. *Central American Writers of West Indian Origin: A New Hispanic Literature.* Washington, D.C.: Three Continents Press, 1984.

———. "The Literary World of Quince Duncan: An Interview." *College Language Association Journal* 28, no. 3 (1985): 281–98.

———. "Popular Black Intellectualism in Gerardo Maloney's *Juega vivo.*" *Afro-Hispanic Review* 5, nos. 1, 2, & 3 (1986): 43–47.

———. *Nicolás Guillén: Popular Poet of the Caribbean*. Columbia: University of Missouri Press, 1990.

Smith, E. Valerie. "A Merging of Two Cultures: The Afro-Hispanic Immigrants of Samana, Dominican Republic." *Afro-Hispanic Review* 8, no. 1 & 2 (1989): 9–14.

Smith-Fernández, Alberto. "Panamá, la patria nuestra." *Afro-Hispanic Review* 3, no. 1 (1984): 3.

Spain and the Americas: Literary and Cultural Cross-Currents (Latin American and the United States). Special issue. *Letras peninsulares*. Forthcoming.

Steiner, Stan. *The Islands: The Worlds of the Puerto Ricans*. New York: Harper and Row, 1974.

Stepto, Robert. "The Aching Prodigal: Jay Wright's Dutiful Poet." *Callaloo* 6, no. 3 (1983): 76–84.

Stimson, Frederick S. *Orígenes del hispanismo norteamericano*. Mexico City: Andrea, 1961.

Stone, Chuck. "The National Conference on Black Power." In *The Black Power Revolt*, edited by Floyd B. Barbour. New York: Collier Books, 1968.

Sunquist, Eric J. *To Wake the Nations: Race in the Making of American Literature*. Cambridge: Harvard University Press, 1993.

Tate, Claudia, ed. *Black Women Writers at Work*. New York: Continuum, 1983.

Taylor, Clyde. "Black Writing as Immanent Humanism." *Southern Review* 21, no. 3 (1985): 790–800.

Thomas, Piri. *Down These Mean Streets*. New York: Knopf, 1967.

Tillery, Tyrone. *Claude McKay: A Black Poet's Struggle for Identity.* Amherst: University of Massachusetts Press, 1993.

Trindade, Solano. *Cantares au meu povo (poesia).* Sao Paulo: Editora Fulgor, 1961.

Troupe, Quince. "These Crossings, These Words." *Callaloo* 1, no. 3 (1978): 87.

Truque, Carlos Arturo. "Mi Testimonio." *Afro-Hispanic Review* 1, no. 1 (1982): 17–22.

Truque, Yvonne América. *Proyección de los silencios.* Montreal: Centre d'Etudes et de Diffusion des Amériques Hispanophones, 1986.

Turner, Darwin T. "Frank Yerby as Debunker." In *The Black Novelist,* edited by Robert Hemenway. Columbus: Charles E. Merrill Publishing Co., 1970.

———. "W. E. B. Du Bois and the Theory of a Black Aesthetic." *Studies in the Literary Imagination* 7, no. 2 (1974): 1–21.

Valcárcel, Emilio Díaz. *Harlem todos los días.* San Juan: Editorial Huracán, 1978.

———. *Hot Soles in Harlem.* Translated by Tanya T. Fayen. Pittsburgh: Latin American Literary Review Press, 1993.

Vallejo, César. *Crónicas.* Tomo I: 1915–1926. Mexico City: Universidad Nacional Antónoma de México: 1984.

———. *Desde Europa: Crónicas y artículos (1923–1938).* Edited by Jorge Puccinelli. Lima: Ediciones Fuente de Cultura Peruana, 1987.

Vance, Donna Williams. "Ntozake Shange Finds the Poetry in Sisterhood." *USA Today,* 6 December 1994, 50.

Wagner, Jean. *Black Poets of the United States.* Urbana: University of Illinois Press, 1973.

Walker, Alice. *The Color Purple.* New York: Harcourt Brace Jovanovich, 1982.

———. *In Search of Our Mothers' Gardens.* New York: Harcourt Brace Jovanovich, 1983.

Walker, Michael. "The Black Social Identity in Selected Novels of Nelson Estupiñán Bass and Adalberto Ortiz." Ph. D. diss., University of California, Riverside, 1977.

Ward, Francis, and Val Gray. "The Black Artist—His Role in the Struggle." *The Black Scholar* 5, no. 2 (1971, 23.

Watkins, Mel. "Sexism, Racism and Black Women Writers." *New York Times, Book Review* section, 15 June 1986, 34–37.

Watrous, Peter. "Harlem of the '20s Echoes in America Today." *New York Times,* 22 January 1989, NR H5.

———. "Bilingual Music Is Breaking Down Cultural Barriers." *New York Times,* 2 September 1990, A19.

"We'll Film Own Tales, Blacks Say." *Gazette* (Montreal), 7 November 1989, C1.

White, Clement. *Decoding the Word: Nicolás Guillén.* Miami: Ediciones Universal, 1995.

White, Florence. "*Poesía negra* in the Works of Jorge de Lima, Nicolás Guillén, and Jacques Roumain, 1927–1947." Ph. D. Diss., University of Wisconsin, 1952.

Wilentz, Ted, and Tom Weatherly, eds. *Natural Process: An Anthology of New Black Poetry.* New York: Hill and Wang, 1976.

Williams, John. *The Man Who Cried I Am.* Boston: Little, Brown, 1967.

———. "My Man Himes." In *Amistad* I., edited by John Williams and Charles F. Harris. New York: Vintage Books, 1970.

———. "Barcelona Beckons," *Emerge.* March 1992.

Williams, Juan. *Eyes on the Prize: America's Civil Rights Years, 1954–1965.* New York: Viking, 1987.

Williams, Lorna. *Self and Society in the Poetry of Nicolás Guillén.* Baltimore: John Hopkins University Press, 1982.

Williams, Shirley Ann. "Some Implications of Womanist Theory." *Callaloo* 9, no. 2 (1986): 303–8.

Wilson, Carlos Guillermo ("Cubena"). *Pensamientos del negro Cubena.* Los Angeles: Author, 1977.

———. *Chombo.* Miami: Ediciones Universal, 1981.

———. "Sinopsis de la poesía afro-panameña." *Afro-Hispanic Review* 7, no. 2 (1982): 14–16.

————. "Afro-Hispanics: A Challenge for Multicultural Education." In *Schools in Crisis: A Socio-Psychological View*, edited by Alfred Lightfoot, 78–97. Lexington, Mass.: Ginn Custom Publishers, 1985.

————. *Short Stories by Cubena*. Translated by Ian Smart. Washington, D.C.: Afro-Hispanic Institute, 1986.

————. *Black Cubena's Thoughts*. Translated by Elba D. Birmingham-Pokorny. Miami: Ediciones Universal, 1991.

————. *Los nietos de Felicidad Dolores (novela)*. Miami: Ediciones Universal, 1991.

Wright, Ellen, and Michael Fabre, eds. *Richard Wright Reader*. New York: Harper, 1978.

Wright, Jay. *The Home Coming Singer*. New York: Corinth Books, 1971.

————. "Introduction." *Play Ebony, Play Ivory: Poetry by Henry Dumas*. New York: Random House, 1974, xvii-xxiii.

————. *The Double Invention of Komo*. Austin: University of Texas Press, 1980.

————. "Guadalajara." *Callaloo* 9, no. 1 (1986): 140–41.

————. "Guadalupe-Tomanzín." *Callaloo* 9, no.1 (1986): 130–37.

————. "Tlazoltéotl." *Callaloo* 9, no. 1 (1986): 138–39.

————. "Daughters of the Water." *Callaloo* 10, no. 2 (1987): 215–81.

————. *Selected Poems of Jay Wright*. Edited by Robert B. Stepto. Princeton, N.J.: Princeton University Press, 1987.

————. *Boleros*. Princeton, N.J.: Princeton University Press, 1990.

Wright, Richard. "How Jim Crow Feels." *True: The Man's Magazine* (November 1946): 25–27, 154–56.

————. *Black Power*. New York: Harper, 1955.

————. *Pagan Spain*. New York: Harper, 1957.

————. *White Man, Listen!* Garden City, N.Y.: Doubleday, 1957.

Yarbro-Bejarano, Yvonne. "Cuban Theater Today: Report on Third Festival of Latin American Theater Today." *Metamorphosis: Northwest Chicano Magazine of Art and Literature* 5–6, nos. 2-1 (1984–1985), 44–51.

Yerby, Frank. *The Golden Hawk*. New York: Dial Press, 1948.

————. *Floodtide*. New York: Dial Press, 1950.

————. *Odor of Sanctity*. Dial Press, 1965.

Young, Al. *The Song Turning Back Into Itself*. New York: Holt Rinehart and Winston, 1975.

————. *Who Is Angelina?* New York: Holt Rinehart and Winston, 1975.

Young, Ann Venture. *The Image of Black Women in 20th Century South American Poetry: A Bilingual Anthology*. Washington, D.C.: Three Continents Press, 1987.

Zapata Olivella, Juan. *Panacea: Poesía liberada*. Cartagena: Ediciones Capricornio, 1976.

————. *Historia de un joven negro*. Port-au-Prince: Edition le Natal, 1983.

————. *Pisando el camino de ébano*. Bogotá: Ediciones Lerner, 1984.

————. *Entre dos mundos*. Bogotá: Plaza y Janés, 1990.

Zapata Olivella, Manuel. *Corral de negros*. Havana: Casa de las Americas, 1962.

————. *Changó, el gran putas*. Bogotá: Editorial la Oveja Negra, 1983.

————. *Lève-toi, mulâtre*. Paris: Puyot, 1987.

————. *Nuestra voz: Apuntes del habla popular latinoamericana al idioma español*. Bogotá: Ecoe Ediciones, 1987.

————. "Negritud, indianidad y mestizaje en Latino America." *Présence africaine* 154 (1988): 57–66.

————. *Chambacú, Black Slum*. Translated by Jonathan Tittler. Pittsburgh: Latin American Literary Review Press, 1989.

————. *Levántate mulato!* Bogotá: Rei Andes, 1990.

Index